WRITERS in REVOLT

WRITERS

in

REVOLT

The Anvil Anthology

Edited by JACK CONROY
and CURT JOHNSON

LAWRENCE HILL and COMPANY

New York • Westport

Selection and notes © copyright 1973
by Jack Conroy and Curt Johnson

Introduction © copyright 1973 by Jack Conroy

ISBN clothbound edition: 0-88208-025-3

ISBN paperback edition: 0-88208-026-1

Library of Congress catalog card number: 73-81748

The selections in this book first appeared
in *The Rebel Poet, The Anvil* and *The New Anvil.*

First edition: November 1973
Lawrence Hill & Co., Publishers, Inc.

Manufactured in the United States of America

1 2 3 4 5 6 7 8 9 10

Contents

POEMS

Contents

Introduction

JACK CONROY

Keith Preston, long a columnist on the Chicago *Daily News,* wrote in the early 20s a short poem called "The Liberators" in which he observed:

> "Among our literary scenes,
> Saddest this sight to me,
> The graves of little magazines
> That died to make verse free."

Almost every critic and author acknowledges the debt of writers and readers to the so-called "little" magazines. Historically, the small literary periodical has been edited by a person or a group in rebellion against the stultifying formalisms imposed by those organs of expression finding it necessary or expedient to tread warily lest they step on sensitive and corn-encrusted toes of conservative readers or potential advertisers.

The rebellion of the 20s was directed principally against the fetters of form and language taboos. There was a time when some avant-garde editors regarded the use of capital letters or punctuation as a reactionary affectation. And the daring young men and women often led forth with four-letter words calculated to curl the hair of staid readers.

In spite of occasional interference by the postal authorities or other official or unofficial would-be censors, the little magazines of the 20s were generally regarded by the watchdogs of public morals as manifestations of a mild insanity and transitory youthful exuberance. The rebels were annoying but held to be not especially dangerous—Hallowe'en pranksters in the world of letters.

Not a few artistically-inclined American youngsters found the atmosphere of Paris more stimulating to their creative processes. Some of the expatriates were supported by indulgent parents; others found jobs of various sorts. The favorable rate of exchange made living temptingly inexpensive. Far from being ineffectual and frivolous dilettantes, the more vigorous and capable of the exiles created significant works of literature and art. The little magazines of the 20s did strive with some success to espouse new freedom of language and form—the right to use such unvarnished language as we see in common use today. Yet, I recall when H. H. Lewis, the rambunctious Plowboy Poet of the Gumbo, was considered too bold for publication even in the radical *New Masses* when he submitted a two-line critique of a la-de-dah volume of verse by Carl John Bostleman called *April Comes Early:*

" 'April comes early,' hear the poet bawl,
Jazzing a Muse that never comes at all."

The euphemism for a word now widely used, especially by black poets, in connection with "mother," was then adjudged to be too raw.

Then came the 1929 collapse of the United States financial structure. Even in the studios along the left bank of the Seine in Paris, the sound of agonized groans of ruined investors, the thud of stock broker suicides jumping from 18-story windows, the reverberations of banks bursting in air, could be heard. Bonds dwindled in value, and bank accounts shrank when funds from transatlantic sources dried up, so that living in Paris wasn't so easy and cheap after all. Soberly, most of the expatriates came home to economic chaos and hard times.

Book and magazine editors ordinarily print with an eye to profit. If they don't, they're not likely to be in business long. Nobody wanted to read about the Depression, or at least most editors and publishers thought that nobody did. Dummies representing Old Man Depression were encased in coffins and buried by grinning morticians and ironically weeping Rotarians. The large-circulation magazines echoed what appeared to be a desperate determination on the part of the public just to disregard the more distressing manifestations of want and woe. Just disregard the Depression, they said in effect, and maybe it'll go quietly away.

Then angry and shabby Jeremiahs in a score of American cities began to gather together pennies, cajole printers, commandeer mimeographing machines, and to issue publications fired with revolt against a system that could permit men, women and children to face starvation in the richest country ever inhabited by human beings.

Few of these magazines of revolt survived for more than two or three issues. *The Anvil,* first printed in a Minnesota cowbarn, was the pioneer of proletarian magazines devoted solely to creative work—fiction and verse—and lasted through more issues than any of the rest. *Left Front* in Chicago, *Left Review* in Philadelphia, *Leftward* in Boston, *New Force* in Detroit—the list is a long one. The John Reed Clubs often provided a nucleus for young writers determined to establish organs through which their voices could be heard. Within two or three years after the Depression had reached its depth, a score of "little" magazines, most of them devoted to proletarian literature, had sprung up.

Editors and publishers began to realize that people *would* read about such unpleasant things as unemployment and hunger. Much of the material in the proletarian magazines was inexpert in a technical sense, a great deal of it was artistically awkward. But its immediacy and sincerity struck a responsive chord. The established periodicals gingerly experimented with proletarian fiction. Publishers included some examples in their lists.

The Anvil had been preceded by *The Rebel Poet,* whose modest debut was as a four-pager on rough paper. The midwife who brought *The Rebel Poet* into actual being was Ben Hagglund, a printer and poet of Swedish ancestry who lived in the wild muskeg country of northern Minnesota, which usually has the dubious honor of recording the lowest temperature readings in the United States during most of the long winters. Ben had a venerable hand press which had been thrown away as unusable, legend had it, by a self-respecting printer during the Boer War. Ben had been printing, editing, and writing to a large extent a poetry magazine called *The Northern Light.* Everything had to be arranged and done via the then slightly more efficient United States Post Office. It was an exchange of letters, consequently, that brought about an agreement between me and Hagglund. Nothing was formal. I'd send Ben whatever I could collect from subscriptions, bundle and bookstore orders, and donations. The latter source of revenue was almost nonexistent. He, in turn, would print when he could buy paper and postage. Often he was compelled to put in a stint on the railroad section, or with hay-baling crews. He published a booklet of his own verse called *Hay-baling Poems.* Peppered with abuse and various accusations from the author, he patiently issued a number of booklets by H. H. Lewis, who was stranded on the parental farm in Cape Girardeau, Missouri.

Lewis and I had been fledgling poets contributing to Noah F. Whitaker's *Pegasus* in Springfield, Ohio. Whitaker duplicated Ben's functions on *The Northern Light,* but when he ripped off a few stanzas of poesie they were always in conventional technique, whereas Ben was hospitable to *vers libre.* Whitaker was an unrelenting foe of free verse, which he always branded as "broken-backed" prose. Carl Sandburg, at that time the foremost exponent of that medium, was Whitaker's favorite target. He invariably spelled Sandburg's name "Sandberg." Noah's fulminations against Hagglund called my attention to the Minnesota editor, a youth of eighteen or nineteen summers, and I unloaded some of my verse on him.

Working in the Willys-Overland plant in Toledo, I became editor of a short-lived magazine called *The Spider,* aimed at college radicals who never in any significant numbers appeared to be aware of its existence. Springfield being comparatively close, I persuaded my nephew Fred Harrison (who is more or less the Ed in my novel *The Disinherited*) to drive me down one Sunday. Whitaker was glad to see us, and after displaying his skill as an old fiddler with such tunes as "Pop Goes the Weasel," he conducted us to his basement. There was the ancient hand press on which he printed *Pegasus,* and nearby was a home-made machine on which he twisted wire into household gadgets such as broom holders. He was a handsome old dog (probably in his middle fifties) with a romantically flowing mustache, a twinkling eye, and a persuasive line of gab. One could readily see that he must frequently find a housewife who would not only buy a broom holder but also a booklet of his poems from the *Pegasus* press. These were illustrated with incongruous and usually inappropriate cuts he had swiped from the composing room of a Springfield newspaper.

The Rebel Poet progressed from four pages to as many as forty, and attracted new poets like Kenneth Patchen. It was the official organ of Rebel Poets, The Internationale of Song. The Rebel Poets had been formed almost four years previously by Ralph Cheyney, a poet and philosophical anarchist who had been jailed during World War I for his pacifistic views. The organization had members in many parts of the United States and in several foreign countries. Local chapters, of which the most active was that in New York City, were in some ways predecessors of the John Reed Clubs. Rebellious magazines in those days customarily opened up with a manifesto of principles, and *The Rebel Poet* was no exception. It stated in part:

"The Rebel Poet wants to be proud of its friends, but prouder of its enemies. A magazine that has no enemies is lifeless, and the character of a publication may be judged accurately by the complexion of its foes. . . . Nothing but general sympathy with our aims is required of members. Affiliated with no political party, we stand unequivocally for the defense of the Soviet Union against the enemies that are massing for attack, we champion the cause of the weak and defenseless, we combat the greed of industrial barons who are converting American laborers into abject serfs,

we decry the spirit of intolerance that endeavors to abrogate the inherent rights of free speech and assembly. . . . We ridicule the musty echoes of the *fin de siecle* slogan, 'Art for Art's Sake,' and inscribe on our banner: 'ART FOR HUMANITY'S SAKE.' "

The New York chapter of the Rebel Poets soon was racked with internal dissension, most of it agitated by Philip Rahv. I had had some correspondence with Rahv, a young translator, and invited him to join the New York group. The all-inclusive liberalism of the magazine distressed ultra-revolutionary Rahv, who in "An Open Letter to Young Writers" appearing in the September, 1932, issue of *The Rebel Poet* pontificated:

"The extreme impoverishment of the working masses, so brilliantly indicated by the Marxian prognosis of the disease and death of capitalism, is now sweeping five-sixths of the world's area with the swift tempo of catastrophe. The exploitative society of capitalism is nearing its end, and the world proletariat is preparing to rise and seize the political power from the infirm hands of the tottering money-grubbers.

"On the literary front, likewise, we are witnessing a parallel process of class division and antagonism. In the course of the last few years we have observed the rise of the proletarian movement in literature, comprising a drastic deviation from the 'nice and waterish diet' of emasculated, unsocial writing, perennially engaged in futilitarian introspection and constipated spiritual incubations."

This turgid polemic wound up with a rousing declaration:

"We must repudiate the prizes of connivance. We must sever all ideological ties with this lunatic civilization known as capitalism."

Rahv soon had a voting majority in the chapter. His only consistent opposition came from Walter Snow, John T. Ackerson, and Leonard Spier. Snow, a newspaperman, poet and fiction writer, sometimes hitchhiked in from Connecticut to attend meetings. John T. Ackerson, under the pen name of George Jarrboe, wrote *The Unknown Soldier Speaks* in the series of Rebel Poets poetry pamphlets published by Hagglund. Spier, the Jimmy Higgins of the New York Rebel Poets establishment, did the mailing, distribution and other mundane tasks necessary for the magazine's existence.

The upshot was that Snow, Jarrboe and Spier resigned when the Rahv faction confronted me with a demand that I relinquish editorship and turn it over to a New York editorial board. The Rahvites insisted that the magazine "identify itself with the *avant garde* of the proletariat" and that a more militant name be chosen. Suggested were *Red Dynamo, Pen and Gun, Advance Guard, Red*

Express, and *Class Front.* Exercising the "executive privilege" conferred on me when I had succeeded Ralph Cheyney as President of the Rebel Poets, I declared the New York chapter dissolved and the magazine suspended. This was only a formality, since the junta had fired Hagglund and driven off workhorse Spier so that continued publication was impossible. (For a more detailed account of these events, see "Jack Conroy as Editor," an article by Professor Michel Fabre of the Sorbonne in the Winter, 1972, issue of *New Letters,* published by the University of Missouri at Kansas City.)

Walter Snow and I had for some time been contemplating the feasibility of a magazine—probably a quarterly—of somewhat larger size and scope than *The Rebel Poet,* one that would emphasize "stories from the mines, mills, factories and offices of America." The indispensable Ben Hagglund was involved, and in May, 1933, he printed 1,000 copies of the first issue. Much of the stuff we published in *The Anvil* was rough-hewn and awkward, but bitter and alive from the furnace of experience—and from participants, not observers, in most instances. Our material naturally invited the jeers of the more esthetic urban and academic critics, but editors—and book publishers, too—began to look with more favor on our motto: "We prefer crude vigor to polished banality." The magazine never presumed to dictate editorial standards for other publications. We simply were plowing a comparatively untilled field, one whose freshness and novelty soon invited the attention of others. *The Anvil* published only short stories and verse, thus keeping aloof from the critical wars raging in the cities—particularly in New York City.

The Anvil circulated rather widely in the United States and even made its way to several foreign countries. Worker-writers trying to capture in a net of words their aspirations and their impressions of the way they made their living might hawk a bundle at union meetings or other gatherings. *These Are Our Lives* was the title of a book of oral histories collected by the Federal Writers Project, and this is what some *Anvil* writers unskilled in oral communication, let alone writing, might say about their own contributions: "Look at us! This is us! We're important." *The New Republic* commented (October 11, 1933):

"The appearance of two little magazines, *Blast* and *The Anvil* must be recorded a straw in the literary wind. Both are mouthpieces of proletarian literature, the first fruits, perhaps, of the critical debates that have been raging for the past months; both, by their simple external appearance, testify eloquently to the difficulties their editors faced in getting them out. Their first issues will hardly excite the enthusiasm of lovers of prose or lovers of fine printing, but they are respectable efforts and they are almost entirely given to the work of young and unknown writers. As such, they suggest a comparison with the little magazines, *Broom, The Little Review* and dozens of others, which flourished and died in the period immediately after the War. The editors and contributors of those magazines were also forced to build up their own publications if they were to have a hearing; editors of established magazines had no sympathy with their technical and stylistic experiments or with their moral and social convictions. Writers took the business of publishing in their own hands, rallied under the banner of Esthetic Independence and from abroad conducted a guerilla warfare against the accepted literary standards and their defenders. The little magazines had an influence out of proportion to their circulations; they launched writers who afterwards came to dominate a good part of the literary scene; they trained editors and educated the audience. The proletarian magazines face the same difficulties as their predecessors, together with those which will always accompany unpopular political opinions, inexperience and drastically reduced resources. One difference is significant. The advance guard magazines of the twenties, railing against American civilization primarily from an esthetic point of view, were edited in Rome, Paris, Vienna and half the capitals of Europe. These new arrivals, preaching the international revolution, hail from such plain American addresses as Mount Hope Place, Brooklyn, and Moberly, Missouri."

Blast, which surfaced in September, 1933, was one of the several proletarian magazines that followed the lead of *The Anvil* within a short time. It was edited by Fred R. Miller, a member of the Rahv faction in the New York chapter of Rebel Poets.

The Anvil not only introduced new writers like Richard Wright, whose first work to appear in a national magazine was published in the magazine, but also ran the stories of well-known writers that they had been unable to have printed elsewhere. An example is Erskine Caldwell's "Blue Boy." I was glad to run this after it had been considered two raw for large-circulation magazines to which he was contributing. In "Blue Boy" a Southern planter is throwing a big hog and hominy dinner for neighboring planters and their dames. After dinner, he sends for Blue Boy, a deformed and half-witted Negro who is a sort of court jester. He orders Blue Boy to perform various tricks for the amusement of his guests, then, as a climax, he orders him to "whip that blacksnake." Blue

Boy then masturbates. Since they do not regard the entertainer as completely human, the obscene act is not very shocking. Everybody agrees that the host is indeed a benign master. Though the idiot has no practical monetary value as a field hand, he is kept as a source of more fun than a barrel of monkeys. Another Caldwell story I published seemed to have violated certain editorial taboos other than sexual. This was "Daughter," about a Negro sharecropper who murdered his daughter because she was always hungry.

Aspiring writers who had never before ventured west of the Hudson River began to invade the Midwest, notebook in one hand and pencil in the other—listening, looking, and scrupulously setting down impressions. These were ordinarily whirlwind pilgrimages. Few could afford a long stay. Bus fare was cheap, but money was scarce as hen's teeth. Hitchhiking was difficult, for during these hard times more and more kind-hearted motorists who picked up hitchhikers were being robbed or even killed. Riding the freights, once the favorite mode of transportation for the penniless, was getting difficult with railroad bulls being extremely zealous in chucking hoboes off trains.

The results of material-seeking excursions by budding writers were often odd and lopsided. One sympathetic visitor noted that young husbands in the poverty-stricken boondocks of Missouri and Arkansas were fully aware that their wives grew old before their time. Why? Because they habitually referred to even teen-age wives as "the old lady." All this meant, actually, is that a customary form of address was being used—it really did not refer to the appearance of age. It might be applied to the blooming bride of a billionaire.

Many of the attempts to set down the vernacular led to similar and even more ludicrous misinterpretations. It was not unknown for a crane operator to bawl out his blundering helper in lofty Shakespearean blank verse. Hearing that *The Anvil* was anxious to publish stories by and about Negroes, one would-be contributor fired in one about "Duke Bellington" and "Fats Galler." You don't have to be too much of an old-timer to catch on that these are ingenious pseudonyms for Duke Ellington and Fats Waller. Frequent borrowings were made from the then-popular radio serial, *Amos 'n' Andy,* in which the Negro characters were played by white actors. "Ah's regusted" was a favorite borrowing. A specimen sentence read: "Ah truckses into the tentses and flang mah armses around his neckses."

A spirited and oddly talented contributor was H. H. Lewis.

He was not unknown in the Soviet Union, the object of his un-qualified admiration, and in the United States he had his advocates among critics of repute. One of these was William Carlos Williams. A group of his poems won the Harriet Monroe Award in *Poetry: A Magazine of Verse*—poems which must have caused the genteel founder for whom the award was named to revolve in her grave. Lewis, who never strayed from his role as a lowly farmhand, was given to comic self-abasement, as when he wrote:

"How can I struggle through toil and strife
Looking up a mule's pratt the rest of my life?"

As a reply to some finicky souls who were offended by the barnyard flavor of much of his verse, he replied: "Here I am, hunkered over the cow-donick, earning my dollar per and realizing with the goo upon overalls how environment works up a feller's pants-legs to govern his thoughts." People were not so conscious of body odor problems at that time, not having been subjected to straight-talking television commercials on the subject. So Lewis was somewhat prophetic in his campaign against what he called "dailybathism," particularly as it affected the female of the species. "Deodorized she-babbits all stink alike," he complained, and added: "I crave the natural B. O." He worked at many a menial job in his time when he took a fling from the home farm as a hobo, but thought he had struck bottom when he was compelled to take a job shoveling out backyard privies not attached to a sewer. He memorialized his low estate in several stories and poems.

As the circulation and connected-work of *The Anvil* increased, it became desirable to add a New York editor and a business manager in St. Louis. Will Wharton, a poet who called himself "the comfort station balladeer," worked zealously and efficiently. Walter Snow, in New York, where "the action" was, proved to be a skillful publicist and also an altruist when he regularly kicked in a goodly portion of his meager salary as a newspaperman to keep the frail financial bark of *The Anvil* afloat.

The Anvil lasted from 1932 to 1935, when it was swallowed in an ill-advised merger with *Partisan Review*. Philip Rahv, aided and abetted by Wallace Phelps (now William Phillips), had managed to seize *de facto* control of the official organ of the New York John Reed Club. Its circulation was only a fraction of that of *The Anvil;* it was heavily in debt to its printer. *The Anvil,* because of its independent editorial policy, had never won complete approval from the Communist Party cultural apparatus, though the CP string of bookstores did distribute the magazine. Alexander Trachtenberg, head of International Publishers and a member of the

Communist Party's Central Committee, evidently found arguments for a merger of *The Anvil* and *Partisan Review* persuasive, inasmuch as the new magazine would be brought directly under CP hegemony and, unlike *The Anvil,* could devote a large amount of its space to the dialectical gymnastics so dear to the hearts of the New York intelligentsia who, as Will Wharton put it, had "a leanin' toward Lenin."

While Hagglund was printing *The Anvil,* the expenses were moderate. But when the print order increased drastically, it seemed expedient to patronize a much more expensive New York printer. The print order eventually reached 5,000, but inasmuch as many of these were placed on a "sale or return" basis returns increased accordingly. The printer had been paid for these unsold copies. Snow had reached the limit of his donations; Conroy was broke in the Midwest. Other *Anvil* well-wishers were no more prosperous. A rather explicit threat that rejection of the merger would bring an end to the CP distribution persuaded me that it was time to throw in the towel.

The new magazine was to be called *Anvil and Partisan Review,* and *Anvil* editors Walter Snow and Clinton Simpson were to be members of the editorial board. Neither was given any authority or voice in decisions, and when the magazine's first issue appeared in February, 1936, the title was reversed to *Partisan Review and Anvil.* The *Anvil* part was soon dropped altogether. The hybrid, sustained for a time by transfusions from the juicy carcass of *The Anvil,* struggled through six issues with constantly diminishing circulation and negligible impact.

Rahv and Phillips, called by some "the Bobbsey Twins of Leftist Literature," were only temporarily daunted. After a year's interval, they launched a revived *Partisan Review* with a distinctly Trotskyist flavor—or at least an anti-Stalinist bias. This ingratitude seemed sharper than a serpent's tooth to the CP cultural commissars who had arranged the seizure of *The Anvil.* Comrade V. J. Jerome, prominent in the cultural domain, was moved to exclaim in *The Daily Worker:*

"Who in the world of bourgeois letters had ever heard of or given a hoot for Rahv and Phillips . . . amateur literati who mishandled a magazine that started out with all the auspices and forces to make it a success?"

Among the old friends and contributors of *The Anvil* who "stayed away from the merger in droves," as Walter Snow later put it, was Nelson Algren. My job on the Missouri Writers' Project had been terminated by a strike and Algren suggested I try the

Illinois project. The upshot was that I arrived in Chicago on a raw March day and lived with Algren in his store-front studio on Cottage Grove while I was being processed for the project. The stores had been built to accommodate shops catering to World's Columbian Exposition visitors and was called simply the Arcade. Algren's only partly successful battles with the huge rodents infesting the area caused us to re-christen it Rat Alley. A *New Anvil* committee was set up, and a series of benefit parties to raise funds ensued. George Dillon, a Pulitzer Prize poet then editor of *Poetry: A Magazine of Verse* became active and was a speaker several times at fund-occasions. So were Stuart Engstrand, Langston Hughes, Peter De Vries, Stephen Stephanchev, Richard Wright, Shaemas O'Sheel and others who appeared to read from their works.

These cultural activities netted some revenue, but not enough to launch the first issue—even with Hagglund called back to the colors as printer. More money was raised from the staging in several Chicago locations of *The Drunkard's Warning, or Chicago by Gaslight*. This melodrama was the tear-jerking tale of James T. Barrelhouse, "a minor triologist and puissant polemicist" whose enslavement to strong waters had not only made a sodden wreck of him but had blighted the lives of his noble wife Phyllis and their small daughter Lily. Algren grew impatient of the temperamental antics of the actress cast as Phyllis, and took over the role. The long gray wig he had borrowed from the Chicago Repertory Company gave him a woebegone air of injured innocence that was both pathetic and appealing. I undertook the part of Behemoth Frittertitter, a temperance crank who long had been consumed by an unrequited passion for Phyllis—one that his strict code of propriety forbade him to vouchsafe openly. The play was produced in music hall fashion, with drinks served. Enthusiastic audiences, while booing Barrelhouse and cheering Phyllis and Frittertitter, threw missiles such as beer bottle caps at the performers. These were as likely to land on wronged Phyllis or high-minded Frittertitter as besotted Barrelhouse.

We rented office space from the Institute for Mortuary Research, a public relations service for undertakers (as they used to be called). Algren and I had access to the outfit's letterheads. They were of good quality, but their ghastly blue hue resembled that of a corpse whose embalming had been delayed too long. We used this stationery for amiable rejection letters. Just as *The New Anvil* was inevitably on its last go-round, I received one that thanked me for my "warm note" which had taken "the chill off many a rejection slip." The writer, Jerry Salinger (who later became better known as J. D.), reported he had just sold a story to *Esquire.* He'd be damned, though, if he'd ever send another story to the Institute for Mortuary Research. It didn't sound right, somehow.

William Carlos Williams, Margaret Walker, Jesse Stuart, Stuart Engstrand and Karl Shapiro were early contributors. The featured story in the April-May, 1939, issue was "The Thunder of God," by Frank G. Yerby. Yerby, a young Negro working on the Illinois Federal Writers Project, said it was his first published story "outside of college magazines." His contribution was a realistic tale about Negro students from a "colored" Southern college being forced at gunpoint to work like common laborers on the levee as the river was rising dangerously. Yerby, taking the "G" out of his name, became rich and famous when he abandoned social realism for fast-moving historical novels with just the right spice of sex for popular consumption. Another young Negro, Willard Motley, worked with me on the Civil Defense branch of the Illinois Writers Project. He showed me a short story called "The Beer Drinkers" which I surely would have published had *The New Anvil* been able to continue. For some reason, Willard gave up the short story for the novel, and achieved both financial and critical success in that area. We remained friends until his death in Mexico in 1965, and one of my treasured mementoes of the *New Anvil* experience is a copy of *Knock on Any Door* inscribed by Willard to me as "one who has unselfishly and without envy helped more aspiring authors than anyone I know."

Hagglund had printed 2,500 copies of the first issue of *The New Anvil,* but only about 2,200 of these were sold. Print orders shrank as circulation diminished. An urgent appeal for financial help from readers printed in the sixth and last issue (May-June, 1940) elicited only a ripple of response. The main business of the country's intellectuals seemed to be the defeat of Hitler. Most of the magazine's support had been in the Midwest, and it proved to be pitifully inadequate.

The intransigent spirit of *The Anvil* and *New Anvil* did not perish from the earth, however. It has been manifested in the astringent impudence of Curt Johnson in his magazine *December* and in various other literary reviews. Up in Minnesota, Jack Miller launched in 1972 the *North Country Anvil.* Editor Miller modestly proclaimed:

"While we hope to introduce some important writers and break a little literary ground of our own, we're starting from point zero and hardly expect to carry on into the blue from the heights *The*

Anvil reached. But I'll tell you this: we do claim to be in the tradition, literary and human, of Jack Conroy."

While such rebellious magazines as *North Country Anvil* have some advantage in technical facilities (such as photo-copying, etc.), while Hagglund laboriously set the original *Anvil* by hand, letter by letter, and strained his muscles running off the separate sheets on a handpress, there are also disadvantages. One of the most ominous is the computerizing of publishing, both magazine and book. An old *Anvil* contributor wrote me recently from Hollywood that she had asked for a certain book in a bookstore there and was told: "We order by computer now. Do you really want this book all that much? We'll have to order through computer service in Minneapolis and it'll be at least eight weeks before we can get it." Computerized ITT, which tried to throw a sprag in Allende's wheel down in Chile, has taken over a number of venerable publishing houses, including Putnam's. So the dehumanizing process forecast in Karel Čapek's play "R. U. R." ("Rossum's Universal Robots") back in 1920 is gaining control of the publishing industry. Report is that one book was remaindered by a computer even before it was published. And with the editorial department of large magazines in one place and the subscription facilities in another, the lines of communication are blurred. It takes about two months to get a magazine coming your way after you subscribe, and if the computer goes awry there may be ludicrous complications A friend of mine signed his name with an initial for the given name one time and with the full name another. In the maze of de-personalized confusion ensuing after he complained about not receiving his magazine promptly enough after subscribing, he eventually began getting a copy for each of his signatures, each name surmounted by a row of cabalistic letters and figures, evidently his computer identification, and now he cannot get the extra copy stopped. Periodically, too, he gets a bill for the extra.

For his untiring labors in assembling the material in this anthology and for his editorial acumen, I must first of all thank Curt Johnson. My gratitude, too, to Professor Michel Fabre of the Sorbonne for his heroic work among the files stored in confusion in the catacombs of my home here in Moberly. He brought order out of chaos. Also, a grant from the Louis M. Rabinowitz Foundation for the preparation of my in-progress autobiography was of sustaining assistance during the period of compilation.

MOBERLY, MISSOURI, MAY DAY, 1973

A Holiday in Texas

NELSON ALGREN

On the Double-O ranch a great holiday was in progress, for Boone Terry, its owner, had returned. For eighteen months he had lived in the Argentine; but now he had come back home to Texas. A great dinner was being spread on a rough board table in front of the house, and every hand on the place had been invited to come.

In the bunkhouse, in the morning, each man scrubbed his face till it shone like a polished apple; then each combed his hair tight back on his head. And, right before noon, all fifteen hands went up to the big house together. There the Mexican serving girls had almost finished spreading the table. Baskets of fruit overflowing, bowls of chicken broth steaming, venison in great long platters and brown mackerel from the mountain streams—the men were abashed. They stood about with their great hats in their hands, looking to be almost as uneasy as they felt; for it was still too early to sit down, and Boone had not yet shown himself. Some sought to conceal their self-consciousness by inventing jokes about the Mexican servant girls, and then laughing at such jokes themselves; but most stood silent and just grinned foolishly at the great table, or pointed surreptitiously at the great pails under the benches, where long-necked bottles swam in ice.

Finally Boone himself came out, and for all his eighteen months among those foreigners, he looked right now more like a West Texas cattle king than ever—sunburned more deeply than when he had left, tall as the doorway in which he now stood smiling, roaring a greeting at them like the roar of one of his own prize red bulls.

The men cheered, and those who knew him best approached and shook his hand; then he came off the porch and shook hands with those who hadn't come up—fifteen mighty handshakes; and whenever he shook the fist of some hand that had been taken in on his absence, he introduced himself in a booming bass and gave the newcomer's hand an extra wring. He made everyone feel smaller than himself, somehow; deliberately he seemed to make

I

you feel smaller, for he gave the impression always of trying to speak louder than he was spoken to, and of wringing your hand harder than you could wring his.

Boone motioned the men to the table, and, after they were all seated, stood on a chair at the table's head and spoke to them as tho he was addressing fifteen hundred congressmen instead of fifteen cowhands.

"Lissen!" he boomed, "You boys go right ahead eatin' now. First thing I want to say is: ain't nobody on th' Double-O gonna call me 'Mister.' " Some of the men were surprised at this, since all had been addressing him by his first name as a matter of course. "Ah was 'Boone' when ah lef' an ah reckon ah'm still plain ol' 'Boone.' Ever' man workin' fo' me was mah frien' when ah lef'—an' now ah've come back to mah frien's. We're all a-workin' together f'om this day on 'cause we're all of us frien's an' brothers—one big family o' boys—Boone Terry's boys"—here he paused, and his voice became more solemn—"an' they ain't one of you boys mite less dear to me than mah own boy Hank . . . th' uncut young mav'rick." This last remark drew a hearty roar out of the men, Boone said it so unexpectedly.

"Now men—right now ah'm startin' things off this-a-way—end of each month hereafter, spring or fall, ah'm givin' a ten-dollar bonus t' th' man whose work's steadiest through th' month, an' ah'll be the jedge o' what steady work is. We're all goin' pull together hereafter, stead o' separate-like like we been, shoulder-to-shoulder, all o' us pullin' fo' th' same goal. Ten bucks, cash down on the barrelhead."

Wayne Hafey, the new foreman of the branding unit, stood up at the other end of the table and said, quietly,

"Reckon that deserves considerable sort o' cheer, don't it, boys?"

Everyone was eating and drinking, but they stopped for a moment to bawl out a cheer for Boone.

Boone smiled hugely, and his big ears grew pink. Then he held up his hand for quiet.

"Somethin' else, fellas—ain't nobody goin' git laid off when th' work's all done this month. Ah'm keepin' ever' man on t' make fence."

This was generosity unheard of—incredible. Not a man laid off when the cutting and branding were done! The men could scarcely believe what they had heard. Was he lying to them to get more work out of them in the coming weeks? Was he holding out to them a promise to which they could not hold him?

Someone near Wayne Hafey shouted,
"Write that down!"

Boone's voice had once more dropped from a booming bass into a solemn monotone. Evidently there was still something else to come. The men became quiet, some glanced at him uneasily.

Out of his hip pocket he drew a little red leather-bound booklet, thumbed its pages hasitly, then inserted a finger to hold a page while he asked them to stop eating. He wanted to read something to them, he said, and he said it so solemnly, and the men gulped so hastily, and the quiet was suddenly so intense, that Boone was taken by surprise; he looked apologetic, as though he had promised something he couldn't give and was being taken up on it. Diffidently he mumbled, "Only a poem." Then he recovered himself, and in a loud voice through which wound sickeningly a stream of piety heavy and dark, recited, for all their ears:

"Tis fine to see the Old World, and travel up and down
Among the famous palaces and cities of renown,
To admire the crumbling castles and the statues of the kings,
But now I think I've had enough of anteekwated things.

"So it's home again and home again, America for me,
My heart is turning home again, and there I long to be. . . ."

At this point he lost the place, and was several moments in recovering it. Then he finished with a robust shout *"America fer me!"*

There was a brief silence. Then as though released by a signal, a dozen voices roared:

"You're th' man fer us, Boone Terry!"

"America fer me!"

"Boone Terry fer us!"

After that, for over an hour, every man drank, cheered, laughed and swore. None felt restraint any more. The ice was broken into fragments as small as those still afloat in the beer pails. Wayne Hafey took off his shirt, despite the coolness of the weather, and sweat was pouring down his face and trickling into the dark matting of the hair on his chest. He was eating so much and eating so rapidly that his eyes were starting out of his head and darkly a blue vein bulged in his forehead's very center. All those about him were laughing and encouraging him to eat yet more, giving him the remnants remaining on their own plates. Wayne had a reputation of being the biggest eater on the ranch, if not the biggest in the county, and he was availing himself of this splendid opportunity to establish his reputation once and for all. With every mouthful he was taking pride; he was determined that none should outdo him. Yet all the others had finished eating and he still kept on, pausing not even to drink from the beer at his side. His belly was paining him fearfully, but the men kept egging him on. . . .

The men were lying about on the lawn. Some were drunk. One called out, "Git Scotty Naylor t' give us a tune." But Scott Naylor and his guitar were nowhere near by, that anyone could see.

The men were tired of watching Wayne Hafey and of urging him to eat; so, at last, when everyone had deserted him to stretch out on the lawn, he stopped. Standing up then, he spoke, with the half-swallowed piece still in his mouth.

"Sure—ah ain't no ninny-gut—ah work lak a man an' ah eat lak a man an' ah drink—an' ah . . . lak a man." Everybody roared at what Wayne said. Boone, drunk as a lord, cheered him wildly, sent an empty whisky bottle crashing against the side of the house, and, standing up on a chair as before, called out, while he pointed at Wayne and the chair rocked perilously,

"That's th' kind o' talk what takes men—Texas men—takes a Texas cracker t' show 'em every time, eh boys? T' show 'em—t' show 'em."

Some of the men observed that he was not quite as drunk as he appeared to be, and watched him with interest, urging him to say more.

"Speech!"

"More poe-tree!"

"Read th' gospel now, y' renegade son-of-a-bitch!"

Nobody knew who it was that said this, and Scott Naylor, the only one likely to say it, was nowhere about. But Boone was too anxious to speak again to care, even if he heard.

The chair was rocking like a boat beneath him, yet on it he somehow raised himself to his full height, and it ceased then to rock.

"Boys! Look at me! Ah was bo'n in Deaf Smith county an' mah pappy kicked me out afore ah was ten—git on out now, ye little devil he says—been feedin' y' long 'nough—go ride yo're own cayuse. Ah been ridin' mah own cayuse ever since, boys—an' making a sweet job of it, too—ah hired out on th' old Bar-7, ah was beat an' ah was starve—boys!—when ah was 20 ah didn't have a pot to pitch in—an' look at me now, boys—ah jes' brung 4500 head back f'om th' South, ah got 4000 mo' in behind thet Mesquite yonder clear all th' way down t' th' river—ever'thin' f'om here clear down t' th' river is mine now boys—ever stop t' think what a slice o' ol' Presidio belongs t' Boone Terry? An' boys ah'm here t' state ah'm a Mexican-lovin' bastard ef ah don' own th' whole shebang one day—all of it, boys!—Whole goddamned Presidio!—Th' whole horsegut county! Ever' acre f'om here t' th' river. Ever' acre—an' ever'thin' on it—"

Abruptly the chair wheeled and swerved beneath his flailing arms, and he had to step off it to avoid falling.

While he stooped, to straighten the chair, someone behind him said quietly,

"Go on, y' ol' pirate, tell us some more."

But this time he didn't climb back on the chair. He stood leaning against the littered table, and his eyes were ablaze. Then his great fist smashed down against the bare wood and he began bawling at them in the drunken belligerent fashion of a half-blinded bear.

"Any you boys know anyone got so much as me?—As me, Boone Terry? Any one o' you, eh?" His eyes squinted, as though he could no longer distinguish them clearly.

No one answered, they were all afraid of him, he answered the question himself.

"No!—Yo' goddamned stinkin' well right know they ain't—ah'm th' big bull o' the Big Bend country, tha's what ah am!—bigges', toughes' bull in th' whole state o' Texas—ever'thin'—ever' acre an' ever'thin' in it—ever' man, woman an' chil'—where'd you bastards be if it weren't fo' me, eh? Who'd feed such a lousy crew like you anyhow? Ever' goddamned man o' you stinks t' heaven, ah kin kick the gut out o' any six o' you with 'un han' behin' me—ah was bo'n in Deaf Smith county an 'when ah was 20—"

But the men were weary of listening. Half were too drunk to understand what he was saying, but banged their tin cups on the wooden table for applause whenever he stopped, their eyes half-glazed looking straight ahead. A few were laughing at Boone; some were silent, even some who were sober were silent.

Suddenly Wayne Hafey stood up, waved his hand at Boone, and Boone sat straight down on the ground, as though Wayne had struck him. He looked about him in a huge and round surprise, his face suddenly looking weakly fat, like a eunuch's face, as though he were helpless to understand why there was no chair under his buttocks.

Wayne Hafey was speaking, and everyone was looking at him.

"Now, boys," he said, "let's all sing somethin' afore we go back t' th' ranch house."

Immediately a dozen drunken voices broke out in a dozen drunken tunes.

"Shut up—we gotta sing together!"

There was instant silence, save for the incessant stupid banging of the tin cups on the bare wood. But Wayne was determined to get order. "Where's Scott Naylor?" he asked.

Everyone began searching and calling for Scott Naylor and his guitar. Then someone pointed him out and laughed. Scott was sitting alone in the shade of the big barn 100 yards distant, munching a big piece of bread and looking so forsaken that every man who was still able to see distinctly had to laugh at the sight. He was sitting cross-legged with his Stetson on his knee, chewing without enthusiasm; but his guitar was not by.

They called to him to come to the house and fetch his guitar along; but he would not move, they had everyone of them to come down to where he sat, and the guitar had to be brought to him from where it hung in the ranch house before he would play and sing for them.

"Scotty! Wake up! Sun-up!" someone roared this in his ear. For Scotty had such a dreamy far-away look in his eye that it seemed necessary to rouse him before he could sing.

He began to strum idly then, and their voices died down a little, for they knew he would not sing while they talked and laughed loudly. Boone came lumbering up after everyone else, his open collar revealing his bull neck, an expression of amiable curiosity on his big face. The men put their arms about each others' shoulders and stood in a friendly little circle together, for it was in this fashion that they most enjoyed listening to Scott. Boone rested his chin in the crook of somebody's elbow and gawked mildly over at the slim boy seated with the guitar.

> "The round-house in Cheyenne is filled every night
> With loafers and bummers of most every plight;
> On their backs is no clothes, in their pockets no bills
> Each day they keep starting for the dreary Black Hills."

> "Oh, I love my boss, and my boss loves me—
> And that is the reason I have no money."

> "I went to the boss to draw my roll,
> He figgered me out ten bucks in the hole.

"So I'll sell my outfit as fast as I can,
And I won't punch cows for no damned man."

The men interrupted him, asking for some livelier tune. So Scott went on to another song, a song none there had ever before heard, a strangely stirring song that at first compelled them to listen, and then made them all feel oddly uneasy.

"Rise up, fields and workshops,
Rise up, workers, farmers,
To battle! March onward
March on, world-stormers! . . ."

The men were silent. The song troubled them, they did not know why. And so, because he would sing no other, but kept strumming this one over and over, one by one they wandered off and returned to the ranch house. Only Big Boone remained behind, his fat face, foolish now with drink, beaming happily down at the thin-faced boy who sang so sweetly for him. Boone slid clumsily down beside the singer, and listened long to the song. It was something about a war somebody was having or was going to have pretty soon, and it lulled him gently, so that he soon slept.

And, when he slept, the boy Scott rose slowly, spat once on the ground at the boss's feet, and walked slowly away from the big white house down toward the ranch house, where already the shadows were lengthening toward night.

The Anvil May-June 1934

Within the City

NELSON ALGREN

Each day I go down to the dime burlesque, to watch the mulatto girl. She dances third from the left, her eyes half closed, while old men lean forward in their seats. This is deep in the heart of the city, where every man seems to go alone and every woman walks quietly. The mulatto girl dances slowly, without effort, with the stage-dust rising uneasily beneath her bare feet. Ten hours a day she breathes this dust, and on Saturday nights puts in an extra two hours. This is a vast and terrible city, with small lights burning all in a row. Within their gleam the ragged men wait, the men from the farms that are mortgaged now and the men from the mines that long since closed down. The men wait in a row beneath the lamps, and the mulatto girl sways slowly.

On South State Street are many rooms, and in each one somebody lives. Someone who sells razor blades to live, or who works in a button factory, or who dances in a burlesque house. The mulatto girl lives in such a room, three flights up and two doors to the rear. There is no running water here, and in summer the smells hang in the air all down the winding staircase. She walks up slowly, her hands on her hips, counting the steps as she walks. I think that when she reaches the top she pauses and thinks, I am alone in this city now, and all about me are the alone men. They lean forward in their seats, or watch beneath the street lamps, or sit with bowed heads in the saloons.

In summer, in Chicago, on South State, there is only the heat, and the dancing women, and the bowed men in the saloons.

When winter comes there will be lines in front of the missions, and a tapping from the rooms. For five winters now South State has gathered its breadlines. This winter the lines will curve down Harrison toward Clark, and the salvation armies will gather them, and the missions will gather them, and the houses will gather them. The little signs will flicker, on and off, and men will pass and repass. The men who are recruiting the boys for the army will be recruiting somewhere else, and snow will lie quietly, and hunger will follow. This is Chicago, its hunger, its savagery, its terror.

Once I walked with the mulatto girl, and she told me of herself. She had been born in East St. Louis, in the grey winter war days, and had come to Chicago when she'd been three. She remembered early days in a south side school, she recalled the race riots of 1917. When she'd finished high school she'd gone to work, and had been working, on and off, ever since. She spoke quietly, all down South Dearborn. All her ways were quiet.

And when I left her it seemed to me that this city will one day flame into revolt from the quiet ways of such beings as this mulatto girl: that all the daughters of the poor will rise, their voices no longer docile, and that day is not far.

The Anvil Oct.-Nov. 1935

Dry Summer

The two little girls—Ronny and Myra—had gone off to gather currants along the creek. Their mother had called after them about the snakes, and they had swung the syrup pails back and forth in the sun until they flashed like mirrors. Daily excursions into the currant bushes had stripped the plants of their fruit, so that the little girls walked farther this day than any day past, determined to fill the tins. Ronny, the younger and taller, who could throw a stone with fine accuracy, had been asked to bring home a rabbit. This she recoiled from doing, and her parents, feeling tender towards animals and birds, were reluctant to mention the possible food. Cottontails, which were better to eat, and which sprang up from the shade of every bush and rock in the yard, were forbidden game until it became necessary to kill them. New ones did not appear and the little girls were sad at the loss. But there was a kind of relief among them all that no more cottontails would be stoned; a wordless agreement: the freedom and safety of young things, that had learned to feel unafraid in the yard. Myra carried a piece of green cloth for the rabbit if Ronny struck one. That green presence kept the little girls from being gay.

Back in the small tar-papered house, Julia, the young mother was baking bread with the last of the flour. She smiled a little at the hopeful "starter" she had saved out in the mason jar; and went on about the ritual of careful watching of bread, and of windows, from which she could see Ronny and Myra trudging along the yellow sand of the creek bed. To the north of this timid house, immediately rose a rock wall, above which rolled the smooth tablelands of Eastern Colorado. It was no good to look out the north windows. To the south a half-dry creek made a wide crescent along a narrow strip of alfalfa, curved along the edge of the sloping grassless yard and on past the barn, keeping close to the high rock wall. Here the creek banks were etched wide and steep from the heavy flow of brown water that rushed each spring down from the mountain country. Each year the yard grew less and the banks were cut in nearer the house. This spring the deluge had roared wildly down the small dry-land stream, sucking the earth away from the willow trees. There they clung to the bank with half their roots exposed to the sun, drooping and bending pitifully. Above the willows stood the pump within five feet of the bank. Next year, she thought, the water would lash the pump from the shallow well-socket and it would go bobbing up and down helplessly in the dark torrent, and be gone. Nothing they could do would save the well.

Julia finished the baking and went out into the yard with a small basket, in which to put what tender young stems of alfalfa she could find in the narrow strip beyond the fence. The alfalfa did not belong to this farm, the owner lived four miles distant, but to-morrow there was work to be done and food to be had. Besides that, few of the plants were fit for greens at this lateness, and the young mother had to look a long time through the fragrant crop to find enough. She could smell the cool of shade and early dusk rising up over the land when at last she finished.

There was a pleasant lonely sound of wagon wheels on the road above the ledge. The woman turned into the field again, cutting armsful of alfalfa, which she threw over the fence into a great heap. This she carried off to the barn and filled the mangers. Once she stood quite still against a harness rack and thought of the good homely odors of stables, mingled with that of the purple blooms on the alfalfa.

She watched the horses wearily but effortlessly enter the yard, the wagon seeming to come along of its own volition. Dip and Sandy looked unsuited in harness, but Dip's shambling grey mate, Bett, had died, and the alert sway-backed pony had gone stubbornly before the wagon beside this patient old man of a horse. The husband drew the team to a stop and leaped down onto the ground. His blue eyes were sullen and he was impatient with the horses.

"What did they say at the store, Ron?" she asked, wishing intensely she had not spoken.

He waved an angry arm toward the empty wagon and swore at the country, at dry-land farming.

"No rain, no credit," he bitterly mumbled after a while, and slapped the horses' behinds, sending them off down the path to the water tank. While he was hanging the harness on the pegs, he noticed the alfalfa ready for the horses.

"Good girl," he called out to her. She felt quite happy for a moment.

Ronny and Myra had stopped below them to look at the rock

wall freckled with the small mud pocket-nests of the swallows. The birds were getting to bed in a wild chaos of sound. The little girls climbed up the bank and past the willows, carrying a full pail of currants, four new gourds for playing, and something in an old cloth.

"Hello-o-o, my boys," laughed Ron, "Here, I've brought the candy!"

He handed over a small bag, and Myra, less shy, passed it among them, then asked:

"You got credit, Papa?"

"We get it Saturday," he answered.

There was a moment of silence in which the little girls knew the truth, and the parents watched them know it.

"Hey, Ronny, what's that you've got there? Another rabbit! You've got an arm, my boy." Ron was proud.

Ronny stood pale and silent, holding the dead rabbit wrapped in his stained shroud. Dumbly she handed the still fur and cloth to her father, and broke past him, running blindly toward the house. Far up into the dusk a screen door slammed. Myra was half way up the path fleeing through the curtains of the night to Ronny. Suddenly she turned off the path into the rock room with the red berry tree, and flung herself on the ground. They could not weep together.

Ronny and Myra could eat none of the rabbit. The father was almost angry, knowing their hunger, and the young mother spoke gently to them of the cycle of killing for food. As if their minds met now and flowed on in a common stream, the little girls sat with tight aching throats, seeing nothing before them but the swiftness gone out of a wild thing suddenly and finally. Quietly, to hush the urging of their parents, the children began to eat slices of butterless fresh bread, and a large helping of greens. The currants exploded in soft muffled sounds in a kettle on the stove. They were for the morrow, but the young mother could spare a few for the little girls.

Since Ron was going to hoe the watermelon vines the next day and Julia and the little girls were to shock cane, the horses were free to graze the wide mesas of buffalo grass. The small family went up the steep road and out on the flatlands to the fields, Ron swinging a water jug wrapped and sewed with burlap, and soaked through to keep the water cool through the long day of heat. He left them at the fence to go to the melon patch. The young mother with Ronny and Myra turned into the cane field, their huge knives flashing in the sun. Each took a row for his own and worked rapidly along its length, leaving the cane in bundles at intervals, later to be laid in shocks that reminded Ronny and Myra of te-pees. Sometimes they grew tired and thirsty at the far end of the field and would have to work the half mile back before getting a drink. Then they would chew the cane juice from the slender stalks, and if they were very tired, Myra would walk in the clearing, imi-tating persons she had seen in the town, making Julia and Ronny laugh until they were too weak to work. While they were resting, Myra would run back to her neglected row and cut fast to catch up with the others. Ron finished his hoeing and came over to help them. He left a headless snake with six rattles dangling on the top wire of the fence; then started down a row chopping cane with his hoe.

In the afternoon dark clouds rolled high against the northwest sky, and a great stillness fell down on the prairies. The suppressed wind held an effort to rain, but no rain came. Electricity so filled the air that the cautious little family left their steel cane knives in a tool box at one end of the field and started across the still plain homeward. Before they had gone far a scanty rain fell on them, wetting only the surface of the dry earth.

That night the kildeers were flying and crying wildly over the creek bottom, accompanying the quiet meagre meal. Afterwards Ron went down to the barn to make sure about the horses, and there was old Dip drooping stolidly alone beside the water tank, and uncouth Bounce with his black tail between his legs restless and whining. Ron walked away in the deep shadows with the dog running ahead, too anxious to discover new smells brought out by the shower.

The little girls were washing their feet in preparation for going to bed when Ron returned. There was something in the hopeless finality of his look and the despair in his shoulders that frightened the three in the house. They seemed to draw together, without moving, against what he was going to say. The brown pony had fallen over a cliff and broken his neck; Ron wanted the shotgun.

"Sandy!" cried Myra.

"Sh-h-h," whispered Ronny and touched her sister for silence. They looked at each other, frightened, with the picture of the dying horse between them, hurt and still in the summer dusk.

Ron took the gun and went out.

"Only enough rain in this goddamned country to let a horse slip and break his neck!" he choked, bitterly, "I'm through!" He turned on them in the doorway as if they had killed Sandy.

"Why don't you say something?" he shouted. "All you do is sit

there and look hungry . . . all of you . . . every day . . . hungry.
Do you think I like to look at you kids getting skinny and big-
eyed? Do you? Do you know what I'm going to do! No, you
don't . . . you can't get your minds off your empty bellies long
enough!" The door slammed sharply, and they in the house heard
him sobbing and stumbling away to shoot Sandy. And all the
time there was that sad lonely song out in the night of the kildeers'
wild crying.

No one dared wonder audibly what the father intended to do.

"Mamma," defended Myra, "we've all worked in the field, and
we were still about being hungry."

"I know," Julia said quietly.

Ronny startled them with a strange mature conclusion.

"I think papa is mad."

"Whatever on earth makes you say that, child?"

"I heard him say he'd go mad with another month of this life,"
repeated Ronny, soberly ending the talk between them.

Then through the room and among them crawled the obscure
thought.

The next morning when Ron had not returned, and the early
day had cleared away the shadowy fears of the night, Julia spoke
to Ronny of her money. When Bett had died, the men had cut
two silver quarters from her shoulders, and given them to Ronny
and Myra, to whom they had been promised a long time. The
little girls had put them away in a fold of flannel, associating them
darkly with the dead mare. Death was so mysterious to them that
the knowledge of the money lay in their minds in a blind pool of
wonder. They feared and were fascinated by the small white box
that contained the coins. When her blackened quarter had to be
spent for a pound of rice, the emotion Myra felt was the same as
when she wore the coat made from her dead aunt's dress. She
handed the box over, not wishing to touch the coin; and could not
watch her mother shop for fear of seeing the money spent. That
night she thought of Bett and cried. Now, Ronny must give up
her silver coin . . . give up all that remained of Bett, save the
strong white bones that ghosted a hollow to the eastward.

Julia and the little girls walked over the six miles of prairie that
separated the stubborn farm from a store and post office, pausing
sometimes for any sign of a walking man, and going on with
quiet misgivings. After the mother talked awhile with the store-
keeper, she bought a small portion of flour and a bag of potatoes,
the latter which had to be divided for the little girls to carry.
Myra sat a long time on a bean barrel in front of the candy case

until the old man handed her a tiny red and white rectangle. Ashamed for the old man, Myra motioned to Ronny, and the two went outside to share the sweet. It was worth the trip, the two agreed wordlessly. The coin was spent, and Julia had a fresh white band on the finger where her wedding ring had been. So they walked toward home. The gathering dusk was already stitched with the mournful cries of the coyotes when the three weary ones stood within the house again waiting for a sound of Ron. Julia sighed and lighted the lamp.

It was difficult to get to bed without talk of the father. When Julia thought the little girls were asleep, she crept out of bed and bolted the door, then stood a long moment by the window straining her eyes through the hazy sheen of night. Fingers of light from a thin moon were groping along the floor. The little girls, awake and tense with the mystery of their father's absence, watched Julia covertly, saw the shining tears on her face as she turned back to bed.

They must have slept, for they were awakened by a wild pounding at the lock, and Ron's trembling voice. He was standing close by the house, knocking at his own door like a stranger. Julia was out of bed. Ronny and Myra had covered their heads; small sounds of little lost creatures came from their bed.

Then through the room and among them crawled the obscure thought.

There was a listening stillness outside, then Ron's voice again.

"I have a calf," he whispered loudly, trying to make Julia hear through the door.

She screamed, and stood against the pane, terrified, frozen.

"For God's sake, what's the matter?" he mumbled quizzically.

The woman relaxed.

"What—what—," she asked, "You have a—?"

"A calf," he shouted, "A calf—to eat—*eat!*"

She opened the door.

"We'll have to skin it tonight. I had to steal the poor little thing. I had to kill it. God. The poor little. . . ."

He was crying.

The Anvil Sept.-Oct. 1934

Telephone Call

J. S. BALCH

The door opened for a moment and some of Mrs. Prince's grief escaped, bolting with the tomcat into the backyard. Then Fanny came out, closed the door, and walked slowly down the steps. Mrs. Jacobs, scrubbing clothes on the other porch, looked at her. The crazy boy's mother, Mrs. Savini looked at her. Even old Mrs. Jackson, the deaf *schwartzer,* heard something and looked up.

"Is mama sick?" Mrs. Jacobs asked.

"No," Fanny said, "Mrs. Jacobs," she wet her lips, "mama says kin she please borrow a nickel till Saturday?"

Mrs. Jacobs was immediately and intensely embarrassed. "I ain't got not a penny in the house," she wailed. "May I die if I got one penny even."

Men from the fire-station had water-hoses trained on Ethel and Sarah and the other children. "Come on, Fanny! Come on!" they shouted as she passed. It was a very hot day and on such days there was no greater fun than "swimming in air through water," as this game was called. It was better even than ice cream or all-day suckers. "I can't," Fanny said, "I got to call on the telephone." She dodged but got a little bit wet.

Mr. Smolefsky's face was pitted like a bad apple. His daughter sang love songs at the school affairs, and she was also in the store.

"A nickel, huh!" Mr. Smolefsky said. "Why not a dollar or ten dollars? You people sure got your nerve."

"We ain't runnin' no grocery business for charity," his daughter shrilled. "Tell your ma she should settle what she owes first."

The drug store boss was in the back, joking with someone. The clerk was waiting on trade.

"What is it, little girl?" he asked at last.

"My mama says kin you please lend us a nickel for the telephone. My mama wants to call up my daddy. He stays at the City Relief Farm. My daddy's name is Mr. Prince."

The clerk frowned.

"All right," he said.

Fanny watched him dial the number.

"Hello. City Farm? Let me talk to Mr. Prince. P-r-i-n-c-e. Prince. . . . What's his first name, little girl? . . . Abe. A-b-e. He's one of the workers, I guess. Yeah, she says it's important. . . . Hello, Abe? Just a minute. . . ."

Fanny craned her neck. "Hello, daddy dear. This is Fanny talking. Mama says come home right away. The baby won't wake up. . . . Can you hear me, daddy? . . . The baby—"

She burst into tears and the clerk had to finish the conversation for her.

The Anvil Jan.-Feb. 1934

Love Story

MILLEN BRAND

On the stone embankment of the Anacostia River opposite the Navy Yard a girl, dressed in a thin sweater and skirt, was fishing for carp. She had walked to the Anacostia side across the long bridge from Eleventh Street. She had been there all afternoon.

It was late fall, the wind was cold and numbed her fingers. It came off the river in gusts, clasped her, then went on back across the vacant flats and she could hear it as it shook the trees on Nichols Avenue. Near her the bridge laid its shadow on the river. She saw the reflection of a bus from Congress Heights crossing into the city.

She had to catch a carp. She watched the water. It moved smoothly along the stone embankment, only an arm length down. Its dark mass was alive; it reflected the city of Washington, opposite. It reflected her, herself—a small figure.

A little after six the sun set quickly, as it does in the fall. For those few minutes there was splendor; light outlined in a cape of black the mass of trees at the river's bend, towered and dropped fire and embers on the river. Then it was dark.

Out of the darkness a single light appeared, a light that can be seen from many places, from Anacostia, from the National Soldiers' Home, from Georgetown—the glowing white rotunda of the Capitol.

Her fish lines quivered. She watched them closely. With the dark the wind became stronger. She put another stone on her bag of meal, on a buttress.

The water now looked black.

A while after sunset a man wearing a mackinaw walked out of the darkness behind her, his steps softened by the grass. She only noticed him when he stood beside here. "Hello," he said.

"Hello"

"Gettin' anything?"

She didn't answer at first, then said, "A few cats."

"Sister—"

She said nothing.

"Sister, I'm hungry."

She showed him the string and he pulled the catfish up. "Take a couple," she said.

"Thanks," he said. He hesitated. "Anything I can do for you?"

"No—"

A short distance up the river, this side of the bend, there was a dredge clearing the channel, working night and day.

"Kind of funny time to be fishin', sister," the man said.

She did not answer.

"Ain't you cold?"

"No."

He put the cats back in the water and took off his mackinaw. "Put this on," he said.

She put it on and felt warmer. The man now had only a thin shirt on.

She watched the lines. Whenever they stopped quivering, she pulled them in and rebaited them, wetting meal and fastening the lumps of dough on.

"Sister, I wish I could do something for you," the man said. "You fishing for carp?"

"Yeah."

"I know a good place to sell it. Get a dollar maybe." he said, "Alone?"

She turned and looked at him steadily.

"Yeah, I thought so. It's worse than hunger, ain't it?" he said.

One of the lines jumped. She put her hand on it and a moment later there was a strike and she pulled back and then she felt nothing and when she almost thought she had missed it, the carp began to run. It was a big one and she let the line out, slowing it as much as she could until the fish began to tire. She had only pulled back a few yards of the line when it began to run again, the line burning out between her fingers. "Watch it," the man said. The line slackened. She pulled in, and again the fish ran. After ten minutes she had it tired. It was so tired it floated belly up as she dragged it along the top of the water. "Look out now," the man said. She drew the carp in close and started to lift it. At the moment she began the swing, the carp gave a last jerk, tore loose, and slipped down into the black water.

"Hell," the man said.

The girl looked steadily at where the fish had disappeared. Finally she took off the mackinaw and gave it back to the man. "Don't wait no longer," she said.

He stood still.

"Take the cats," she said.

"No. I guess you need them."

"No, I don't need them. You can have them all."

"What do you mean, I can have them all?"

"Go away—"

"Why should I go away?"

He saw. She was staring at the water.

"So that's it," he said.

"What if it is?"

He stood beside her. "Two of us could be broke, two of us could be hungry, but we couldn't be alone, sister."

She hardly moved.

"And I can cook cats," he said.

The New Anvil Dec. 1939

Now He Is Safe

ASHLEY BUCK

The wind blew hard out of the late autumn day. It came fast over the fields, the tall grass bending low and only becoming upright with the diminishing of the wind. From the fields it struck the highway, sweeping the cement clean, leaving it cold and strangely quiet. In the west a huge sun hugged the horizon, waiting to die, hungering for the night. The woman came upon the road from the west, seeming to step out of the sun. The wind whipped her cheap calico dress furiously about her body as though it were ready to hurl her into the center of the lingering ball of fire. She stood there like a storm-struck tree, shattered, swaying, but rooted to the earth. She only knew that her hands were cold and looking at them she saw they were still damp between the fingers where the wind had not touched them. She opened her fingers wide, holding the hands before her eyes, staring at them with dumb amazement, like a fighter punch drunk from a blow. The surprise drunkenness went away and the hands fell heavily to her sides. Clear thinking returned, far away, coming slowly over her whole being, settling in her eyes, bringing an aching thankfulness. The roads and fields came plainly before her. She knew them and began walking southward. For the first time she felt the wind hurting her body. A short while ago, when she came from town, she had not felt it, and the going then was much harder than now. Now she was empty-handed, nothing in her fingers but the cold from icy water wind-dried. There was nothing warm nor filled with life to cling to as there had been. There would never be that to hold to anymore. That was gone. It had not known, and whatever pain or suffering there was had been the unconscious kind, not realized or felt through the brain; not anything like the earlier drawn-out suffering, and life had ended quickly and without crying. She would have done it another way —at their room—but there was no gas. The woman knew all this and going over it again and again, found herself blameless.

Automobiles came like many colored ghosts, streaking into old unknown horizons, dissolving into the dark day. The woman moved hurriedly, an exhausted forced walk. She couldn't remember when she had ever been so tired. She heard the car beginning to stop behind her and did not care who it might be. It did not matter what they wanted or what they would talk about . . . only it would be better if they didn't talk, but remained silent and let her off in the town. The car was beside her now and she heard the voice above the noise of the motor: "Wanna lift?" She did not answer, but got into the car. It was a sedan, new and warm. Several suitcases were piled in the rear. The radio was playing "Beale Street Blues." The driver was a big man wearing a huge brown coat. He smoked a large black cigar. His face was moon-shaped, close shaved and heavily powdered. She saw his eyes go over her body as she stepped into the front seat.

"Where ya goin'?" he asked.

"The next town—Roxbury."

"How far is it?"

"Four or five miles."

"It's a hell of a cold day to be runnin' around dressed as light as that," he said.

"Yes," she said dully.

He turned his eyes from the road, watching her closely, shutting off the radio.

"Haven't ya got a coat?"

"No."

"That's a hell of a note." He pulled a bottle of whiskey from the side pocket of the car. "Have a drink. It'll warm ya."

"No, thanks."

He tipped the bottle to his mouth, driving with one hand, the cigar stuck between fat fingers. They rode in silence, the wind howling against the windshield, the man glancing often at the woman. She felt what he was going to say even before he said it:

"You're too damned pretty to be without a coat."

"Please," she murmured.

"O.K., sister. I only wanted to help ya out. I'm a guy that is frank. I put all my cards on the table. Why delay things? Get down to the facts is my motto. Now, I got a few bucks to throw around and I'd just as soon throw 'em on you as on some of them baby faced dumb-bells I know in Philly or New York." He lowered the window, tossed the cigar away, cleared his throat and spat upon the highway. "What kind of place is this Roxbury? How big is it?"

"About five thousand," she said. She wasn't listening to words, only hearing them and answering without thinking. Again she felt the water drenching her hands, saw the faint bubbles mingling with the tiny storm-rippled waves—so very faint with little of life to break the steady wind-struck evenness of the pond's surface. And when the bubbling stopped it seemed her hands had frozen and were no longer her own. But it wasn't the hands, or the cold, or the water. It was the heart within herself. That heart had begun to die with the first unnatural movement of the water, a thing not belonging to the pond and really not a part of it, and that heart had slowly continued to die until the last bubble—until the pond had served its purpose. And now it was completely dead and cold as the wind, the pond and the preciousness she had left in the pond. But despite the deadness the heart knew a great relief. Pride was an awful thing. It was all right for her to go hungry, but not him. Growing weaker day after day, crying for food. Well, he would never be hungry again. If you did not have to, it was better not to grow up in such a world, better to stop living before the world deprived you of what you really needed to live. If you were mature and had seen and been through some of it, and didn't have too much pride, you somehow lived until the end, but what chance had there been for him? Why should he have lived and suffered horribly from the beginning? If there was bravery why did it have to be continually applied in the small things of living?

The man was speaking again: "I can't understand how so many good looking girls are always in these tank towns. Now take yourself f'rinstance. You could be really a swell dresser. You got the body to carry clothes." He took another drink.

"I can walk the rest of the way," she said.

"Now don't get that way. I didn't mean to offend ya. That was a compliment. I know plenty of girls who would love to hear me say that about them."

"Then you tell it to them, mister."

"You're kinda touchy, sister. All small town girls ain't like that. Why, I met a girl back in—"

"For God's sake, mister, either shut up or let me out."

"Now don't get excited. We're almost there. But I'd like to buy ya a coat. I sure would!"

"I won't be needing a coat."

"Wait till the boys hear that one! A dame refusing to allow Old Hartley to buy her a coat!"

The lights of the town were like stars low to the earth. The woman saw the dome of the Cadwell Building. Six stories high, the pride of Roxbury. Carl had worked on that building: Assistant Chief Carpenter. The year since he had died seemed a lifetime.

Carl had built a lot of houses they were now passing—built them and lost them. At one time they had been happy and the people who lived in Carl's houses had been happy too. That time seemed so long ago. Carl would not blame her for what she had done on this day. They were both together now. Safe. Nothing could touch either of them. Carl had been a good man. Maybe the man beside her was good; perhaps he had only lived too long in cities. When her mind drifted from what she had just done, she knew he wouldn't tell the boys about her or about the coat, and if he did, he would not tell it exactly the same. She knew when men are together and they tell how they speak to women it is seldom as they reveal it. Men, even the coarse ones, are different with women and they speak differently, and whether the men are rough or gentle it is never like they tell it to each other.

They were now entering the suburbs. She knew where she was going when she left the car. There would never be that cold room to sleep in again. They could do what they wanted with her. They had not done anything when she really needed it. Now let them take care of her. Let them nourish that part of her which had not died with the heart, that unimportant part which all others saw.

"I wish you'd drive on to Baltimore with me," the man said. "We can make it in three hours. I'll buy ya everythin' from hats to shoes."

"I'll get out here."

The man grinned: "Someone'll miss ya if ya don't report, huh? Is that it?"

"No. No one will miss me. I'll get out here."

"All right, baby, but don't say I didn't warn ya. It'll be a lot colder than this when winter sets in." He looked at her.

"Will you please let me out," she said wearily.

"Right this minute, baby. Right this minute."

He drew the car to the curb and opened the door for her, speaking less harshly than before: "I like ya, sister. You're real nice, but you're all upset about somethin'. I hope ya didn't let me bother ya none." The liquor began talking. He was filled with his own importance, rashly generous and well-meaning: "To show ya what kind of a guy I am, I'll buy that coat right now and it won't cost ya one thing—I'll give it to ya."

She was on the street now, one hand clutching the opened door. "Don't be so damned good! To hell with your goodness. I'd have done it yesterday or this morning for less than what a coat cost!" She started to run up the street, sobbing, all the pain of weeks rushing to her eyes, shaking her body. She ran up the steps into the warm room, in front of the large desk. Through a mist she saw the blue uniform, the brightly polished buttons and silver shield. She began speaking hurriedly, jerkily, the words wrenched from her pulsing stomach. The blue-brass neatness raised a hand. She went on, insanely, unable to stop, wanting to get it all out of her. She saw the hand come downward, heard a bell ring. Another man entered the room, placing hands upon her shoulders. The hands were a soothing impact, his words effortless, bringing confidence. She continued, more calmly now, proud, her words uttered with great dignity, her body beautifully poised. The men became all order and attention. Pencils began to move. Words started to flow from each of them. . . . It seemed a long time until she was alone in the room built of iron and stone. She had been fed, Carl and his son were safe . . . and it was warm.

The New Anvil July-Aug. 1940

Daughter

ERSKINE CALDWELL

At sunrise a Negro on his way to the big house to feed the mules had taken the word to Colonel Henry Maxwell, and Colonel Henry 'phoned the sheriff. The sheriff had hustled Jim into town and locked him up in the jail, and then he went home and ate breakfast.

Jim walked around the empty cell-room while he was buttoning his shirt, and after that he sat down on the bunk and tied his shoelaces. Everything that morning had taken place so quickly that he had not even had time to get a drink of water. He got up and went to the water bucket near the door, but the sheriff had forgotten to put water in it.

By that time there were several men standing in the jail yard. Jim went to the window and looked out when he heard them talking. Just then another automobile drove up, and six or seven men got out. Other men were coming towards the jail from both directions of the street.

"What was the trouble out at your place this morning, Jim?" somebody said.

Jim stuck his chin between the bars and looked at the faces in the crowd. He knew everyone there.

While he was trying to figure out how everybody in town had heard about his being there, somebody else spoke to him.

"It must have been an accident, wasn't it, Jim?"

A colored boy hauling a load of cotton to the gin drove up the street. When the wagon got in front of the jail, the boy whipped up the mules with the ends of the reins and made them trot.

"I hate to see the State have a grudge against you, Jim," somebody said.

The sheriff came down the street swinging a tin dinner pail in his hand. He pushed thru the crowd, unlocked the door, and set the pail inside.

Several men came up behind the sheriff and looked over his shoulder into the jail.

"Here's your breakfast my wife fixed up for you, Jim. You'd better eat a little, Jim boy."

Jim looked at the pail, at the sheriff, at the open jail door, and Jim shook his head.

"I don't feel hungry," he said. "Daughter's been hungry, tho— awfully hungry."

The sheriff backed out the door, his hand going to the handle of his pistol. He backed out so quickly that he stepped on the toes of the men behind him.

"Now, don't get careless, Jim boy," he said. "Just sit and calm yourself."

He shut the door and locked it. After going a few steps towards the street he stopped and looked into the chamber of his pistol to make sure that it had been loaded.

The crowd outside the window pressed in closer. Some of the men rapped on the bars until Jim came and looked out. When he saw them, he stuck his chin between the iron and gripped his hands around it.

"How come it to happen, Jim?" somebody asked "It must have been an accident, wasn't it?"

Jim's long thin face looked as if it would come thru the bars. The sheriff came up to the window to see if everything was all right.

"Now, just take it easy, Jim boy," he said.

The man who had asked Jim to tell what had happened, elbowed the sheriff out of the way. The other men crowded closer.

"How come, Jim?" he said. "Was it an accident?"

"No," Jim said, his fingers twisting about the bars. "I picked up the shotgun and done it."

The sheriff pushed towards the window again.

"Go on, Jim, and tell us what it's all about."

Jim's face squeezed between the bars until it looked as tho only his ears kept his head from coming thru.

"Daughter said she was hungry, and I just couldn't stand it no longer. I just couldn't stand to hear her say it."

"Don't get all excited now, Jim boy," the sheriff said, pushing forward one moment and being elbowed away the next.

"She waked up in the middle of the night again and said she was hungry. I just couldn't stand to hear her say it."

Somebody pushed all the way thru the crowd until he got to the window.

"Why, Jim, you could have come and asked me for something

for her to eat, and you know I'd have given you all I got in the world."

The sheriff pushed forward once more.

"That wasn't the right thing to do," Jim said. "I've been working all year and I made enough for all of us to eat."

He stopped and looked down into the faces on the other side of the bars.

"I made enough working on shares, but they came and took it all away from me. I couldn't go around begging after I'd made enough to keep us. They just came and took it all off. Then daughter woke up again this morning saying she was hungry, and I just couldn't stand it no longer."

"You'd better go and get on the bunk now, Jim boy," the sheriff said.

"It don't seem right that the little girl ought to be shot like that, Jim," somebody said.

"Daughter said she was hungry," Jim said. "She'd been saying that for all of the past month. Daughter'd wake up in the middle of the night and say it. I just couldn't stand it no longer."

"You ought to have sent her over to my house, Jim. Me and my wife could have fed her somehow. It don't look right to kill a little girl like her."

"I'd made enough for all of us," Jim said. "I just couldn't stand it no longer. Daughter'd been hungry all the past month."

"Take it easy, Jim boy," the sheriff said, trying to push forward.

The crowd swayed from one side to the other.

"And so you just picked up the gun this morning and shot her?" somebody said.

"When she woke up again this morning saying she was hungry, I just couldn't stand it."

The crowd pushed closer. Men were coming towards the jail from all directions, and those who were then arriving pushed forward to hear what Jim had to say.

"The State has got a grudge against you now, Jim," somebody said, "but somehow it don't seem right."

"I can't help it," Jim said. "Daughter woke up again this morning that way."

The jail yard, the street, and the vacant lot on the other side was filled with men and boys. All of them were pushing forward to hear Jim. Word had spread all over town by that time that Jim Carlisle had shot and killed his eight-year-old daughter, Clara.

"Who does Jim share-crop for?" somebody asked.

"Colonel Henry Maxwell," a man in the crowd said. "Colonel Henry has had Jim out there about nine or ten years."

"Henry Maxwell didn't have no business coming and taking all the shares. He's got plenty of his own. It ain't right for Henry Maxwell to come and take Jim's, too."

The sheriff was pushing forward once more.

"The State's got a grudge against Jim now," somebody said. "Somehow it don't seem right, tho."

The sheriff pushed his shoulder between the crowd of men and worked his way in closer.

A man shoved the sheriff away.

"Why did Henry Maxwell come and take your share of the crop, Jim?"

"He said I owed it to him because one of his mules died a month ago."

The sheriff got in front of the barred window.

"You ought to go to the bunk now and rest some, Jim boy," he said. "Take off your shoes and stretch out, Jim boy."

He was elbowed out of the way.

"You didn't kill the mule, did you, Jim?"

"The mule dropped dead in the barn," Jim said. "I wasn't nowhere around. It just dropped dead."

The crowd was pushing harder. The men in front were jammed against the jail, and the men behind were trying to get within earshot. Those in the middle were squeezed against each other so tightly they could not move in any direction. Everyone was talking louder.

Jim's face pressed between the bars and his fingers gripped the iron until the knuckles were white.

The milling crowd was moving across the street to the vacant lot. Somebody was shouting. He climbed up on an automobile and began swearing at the top of his lungs.

A man in the middle of the crowd pushed his way out and went to his automobile. He got in and drove off alone.

Jim stood holding to the bars and looking thru the window. The sheriff had his back to the crowd, and he said something to Jim. Jim did not hear what he said.

A man on his way to the gin with a load of cotton stopped to find out what the trouble was. He looked at the crowd in the vacant lot for a moment, and then he turned and looked at Jim behind the bars. The shouting across the street was growing louder.

"What's the trouble, Jim?"

Somebody on the other side of the street came to the wagon. He put his foot on a spoke in the wagon wheel and looked up at the man on the cotton while he talked.

"Daughter woke up this morning again saying she was hungry," Jim said.

The sheriff was the only person who heard him.

The man on the load of cotton jumped to the ground, tied the reins to the wagon wheel, and pushed thru the crowd to the car where all the swearing was being done. After listening for awhile, he came back to the street, called a Negro who was standing with the other colored men on the corner, and handed him the reins. The Negro drove off with the cotton towards the gin, and the man went back into the crowd.

Just then the man who had driven off alone in his car came back. He sat for a moment under the steering wheel, and then he opened the door and jumped to the ground. He opened the rear door and took out a crowbar as long as he was tall.

"Pry that jail door open and let Jim out," somebody said. "It ain't right for him to be in there."

The crowd in the vacant lot was moving again. The man who had been standing on top of the automobile jumped to the ground, and the men moved towards the street in the direction of the jail.

The first man to reach it jerked the six-foot crowbar out of the soft earth where it had been jabbed.

The sheriff backed off.

"Now, take it easy, Jim boy," he said.

He turned and started walking rapidly up the street towards his house.

The Anvil Nov.-Dec. 1933

Blue Boy

ERSKINE CALDWELL

Two hours after dinner they were still sitting in the air-tight over-heated parlor. A dull haze of tobacco smoke was packed in layers from the table-top to the ceiling, and around the chairs hovered the smell of dried perspiration, intestinal belches, and stale perfume. The New Year's Day turkey-and-hog dinner had made the women droopy and dull-eyed; the men were stretched out in their chairs with their legs uncrossed and their heads thrown back, appearing as if around each swollen belly a hundred feet of stuffed sausage-casing had been wound.

Grady Walters sat up, rubbed his red-veined face, and looked at his guests. After a while he went to the door and called for one of his Negro servants. He sent the Negro on the run for Blue Boy.

After he had closed the door tightly, Grady walked back towards his chair, looking at the drowsy men and women through the haze of blue tobacco smoke and stale perfume. It had been more than an hour since anyone had felt like saying anything.

"What time of day is it getting to be, Grady?" Jim Howard asked, rubbing first his eyes and then his belly.

"Time to have a little fun," Grady said.

Blue Boy came through the back door and shuffled down the hall to the parlor where the people were. He dragged his feet sideways over the floor, making a sound like soybeans being poured into a wooden barrel.

"We been waiting all afternoon for you to come in here and show the folks some fun, Blue Boy," Grady said. "All my visitors are just itching to laugh. Reckon you can make them shake their sides, Blue Boy?"

Blue Boy grinned at the roomful of men and women. He dug his hands into his overalls pockets and made some kind of unintelligible sound in his throat.

Jim Howard asked Grady what Blue Boy could do. Several of the women sat up and began rubbing powder into the pores of their skin.

The colored boy grinned some more, stretching his neck in a semi-circle.

"Blue Boy," Grady said, "show these white folks how you caught that shoat the other day and bit him to death. Go on, Blue Boy! Let's see how you chewed that shoat to death with your teeth."

For several moments the boy's lips moved like eyelids a-flutter, and he made a dash for the door. Grady caught him by the shoulder and tossed him back into the center of the room.

"All right, Blue Boy," Grady shouted at him. "Do what I told you. Show the white folks how you bit that pig to death."

Blue Boy made deeper sounds in his throat. What he said sounded more unintelligible than Gullah. Nobody but Grady could understand what he was trying to say.

"It don't make no difference if you ain't got a shoat here to kill," Grady answered him. "Go on and show the white folks how you killed one the other day for me."

Blue Boy dropped on his hands and knees, making sounds as if he were trying to protest. Grady nudged him with his foot, prodding him on.

The Negro boy suddenly began to snarl and bite, acting as if he himself had been turned into a snarling biting shoat. He grabbed into the air, throwing his arms around an imaginary young hog, and began to tear its throat with his sharp white teeth. The Howards and Hannafords crowded closer, trying to see the semi-idiot go through the actions of a blood-thirsty maniac.

Down on the floor, Blue Boy's face was contorted and swollen. His eyes glistened, and his mouth drooled. He was doing all he could to please Grady Walters.

When he had finished, the Howards and Hannafords fell back, fanning their faces and wiping the backs of their hands with their handkerchiefs. Even Grady fanned his flushed face when Blue Boy stopped and rolled over on the floor exhausted.

"What else can he do, Grady?" the youngest of the Hannaford women asked.

"Anything I tell him to do," Grady said. "I've got Blue Boy trained. He does whatever I tell him."

They looked down at the small, thin, blue-skinned, seventeen-year-old Negro on the floor. His clothes were ragged, and his thick kinky hair was almost as long as a Negress'. He looked the same, except in size, as he did the day twelve years before, when Grady brought him to the big house from one of the share-croppers' cabins. Blue Boy had never become violent, and he obeyed every word of Grady's. Grady had taught him to do tricks as he would instruct a young puppy to roll over on his back when bidden. Blue Boy always obeyed, but even then he was not quick enough to suit Grady sometimes, and it was then that Grady flew into him with the leather belly-band that hung on a nail on the back porch.

The Howards and Hannafords had sat down again, but the Negro boy still lay on the floor. Grady had not told him to get up.

"What's wrong with him, Grady?" Jim Howard asked.

"He ain't got a grain of sense," Grady said, laughing a little. "See how he grins all the time? A calf is born with more sense than he's got right now."

"Why don't you send him to the insane asylum, then?"

"What for?" Grady said. "He's more fun around here than a barrel of monkeys. I figure he's worth keeping just for the hell of it. If I sent him off to the asylum, I'd miss my good times with him. I wouldn't take a hundred dollars for him."

"What else can he do?" Henry Hannaford asked.

"I'll show you," Grady said. "Here, Blue Boy, get up and do that monkey shine dance for the white folks. Show them what you can do with your feet."

Blue Boy got up, pushing himself erect with hands and feet. He stood grinning for a while at the men and women in a circle around him.

"Go on, Blue Boy, shake your feet for the white folks," Grady told him, pointing at Blue Boy's feet. "Do the monkey shine, Blue Boy."

The boy began to shuffle his shoes on the floor, barely raising them off the surface. Grady started tapping his feet, moving them faster and faster all the time. Blue Boy watched him, and after a while his own feet began going faster. He kept it up until he was dancing so fast his breath began to give out. His eyes were swelling, and it looked as if his balls would pop out of his head any moment. The arteries in his neck got larger and rounder.

"That nigger can do the monkey shine better than any nigger I ever saw," Henry Hannaford said.

Blue Boy sank into a heap on the floor, the arteries in his neck pumping and swelling until some of the women in the room covered their faces to keep from seeing them.

It did not take Blue Boy long to get his wind back, but he still lay on the floor. Grady watched him until he thought he had recovered enough to stand up again.

"What else can your trained nigger do, Grady?" Jim Howard

said. "Looks like you would have learned him a heap of tricks in ten or twelve years' time."

"If it wasn't getting so late in the day, I'd tell him to do all he knows," Grady said. "I'll let him do one more, anyway."

Blue Boy had not moved on the floor.

"Get up, Blue Boy," Grady said, "Get up on your feet and stand up."

Blue Boy got up grinning. His head turned once more on his rubbery neck, stretching in a semi-circle around the room. He grinned at the white faces about him.

"Take out that black snake and whip it to a frazzle," Grady told him. "Take it out, Blue Boy, and show the white folks what you can do."

Blue Boy grinned, stretching his rubbery neck until it looked as if it would come loose from his body.

"What's he going to do now, Grady?" Jim Howard asked.

"You just wait and see, Jim," Grady said. "All right, Blue Boy, do like I said. Whip that black snake."

The youngest Hannaford woman giggled. Blue Boy stopped and stared at her with his round white eyeballs. He grinned until Grady prodded him on.

"Now, I reckon you folks know why I don't send him off to the insane asylum," Grady said. "I have a heap more fun out of Blue Boy than I would with anything else you can think of. He can't hoe cotton, or pick it, and he even hasn't got enough sense to chop a piece of stove wood, but he makes up all that by learning the tricks I teach him."

Once more Blue Boy's eyes began to pop in the sockets of his skull, and the arteries in his neck began to pump and swell. He dropped to his knees and his once rubbery neck was as rigid as a table leg. The grinning lines on his face had congealed into whelp-like scars. The Howards and Hannafords, who had come from five counties to eat Grady's turkey-and-hog dinner, gulped and wheezed at the sight of Blue Boy. He began to droop like a wilting stalk of pigweed. Then he fell from his knees.

With his face pressed against the splintery floor, the grooves in his cheeks began to soften, and his grinning features glistened in the drying perspiration. His breathing became inaudible, and the swollen arteries in his neck were as rigid as taut-drawn rope.

The Anvil April-May 1935

Down in Happy Hollow

JACK CONROY

In Happy Hollow and on the hills encircling it the trees with tall, straight boles had been cut long ago for mine props and timber. Some of them had been hewed into railroad ties. The second growth of hickory and scrub oak grew as thick as the hair on a dog's back, and Leo and Robert found it a fine place to play hide-and-seek and redskin and cowboy. A corduroy road made of oak and elm poles, with the bark on, wound through the hollow, first on one side of the creek then on the other. Coal wagons from the drift mines down the hollow and the smaller hollows branching from Happy Hollow creaked along the road, the drivers cursing and lashing their teams, the horses' shoes ringing loudly on the tough wood of the road. Leo and Robert liked to pretend that the coal wagons were wagon trains crossing the prairie, with the boys in the role of bloody savages lying in ambush on the hills. They skulked from tree to tree, sometimes shying stones at the drivers, who swore thunderously and shook their blacksnake whips.

It was in Happy Hollow that Robert and Leo first saw Monty Cass, the Murderer.

Splashing down the creek with their breeches rolled high, the rank-smelling blue mud of the bottom squirting up between their toes and staining the water, they found Monty kneeling by the side of the stream prodding a dry land terrapin with a stick. The terrapin had drawn its feet and legs beneath its shell.

"Derned critter won't crawl fer love or money when it knows you want it to," Monty told the boys disgustedly. "Some way 'r other, it tickles me like all get-out t' see one o' them scoundrels take out a-crawlin' and a-stretchin' his neck."

He gave up his teasing of the terrapin, and rose to his feet. At one time he had been a tall man, but a mine accident had caved his chest in, stooped his shoulders, and raised a hump on his back. He spoke in wheezing gasps, his voice dying in a metallic rasping. He had the long, lean face, straight nose and protruding ears of the farmers thereabout, descendants of the pioneers, but there were blue lumps under the skin on his face where sharp chips of coal had burrowed. Many of the farmers in the vicinity opened small "drift" mines, dug horizontally under the hills, in the winter after the heavy work of harvesting was over. These dilettantes were bitterly hated by the miners who had no other source of income—Irish, Italian and Polish interlopers, overflow from the mines of Pennsylvania and Illinois.

A forelock of Monty's heavy, graying hair dropped persistently over his right eye. He had a habit, when preoccupied, of thrusting the end of his forelock behind his ear.

The boys splashed down the creek, while Monty trotted along the bank, eyeing them brightly and slyly.

"Come down t' the shack, boys. I'll show you a real live horsehair snake, longest and fullest o' life I ever seed."

Leo and Robert had often heard it said that a horsehair, left in water when the signs of the Zodiac were auspicious, would, after a certain period, become a snake. The boys were anxious to find out the truth or falsity of the assertion.

Monty led them down an abandoned road that ran up a ravine. Saplings as thick as a broomstick had grown up in the center, and the ruts, worn by the heavy wheels of coal wagons, were filling with the fallen and rotten leaves of autumn after autumn. Monty climbed a blue slag heap before the timbered mouth of a "slope" mine. "Watch y' selfs!" he cautioned. In some places fire was eating under the crust of slag, and a leg plunging into it would be badly burned before it could be withdrawn. The heavy scent of sulphur and a dank wind from the mouth of the "slope" smote the boys as they reached the summit of the slag heap. The blacksmith shanty was standing, and Monty paused beside the door, waiting for the boys.

"Come in and make yerselfs at home," he invited.

Inside, the rusty anvil was being used for a seat, and a rude table had been built of unplaned oak boards. Pans and a skillet depended from nails hammered in the wall, and a small cot with a corn shuck mattress filled one end of the shack. The boys sat down on the cot, and the shucks rustled harshly. Monty turned to a corner and began searching in a heap of rusty picks and tin cans.

"Well, I declare!" exclaimed Monty, trying to look astonished. "Reckon when I pitched that pick I was a-sharpenin' over here yestiddy I busted the jar and let the water out offen the snake. 'Twas jist as lively as a chipmunk, and here 'tis dead as a mackeral, stiff as a board." He picked up an ordinary horsehair beside a broken fruit jar and regarded it ruefully.

"Never was no snake in the first place. I wasn't born yesterday," jeered Leo. He was fifteen now, and had learned a few things. "Come on, Bob, let's go," Leo said.

"Wait! Wait!" begged Monty, grinning sheepishly. "Reckon that's a hoss on *me!* Sure, I'll own up, it was only a snide about the horsehair snake. I ast everbody that come this way fer a month, and you two's the first one t' even feel cur'ous t' come and take a peep. It was wantin' somebody t' talk to, mainly. About the man I killed. I killed a man. I ain't braggin' about it, no more am I sorry. I mean I'm sorry I had t' kill him, but I had to. Wa'n't no way out o' it. If 'twas t' do over, I'd do the same. But I wish t' the good Lord it had never happened."

The words poured from him in a torrent, as though he wanted to say as much as he could before the boys ran away, as though he was accustomed to seeing people run away before he had his say.

"Don't be a-skeered o' me boys! Fer Jesus sake, amen! I wouldn't no more harm any hair on yer head no more than I would my poor old mother's. Won't you set a while and leave me talk t' you? I'll tell you where t' find a den of polecats where you c'n lay in a bush and watch 'em friskin' around like kittens. Ain't *nothin'* on God's green earth purtier 'n a baby polecat, ain't nothin' more cunnin' and full o' ginger. This is gospel from now on, I'll swear on a stack o' bibles high as any white oak. . . ."

The boys had started to their feet and were edging uneasily toward the door. Monty paused for breath, and picked up two powder cans, setting them side by side.

"Set down! Set down!" he urged. He feverishly poked his fore-lock behind his ear, only to have it fall limply over his eye again. The boys were afraid to refuse, and sat stiffly on the kegs, peering furtively at their feet to see whether the madman had a fuse at-tached to blow them to kingdom come.

"Got t' get it straight in my own noggin," began Monty, flinging his leg over the anvil and resting his hip against the horn. "I go around talkin' t' myself about it, and that's why folks thinks I've got bats in my belfry. When I seed Jess Gotts a-laying there breathin' his last, with my pick buried in his head, and the red blood and grey brains blubberin' out o' his skull, I was sure heartsick and sorry. Hearin' his wife and kid hollerin' and scream-in' didn't help none either. That was back in the days when the union was stronger, before they busted it with the gun-totin' dep-pities from St. Louis and chased the organizers clean out o' these hollers. If the union hadn't been so strong, I'd of got my neck stretched or life in the pen. The jury had some union men on it, and I got off with twenty-five years. I was a model prisoner, and inside o' twelve years, back I come. But sometimes I wisht they had stretched my neck in the first place. They blackballed me in all the tipple mines, and nobody don't want me a'workin' even in their dog holes where you got t' wiggle back t' the face like a snake crawlin' on his belly. I start a slope o' my own ever' fall, but I hate t' go t' town, people always makin' hard and cur'ous eyes at me. So I don't sell much coal, but it don't take much fer me t' live when I c'n put up wild blackberries an' raise a little garden and a hog 'r two fer my meat.

"It's the lonesomeness hurts me most. I took a notion t' go into Green Valley one night and see one o' these here movie pitchers. 'Twas 'bout a murderer, and he was allers a-bein' haanted by the ghost o' the man he killed, and he was allers a-seein' 'Thou Shalt Not Kill' spelled out right in front of 'im. I been imaginin' things sence, and danged if I don't see them words a-spellin' out against the trees on yan hill or in the crick when I'm a-fishin'. Heer'd somebody a-prowlin' around here at night, and took a shot to'rds 'em. Somethin' squealed like a rabbit, and I've 'lowed sence, it might've been that wild girl, Anna Leischer, that lives up Butler Holler. Her father, that blasphemin' old Dutchman, he leaves 'er go anywheres she wants and she roams at night more 'n day time.

"She used t' sashay around that hill there, and tease me. I had most forgot about women, but I got t' studyin' how nice it would be t' get 'er in the shack here. I offered 'er all kinds of purties, but she only laughed and shied puff balls at me. I got along ver' well without even thinkin' what a woman was like till she got t' horsin' around.

"I was right in killin' Jess because he was a scab. The way the miners has been treated sence the union was busted w'd make even a blind man see that. Scabs take the bread and butter from the mouths o' widders and orphans. So they got t' be fought.

"Nobody can't say I aimed t' kill Jess when he tried t' pass the picket line that mornin'. I only wanted t' keep him away.

" 'Jess, don't go! Jess, be a white man!' I coaxed 'im as nice as I knew how. I had been a-strikin' three weeks, and purty ga'nt under the belt. I had a wife and a kid then, as happy a home as ever you clapped your eyes on. They dusted out when I was sent up t' the pen; God knows where they are or what a pass they've come to.

" 'Jess, don't stick no knife in yer brothers' back,' I pled as pitiful as I c'd, willin' and anxious t' do anything or say anything, t' touch his heart and cause him t' dump the water out o' his water deck and turn back from the tipple.

"What I'll allers stick to long as the breath o' life's in me is that it wasn't Monty Cass hittin' Jess Gotts with a pick; it was a union man hittin' a scab, and such things 's got t' be. I brang the pick along mostly t' skeer the scabs, but never aimed t' hit one with it. Leastaways, not the sharp end of it.

"When he wouldn't lis'en to me, and walked off to'rds the mine, I run after 'im and hit 'im. It sure was a horrible feelin' in my arm, in my head and in my stummick when I felt the pick point dig right into his brain.

"I stood right there while they fetched his woman and kid, and them a-pawin' and a-sobbin' over 'im and I never felt much sorry till that.

"If I could dust out o' here som'eres t' where the union is still alive and strong, it wouldn't be so bad. But seems like I took roots here in this holler, seems like this is where I'll cash in my chips."

"Let's not go past Monty's," Leo said two weeks later as the two boys made their way down the hollow. "He'll nail us again and talk our heads off."

They had seen Monty several times since their first encounter with him, and each time he had managed to hold them for an hour or so. They skirted the hill opposite Monty's ravine. They heard and felt the dull rumble of a blast under their feet as they descended toward the corduroy road.

"Somebody under here. Maybe it's Davy and the goblins," said Robert who was always trying to invest every situation with romance garnered from fairy stories.

"Maybe. More likely somebody tryin' to get a few more chunks of coal out of the hill. Been a dozen mines in it a'ready."

They were dismayed to see Monty leaning against a mining car at the foot of the hill and drinking in noisy gulps from a tin syrup bucket. He had taken possession of an old, presumably worked-out, slope mine this time, and was trying to clean up the fallen rocks and dirt, bale out the water, and replace the rotten timbers with sound ones. A large shepherd dog stood nearby, barking excitedly at the mouth of the mine.

"He ain't used t' hearin' the shots," Monty explained, as he took the bucket from his face and wiped his mouth with the sleeve of his overall jacket. "Boy! I struck it rich this time for true. Rover here run a rabbit back in this old slope, and I followed back there. A four-foot vein o' the purtiest coal ever laid under these hills, and I seen a world of it. Don't know why the devil and

Tom Walker somebody give it up, but that's not my funeral.
Don't even hafta pay any royalty! This land belongs t' the Jones
heirs, and they ain't been seen or heerd of in these parts for years.
They 'lowed all the coal was gone offen their land, and it's so
poor a rabbit has to pack his lunch t' get acrost it."

He sat down and poked his forelock behind his ear time and
again. His shirt was open, and Robert saw his caved-in chest with
the cruel weals across it. It always made him sick. Monty wiped
the sweat off his face, and fanned himself with his miner's cap.
His lardoil torch smoked close to the entrance of the slope. In
high humor, he sang:

> *"Oh, I eat when I'm hungry,*
> *And I drink when I'm dry;*
> *If a tree don't fall on me,*
> *I'll live till I die!"*

"I jist put in a shot. Coal'll be a little red for a load 'r two, but
back there a few feet it'll be black as a crow and burn like a pine
knot. Soon's the smoke clears out a mite, I'm goin' back there t'
see what the shot's done. 'Fraid I set it a little toein'. Can't allers
tell jist *how* coal 'll shoot. No two pieces of coal shoots alike; it's
a God's fact."

"Can we go back too?" asked Leo. The boys had never been
to the face of the coal in any of the slopes, though they had
crawled inside the mouth to the gate set across the rails to keep
intruders out. Sometimes rocks fell with splashing noises in water
far back in the mine, and the boys ran out to the sunlight, making
a bright square of the mouth, with their hearts thumping. Icy
drops of yellow sulphur water were distilled on the poles that
timbered the roof, and the boys winced when globules trickled
onto their heads and down their necks.

"No, better not, I ain't afraid fer myself. I've worked in the
mines, man and boy, fer thirty odd years. But if somethin' sh'd
happen t' a greenhorn, I'd feel t 'blame. I do aim t' take you back,
boys, soon 's I git 'er in applepie shape. Looks like the smoke's
cleared out considerable. I'll jist ease back and see how the land
lays."

He shook his lard-oil torch till the flame brightened. The boys
watched the light recede into the mine like a fading star, heard
Monty's hobs ring on the rails, then a faint shout of exultation:
"Boy! purtiest shootin' coal I've seen in a month o' Sundays.
Knocked some o' the props loose, tho. . . ."

His voice ascended to a terrified yell, and the light died suddenly. A mighty whoosh of cold and foul air rushed out of the mine and set the leaves a-trembling on bushes for a hundred feet around. At the same time there was a tremendous rumbling and grinding and the staccato cracking of timbers.

"God a'mighty! He's buried!" Leo shouted.

A weak moaning could be heard after the noise of the cave-in subsided. Clouds of dust were belching from the mouth of the mine.

"He's still alive! Run like hell for help. I'll go back and see if I can help him any," Leo told Robert. "Run on, you little fool! Are you paralyzed? For Christ's sake!" Leo gave Robert a shove that sent him running mechanically down the slag heap, then ran inside the tool shed to look for a torch. He found one, and some matches in a tobacco tin.

The torch shed a wan light, and Leo felt along cautiously with his feet. It seemed to him that his feet were detached from his head and acting independently. His shins struck against the rails and the ends of the cross ties.

When he reached the cave-in, he saw that the whole passageway was blocked and daylight was filtering through the dust motes in the air. The roof had caved in to the grass roots. Leo shouted Monty's name, and heard a muffled answer, but it was hard to tell its direction. The shepherd bounded down the slope, his bark booming and echoing. He sniffed beneath the edge of a huge rock and began barking more loudly. Leo knelt and saw Monty's wild eyes shining beneath the rock. He was so frightened that he dropped the torch and it was sputtering out when he righted it just in time.

"It was a union man killin' a scab, not Monty Cass stickin 'a pick in Jess Gotts' head and makin' a widow and an orphan. People oughter see it thataway," Monty wheezed painfully. "I can see you, boy! Don't leave me alone! Scoot me some water back here. You c'n do it in the deck o' my dinner pail, over by the wall. It's pressin' closer, squshin' me right in the muck same 's a man would mash a worm under his feet."

Leo tried to pass the water deck of Monty's dinner pail under the rock, but there was not room. He seized a rock and bent down the edges. Blood was gushing from Monty's mouth and nose, and it splashed in the water, dyeing it red, before he could gulp a swallow. He did not notice, and plucked avidly at the water with his lips. He could not move his head or use his hands to tilt the deck.

"Might get a prop—Might ease up on me if you c'n get a prise under the aidge," gurgled Monty. "I been in most as bad scrapes and got out. When I got my chest caved in. . . . God A'mighty, Son o' God, Jesus! If you got mercy like preachers claims, lift yer million-ton foot offen me and let me breathe!"

The shepherd climbed up the heap and barked at the daylight. Leo called sharply for him to come down. It didn't seem right for the dog to be jumping on the heap that covered Monty. Like as if that little extra weight would make any difference. I must be going crazy, thought Leo.

He found a long prop, but didn't understand just how to use it. He was afraid that Monty was getting out of his head.

"Some folks don't understand union principles. In them days it was a fight fer more props and better air, fer wash houses so's a man c'd scrub some o' the black offen him before startin' home. . . . I didn't kill you, Jess Gotts; I killed a scab. That's different. . . ."

"Here's the prop. You hear me? Here's the prop. But I don't know how to use it. Can you hear me?"

"Sure I kin. Get a good bite under the aidge. I mean stick it back fur 'nough so's the aidge won't break off, but not too far. Then raise it up purty high and stick a chock fer a heel under the prop fur back as it 'll go. Hardest rock 'r wood you kin find fer a heel. Then heave all you got on the fur end. If you might prise it up jist a *little,* ease it offen me so 's I c'd breathe, then fetch help."

Leo found a billet of oak wood for a heel, selected a thick part of the rock, and threw all his weight on the end of the prop. To his joy, the rock slowly lifted five or six inches.

"Doin' good! Doin' good! Keep it up!" Monty called.

Leo felt himself lifted and hurled through the air like a stone from a sling. He thudded against the heap, and saw the prop cocked in the air before him, the edge of the rock skinning down the bark. When he leaped down the rock had settled so low that he could not even see underneath.

"Oh, God! He's a goner! I killed him!" Leo yelled to himself. He ran frantically around the heap and noticed something he had not seen before. Monty's foot and ankle were protruding. What if I could yank him out? thought Leo, grabbing the foot. It wobbled loosely on the ankle and the gritting of bones sickened Leo. As he lifted Monty's foot, dark blood poured out of the shoe.

It was Leo's first grim contact with the violent aspects of a world he knew he was destined to share. He was cut out for it; had never learned much at school. He belonged with those men who had their fingers clipped off by whirling saws in the sawmill where his father worked, with trainmen roasted and scalded in the telescoped debris of train wrecks. Violence, death, backbreak.

He lay back and began sobbing, but stopped when he heard the rescue party stumbling down the slope. Little Robert had been afraid to come inside with them.

The Anvil March-April 1935

A Good Recommendation

PAUL F. COREY

It was the middle of May and the directory was supposed to go to press in about two weeks. I was the third supervisor on this new system of directory compilation—the stencil system.

All the changes in names and addresses, and the listing of new subscribers were stamped on metal plates like those made for addressograph machines. Every evening the plates embossed for the day were run through a machine which stamped the listings on a long roll of paper. This was sent to the printer.

There were only three supervisors on the directory crew. We had charge of forty-one girls doing the work.

I always got to my desk about ten minutes of nine and scattered my papers about so that I was ready to go to work as soon as the bell rang. Those few minutes before nine o'clock I usually spent looking out our tenth story window above North River.

It was nice and clear that morning. I could see almost to the Forty-second Street Ferry. I watched the ferry boats cross and re-cross, bringing people to work in Manhattan; then I counted the big ships docked along the east side of the channel. About three minutes to the hour a big four-funneled liner came slowly up the stream. It seemed to fill the whole river.

Some of the girls were gossiping at a desk near mine, and I overheard one of them say: "Look! There's a liner."

"That's the Mauretania."

It was Miss Maloney who answered. I could tell by her brogue. She was just over from Ireland six months and still read the "Incoming and Outgoing Ships" every morning.

"It's supposed to dock at nine-thirty," I heard her explain.

It was certainly a swell looking boat, but I don't think I'd care to travel on it. I don't care much about going out on the ocean. They say those boats are as safe as a hotel, but I think I'd prefer land under my feet.

Someday I would like to make the Bear Mountain excursion on the Hudson River Day line. I believe in seeing this country. A lot of people go abroad and travel all over Europe and don't know they've got nice places to see in America. There's lots of good scenery in this country. I'd like to go out to California sometime. I've always wanted to see redwood trees and Yosemite Valley. And there's Yellowstone National Park, I'd like to see that some time.

I got to thinking about traveling that morning. I thought I might be able to someday because I was buying stock in the company and after ten or fifteen years I would have enough laid by to take a little vacation.

Then I began to wonder if my wife was enjoying herself in Poughkeepsie, visiting Mable. I didn't get a letter from her in the morning mail. But I figured there would probably be one waiting for me when I got home in the evening.

The bell rang and I gave a look about the office to see if all the girls were in their units and settling down to work. Mr. Smedley, the second supervisor, was at his desk. He nodded good morning to me and I nodded back. I liked Smedley. He always seemed like a good egg.

Miss Martin was standing by her desk talking with Miss Steuben, the query unit head.

Evelyn Martin was one of the best query clerks we had. She was wearing a pale green dress that made her look slender and pretty. She seemed excited about something.

I made up my mind to ask her to go to dinner with me that evening if I got a chance. I thumbed through a bunch of orders, then got up and went over to where the two were talking.

"How're the 'queries' this morning?" I asked.

"We're way behind," Eve said. "Those girls out on the card rack take weeks to check the order numbers."

"What's the matter with the girls out there?" I asked Miss Steuben.

"They have to check three times and the last check should be against the stencil," she said. "The third time is a duplication of the second check."

"I'll talk to Mr. Smedley about making a change in the routine," I said, and Miss Steuben went back to her desk. "What's the matter with that order?" I asked Eve, snapping the corner of the paper she held in her hand.

"Can't find the 'A' order," she said. "I've got the original, and a 'B' order and there has to be an 'A' order before a 'B' can be issued, and I can't find it. There ain't any record of it in any of the offices."

She sounded like she was about to cry.

"Give it to me," I said. "I've got the answers to a lot of queries like that on my desk. I'll fix it for you."

"Thanks loads," she said and smiled.

She was awfully pretty when she smiled.

"Say, will you go out to dinner with me tonight?" I said. "I know where there's a swell speakeasy. We'll go to a movie afterwards."

"This is so sudden," she said.

"That doesn't make any difference."

"But I'm not dressed for it or anything."

"That doesn't make any difference," I said again. "That's an awfully pretty dress you got on now."

"It's several years old."

"I don't care," I snapped. I didn't like the way she kept stalling. "You look good enough for me."

"I can't tonight," she said. "Some other night."

"I want you to go tonight."

She could have gone just as well as not. She was just stalling so that I would have to stand there and argue. But I don't do that anymore.

"I can't," she said again.

"All right!" I snapped and walked back to my desk.

Before I was out of earshot I heard Mrs. Larkin, the other query clerk, say: "There, you've made Mr. Dodd mad."

I wouldn't ask her again. I made up my mind to that. A woman only got one invitation from me. Anyway, my wife was coming home the next day.

Later on in the morning I talked the question of duplication in checking over with Mr. Smedley and we went out and discussed the matter with Mr. Bruce, the first supervisor. About eleven-thirty we reached a decision to eliminate one of the checks.

By that time I had forgotten all about Eve and my asking her to go to dinner with me. She kept watching me out of the corner of her eye all morning and was awfully nice to me every time we had to talk about anything in the work. But I was through with her. I only ask a girl to go out with me once.

In the afternoon I said to Mr. Smedley, "This book is supposed to go to press in two weeks' time and we won't be anywhere near ready. It'll be a month before the last stuff can go to the printer. Orders come in here and aren't set on the stencils for ten days. That ain't right." I had got an idea for a change and I was going to the mat with it. "An order that comes in here in the morning should be through the works and on the stencil by night," I said.

He agreed with that all right. Then I said: "Now the holdup comes in Miss Steuben's unit. She's a good query clerk but as manager of the editors she's a flop. That unit is too large, anyway. I think we should split the unit and put Miss Steuben in charge of the query clerks only. Both Miss Martin and Mrs. Larkin will do better work then and we'll make Miss Dillingham head editor. In that way we can push both sides faster and bring the routine up to schedule."

Mr. Smedley wouldn't hear of such a change. He argued every possible way against it, and finally I gave up fighting with him. I didn't much care if the book got to press on time or not, only it seemed to me that I saw the way it should be done.

Well, May dragged past and we didn't go to press. The publication date was set ahead two weeks. I was scheduled for one week of my vacation the last part of June, up to and including the Fourth of July. I talked to Mr. Bruce about it.

"We'll be right in the middle of press time," I said. "If you want me to put off my vacation until it's over I'm willing."

"Never mind," he told me. "We'll probably be later than that anyway. Mr. Smedley and I can handle the work."

"I'll put off my week until later," I said again. I didn't want them to feel that I was shirking.

"No," Mr. Bruce said. "Everything will be all right. Don't worry about it."

So when the end of June came along I went up to the country for my week. My wife was over in Jersey visiting her folks. We thought I'd get more rest if we weren't together. I didn't like being in the country very much. The house was old and spongy. It belonged to a friend of ours. He loaned it to me for the week. I had to do all my own cooking. Toward the end of the week I got awfully tired of bacon and eggs.

It was lonesome. There were so few people about. My nearest neighbors were a family of Italians. They lived about a block down the road. I bought my milk from them. It was good Jersey milk. What they didn't sell they made cheese of. I don't care much for milk but it's good for a person.

When I got back to the office the directory was just going to press. Eve warmed up to me and we got chatty again. Both Mr. Bruce and Mr. Smedley asked me if I had a good vacation.

One afternoon several days after I'd returned, Mr. Smedley said to me: "I've found the hitch in the routine."

"You have?" I said. "Good!"

"It's in the editing-query unit," he said. "We've got to split it up and let Miss Steuben just manage the queries."

Then he went over exactly the same plan I had outlined to him about two months before.

I said: "I told you that in the middle of May."

He looked sort of blank and went on to explain in more detail how the split should be made. He was using my idea word for word.

"I told you all that more than six weeks ago," I said.

He started to go on with his explanation, then blushed suddenly and walked back to his desk. He didn't look up when he sat down in his chair. I went on with my check-up on missing orders. It made me sore to think he had been telling me the same idea he wouldn't listen to a while ago. I wondered what kind of a sap he took me for.

When Friday came Mr. Bruce stopped me as I was passing his desk on the way to the men's room. "Mr. Dodd," he said, "we've figured out a way to simplify and speed up the routing on this stencil system and we're not going to need as many supervisors. You came on last so I guess you'll have to give way."

"Oh," I said. I suddenly thought of all the stock I was going to lose and the market going up. And I thought of my wife going to have a baby in September. This is tough, I thought.

"All right," I said, "I hope my work's been all right."

"Your work's o.k.," said Mr. Bruce. "I'll tell you, you're lucky to get out of here. This's an awful hole to get stuck in."

This is tough, I thought.

"Yes, not much of a future here," I said.

"Mr. Dilger wants to see you," Mr. Bruce went on to say. "It's about the same thing. I thought I'd tell you before you saw him. A little bit easier facing the Big Boss if you're wised up beforehand, you know."

I thanked him and went down the long aisle of desks to Mr. Dilger's office, the directory manager.

"Good morning," he said, when I came in. "Have a chair. I suppose Mr. Bruce has told you that we are cutting down the directory supervisory staff," he said.

I nodded.

This is going to be tough on my wife, I thought. Then I tried to think up the story I was going to tell her.

The directory manager continued: "This first trial of the stencil system didn't come off as smoothly as we feel it should, but we have learned enough to reduce the waste time in the routine. As a result we won't need as many supervisors. You can draw two weeks in advance of your salary today, and the money you have paid in on stock. You needn't come in tomorrow morning."

"I hope there has been no question about my work," I said.

"None, absolutely none," said Mr. Dilger. "Both Mr. Bruce and Mr. Smedley have spoken highly of you. We'll be glad to give you a good recommendation whenever you wish it. Good-bye, Mr. Dodd."

I shook hands with him and went back to the directory department. When I looked out of the window by my desk I saw another big liner steaming up the river. It was hard to think what to do in the circumstances. I hadn't been out of a job for five years. My wife will feel awfully bad about this, I kept thinking. Mr. Smedley came over and told me how sorry he was that I was going and that he'd enjoyed working with me. He seemed awfully sympathetic.

That evening, just before I left, Eve Martin came over and said: "I hear you're leaving us. I'm awfully sorry, really." Then she smiled her pretty smile. She was wearing that pale green dress that showed up her figure so well.

As I took the subway uptown I thought to myself, I'll tell the wife just exactly what happened. I'll tell her they're going to give me a good recommendation anyway.

The Anvil Nov.-Dec. 1933

On the Outside

AUGUST W. DERLETH

I can't remember when the boy got on the train. Perhaps he'd been there already when I boarded it and I hadn't seen him, or perhaps he'd changed coaches while I was reading.

I can't even remember what it was that made me see him at last. A thin little fellow, looked to be under twelve. He had sharp black eyes, intelligent eyes, and when I saw him, they were fixed on a prosperous-looking businessman sunk deep in a fur coat. The boy had turned in his seat to look at the businessman and to listen to him.

I had noticed the businessman when I passed him to go to my seat, just a glance, no more. He had been talking for the past half hour with two university students who sat across the aisle from him.

When I looked at the boy and watched him, I began to listen to the conversation. The businessman was talking.

"You fellows," he was saying, "are on the outside. You theorize. That's all very well. But you don't know anything about it. . . ."

"Capitalism," interrupted one of the students.

"Catchwords," cut in the businessman. "I know, I'm on the inside. I have to go through these things. You know nothing but what you read in the newspapers—and God knows what they don't all print."

"Capitalism," said the student patiently, "is bound to collapse within a few decades."

The businessman smiled but said nothing.

"This massacre at Detroit, now," cut in the second student. "What do you think of that?"

"It serves those men right. The only thing I'm sorry about is that it gives them a chance to be martyrs for the martyr-worshiping hoodlums who cause riots and disturbances."

"Riots and disturbances," murmured the first student. "Riots and disturbances. If a man wants bread and goes to get it, that's

50

a riot. If a woman wants milk for her children, it's a disturbance, and dangerous to the peace. Hunger is a crime against society."

"Bosh," said the businessman. "That's an extreme view."

"Hunger," said the second student, "is always extreme."

There was an expression of satisfaction on the businessman's face, and it was not dispelled by the student's bitter words. The man looked away from the students. Suddenly his eyes met the boy's. "You," he said smiling, "what do you think about it?"

The boy looked at him for a moment without answering. "Detroit," he said slowly, "was a hungry place."

Everyone looked at the boy.

"I'm glad we're going away from it."

"Oh, you're not alone, then?" asked the businessman.

"No, pa's along. We're both going. We're going to New York where ma is."

Silence fell. The clicking of the drivers edged into the coach, sounding louder and louder.

"I didn't see your father," said the businessman. "I didn't see him come in. Where's he at?"

The boy made a vague gesture in the direction of the smoking car.

"Oh, I see," said the businessman. He looked speculatively at the boy and asked. "What are you going to do in New York, you and your dad?"

"I don't know."

Silence crept into the coach again and presently the businessman turned away. But the boy continued to look at him, staring at him rather, without once blinking his eyes or shifting his stare. The businessman was conscious of the boy's scrutiny, for he looked up again, fixed the boy with his eyes, and said, "Your dad's been gone some time. He must have a whole box of cigars."

At that, the boy's stare wavered for the first time. He closed his eyes for a moment. "A big box," he murmured. "A big box."

The businessman got up suddenly and stretched himself. "I'm getting old," he muttered.

"No, I'm stiff, too," said one of the students, and came to his feet.

"I tell you what," said the businessman abruptly, looking toward the boy. "Let's go find your dad."

The boy nodded eagerly and jumped from his seat. He went quickly along the aisle, pausing only once to look back to see whether the others were following. On an impulse, I got up, too.

We passed through another coach, in which three men were

sleeping, one with a newspaper spread over his face. Then we came to the smoker, but there was no one in it. The businessman, who was directly behind the boy, stopped, but the boy apparently did not notice, for he kept on going.

"This is the smoker," he called to the boy. Then he turned, said, "Diner ahead, perhaps," and went on.

But there was no one in the dining car either. The boy kept on, and we followed him.

We came to the baggage car. Two men were sitting in it; they looked curiously at us.

The boy stopped and pointed. "There's my pa," he said.

He was pointing at a long box.

The students stared. The businessman drew a sharp gasping breath, and his face coloured.

"They shot him in Detroit," the boy said, his voice sounding loud in the sudden silence.

"Listen," said the businessman jerkily, turning to the boy, "have you had dinner?"

The boy shook his head. "I'm hungry," he said in a slow, dispassionate voice, as if despair of ever getting food had saturated his thin body. "I was always hungry in Detroit. All of us. It used to be better—before they put oil on the stuff in the garbage cans. They wanted to save our health."

One of the students smiled bitterly. "They wanted them to starve healthily," he said.

The businessman said, "We'll fix that in a jiffy," avoiding the eyes of the students. "You come right along and see what Rastus can find for you in the dining car."

He took the boy by the hand and led him quickly out of the car.

One of the students began to laugh harshly. "Using an eye-dropper on a burning skyscraper. My God! what about the millions?"

The Anvil Sept.-Oct. 1933

Desert Incident

Preston dressed and ate, but when he was ready to go he learned that he had fifteen minutes to wait for a bus. Because he could not control his impatience he walked past the line of small cabins to the row of trailers at the end of the camp. The tubercular girl Elizabeth lay on a cot in the sun. Near her on a camp stool sat a boy, tall, broad, and brown of face, but with the betraying tubercular white tightness across his cheeks.

Preston came near them. "Hello," he said to the girl. And he turned toward the boy to include him in his greeting. "I'm going to town. Came over here while I wait for the bus."

The girl sat up. Preston noticed that her body was pretty in its tan, in spite of its thinness. Where she had not tanned her skin was shadowed with blue like snow under pine trees.

Looking at him she said, "You kin do anything you want. Gerald and me never kin do nothin'."

Preston glanced at the boy. He had a low, broad, heavy brow and heavy lashes over deep-set brown eyes. The expression of his face was sullen, and Preston could feel that he was silently echoing the girl's words. In his pity Preston forgot his usual revulsion at their disease and stepped closer, almost touching them.

"But you're going to get well," he said. "The sunshine will make you well."

The girl nodded toward the boy. "He's gettin' well. Sunshine's enough for him. But not me. I gotta have a lung operation and stay in a sanitarium for a year. It'll cost five hundred. And my family can't never save that much pickin' cotton. They can't never get more than twenty dollars set by before they has to spend it."

Preston stepped back. She had spoken furiously, as if he were to blame.

The boy Gerald looked up at Preston. "Don't mind Elizabeth. She's sore today 'cause her ma said she couldn't even sit up until she stopped runnin' such high fever."

Preston said, "Maybe my bus is coming," and went away. When

53

he had gone Gerald asked, "Why were you sore at him? He seems like a good guy."

"Aw, I know how he feels. Like we was somethin' sep'rate. Feels he has to be kind. Let's go for a walk."

"Walk!" Gerald stood up frightened. "Where?"

"Down through the cotton patch in back. See what's on the other side. What's the matter? Are you afraid?"

Gerald sat down, his boyish face turned from her. "No, I'm not afraid. But I don't want to. I'm not chasin' around. I'm obeyin' orders. The doctor says I'm gettin' well."

Elizabeth snarled in answer. "All T.B.'s think they're gettin' well. The doctors just kid 'em. You're dyin'. I'm dyin'. Only I'm dyin' faster." She stood up, tottering a little. "Are ye comin', or are ye scared?" She stood over him, making herself straight.

His eyes traveled up her legs past the blue trunks, the brown band of her belly, the blue and white halter, to her face. Her standing cocksure above him was more challenge than her words. He rose slowly, straightening until his head was above hers. Breathing deeply to broaden his chest he said, "See, I'm gettin' well. I've put on twenty pounds and grown taller."

"If you're so strong why are you afraid to go with me?"

"I ain't afraid." But as he spoke he looked toward his parents' trailer to see that his mother was not watching. "Where do you want to go?"

She stepped away and he followed her, crawling between the barbed wire fence at the court limits and plunging into a field of dry cotton. They walked in separate rows, Elizabeth slightly in the lead. The field had been picked over several times, only a few small dirty bolls showed against the woody cotton stalks. Most of the leaves had fallen. Those that remained were brown and hard. Elizabeth walked with her hands in front of her, bending the woody branches away from the bare parts of her body. Suddenly she stopped, pulled a small boll from a plant, and spread it so that it appeared loose and white.

"This is cotton," she said as if to herself. "I've heard nothin' but cotton since I got sick, and this is the first time I ever picked it."

Gerald stepped into her row. "You had enough, you better go back. Your face is flushed. You'll be runnin' fever."

"I always run fever. I won't go back till I see what's beyond."

They walked on until they came to the end of the cotton. On the other side of a fence stretched a green cool field of half-grown alfalfa. Beyond it the land dropped slowly away for many miles, revealing a patchwork of desert and green farms, then the swift upgrade of a long mountain, shutting off the world to the south.

"Well," Gerald said, "was it worth chasin 'down here for?"

She put her hand on his arm to steady herself. "Help me over to the grass. I can't stand any more. I gotta rest."

They went under the fence. "Let me put my head on your lap, and you sit so that you shade my head." He obeyed her, frightened by her weakness.

"I shouldn't have let you come. Now how'll you get back?" Her eyes were closed. Each breath came swiftly.

They rested without speaking. Then when the startling flush had grown less in Elizabeth's face and her breathing came slow and regular again, Gerald became aware that her hand was passing up his bare arm. The fingers tried to encircle his biceps, then traveled upward, feeling over his shoulder and into his armpit, then under his overall strap to his chest. As he trembled from the pleasure of it he looked at her face, but she did not open her eyes. Her hand dropped away. "You're strong, and your heart's not even beating fast. Maybe you won't die."

"I ain't goin' to die."

She looked at him. Then she raised her hand and laid it against his cheek. "I'm goin' to run away. I was goin' to ask you to go with me. But if you're really goin' to get well you won't go."

He laughed, thinking that she was talking only to tease him. "We can't go away. We're too young. I'm not eighteen yet."

"I'm just eighteen. But that don't matter. When a person just got a short time to live they're old, no matter if they're eighteen or eighty."

"But you'll get well if you don't do more foolish things like runnin' away."

"I won't get well unless I get the lung operation, and pa'll never get the money saved. Three of 'em pickin' every season can't make the $500. I wouldn't mind dyin' so bad if I knew I had done somethin' in life."

She raised herself on her elbows. "Do ye want to kiss me?" And seeing him hesitate she sank back. "Even you're afraid. I gotta eat out of sep'rate dishes, nobody stands close to me but my folks. I thought you was sep'rate like me. But you're afraid, like the rest."

He laughed awkwardly, trying to clear a thickness in his throat. "I ain't a-scared of your germs. I'm just a-scared of kissin' you. I never kissed nobody."

"Neither did I. That's why—" She sat up suddenly and put her slender arms about him, sliding them under the overall straps so that they were against his bare back. Then she kissed him with her hot dry lips. But to him they were tender and soft, and though he wanted to hold her, so much of her back was bare that his sense of modesty kept his arms against his sides.

When she lay back she said, "Now I want more than before for you to run away with me. I want us to go away together and not be beholden to our folks and always afraid to move."

"I'll go," he said, the nerves within him still shaking from her kiss. Then clearing his throat repeatedly he added, "I got $25 saved up in a coin bank."

"I got eight dollars of my own."

"I kin learn to pick cotton."

She pulled him down to her side and they lay in the cool green field, their arms about each other, kissing.

The New Anvil March 1939

Reverend Father Gilhooley

JAMES T. FARRELL

I

Domine, non sum dignis . . . .

Albert Schaeffer, from the sixth grade, sounded the sanctuary bell, its echoes knelling through the hush of Saint Patrick's barn-like church. Heads lowered in pews, and closed fists beat against suddenly contrite breasts. Low sweet organ tones flowed, and Miss Molly O'Callaghan sang:

Agnus Dei, qui tollit pecata mundi,

Agnus Dei . . . .

Communicants slowly and solemnly marched to the altar rail, heads bent, lips forming prayers, hands palmed together in stiff prayerfulness. Father Gihooley, the corpulent, ruddy-faced, bald gray-fringed pastor, choked his Latin, mumbled. Miss O'Callaghan's voice lifted, evoking and spreading through the church a spirit of murmuring contrition, a deep and feelingful Catholic humility.

Oh Lord I am not worthy

That Thou shouldst come to me,

But speak the words of comfort

And my spirit healed shall be.

Father Gilhooley descended from the altar carrying the golden chalice. His Irish blood plunged with pride, pride in his ascent to the priesthood from his lowly Irish peasant origins, pride in his power to change flour and water into the Real Presence, and to carry it comfortingly to penitents and sorely troubled sinners.

Oh Lord I am not worthy

The cassocked acolyte shoved the silver communion plate under the fat chin of the first communicant. The priest extracted a wafer of unleavened bread with his consecrated fingers, crossed it in the air, and placed it on the outthrust tongue, muttering simultaneously,

Corpus Domini nostri Jesu Christi custodiat animam tuam in vitam aeternam.

Eighteen-year-old Peggy Collins knelt at the altar rail, dark eyes closed, her pert round face lifted, her tongue stuck out. She waited, praying please to God and the Blessed Virgin to guide her and aid her and give her the grace and courage to see and to do what

57

was right in the eyes of Heaven. The priest laid the host on her tongue and swept along.

Corpus Domini nostri Jesu Christi custodiat animam tuam in vitam aeternam.

Oh Lord I am not worthy

II

"Gee, I'll have to hurry, I'm going to be late at the office," Peggy Collins said, entering the kitchen, home from the eight o'clock mass.

"Well, the food is here. You can make your own breakfast, and not be expecting me to be waiting on you hand and foot," Mrs. Collins, a beefy and coarsefaced woman, said, frowning as she talked.

Peggy turned on the gas under the coffee pot.

"When you're my age, I hope you won't be expected to slave for ungrateful children."

"Oh Mother, please now! I've just come from receiving Holy Communion. Please, let's not quarrel!"

"And little good it'll do you!"

"Why Mother!" Peggy exclaimed, turning toward her mother with a pained expression.

"Don't talk to me, you that would disgrace me in the eyes of the parish, and before a holy man, a breathing saint of God like Father Gilhooley. Well, you mark my words. There's never the day's luck that will shine on you and yours. I only hope that the day will come when your children won't turn their backs on you the way mine have on me," the mother slobbered.

"Oh, Mother, let's not be silly!"

"So it's silly I am! She with her airs and her primping and powdering and cooing and billing for a black devil of a Protestant. So it's silly I am!"

Peggy poured coffee, buttered a slice of white bread, and sat down at the kitchen table.

"Marry a black devil out of Hell! A Protestant!" the mother exclaimed sarcastically, standing over Peggy with her hands on her hefty hips. "Setting yourself against the wishes of one of God's noble men. Disgracing your home and your hard-working father, and me, your mother, who bore you, and washed your diapers, and raised you."

"I'm not doing anything wrong, and you can't talk to me like that! I'm not a child or a baby any more," Peggy said, struggling to check a flow of tears.

"Why the priest of God won't even marry you. He knows your

ilk. Ah, the day will come! The day will come when you'll regret
what you're doing to your poor mother. And when it does, I only
hope that your heart does not ache as my poor heart aches, and
that the curse of God will not be put on your soul."

Mrs. Collins followed Peggy to her bedroom and to the front
door.

"Go, you whore, and never come back for all that I may care!"

Peggy slammed the door, and went down the stairs sobbing.

III

"Mary, God has given us another Spring day," Father Gilhooley
floridly said, as he expanded comfortably in a chair. His housekeeper set an ample breakfast before him, and he said Grace before eating heartily. As he slowly stirred his coffee, Mary ushered
in a boy of about twelve who stood by the entrance, blushing and
breathless with awe.

"What's the trouble, son?"

"Father . . . can . . . can you give me Holy Communion?" the
boy asked.

"But you know, son, mass is at eight o'clock."

With several stuttering lapses, the boy exclaimed that he was
making the nine first Fridays for a very special intention, and this
morning, the alarm clock had not worked, so he hadn't woke up
until around eight-twenty. He'd run all the way to church, but had
arrived after Holy Communion. He was terribly worried for fear
that his Fridays be broken, and he looked pleadingly at the priest.

Father Gilhooley answered that there were no more hosts and
he couldn't consecrate any because he had already said mass.

"Father, does a spiritual communion count?" the boy said with
timid hope, fumbling with his cap as he spoke. "When I was running to church, all the way, I tried to think of God and holy
things, and keep my mind on them and imagine that I was receiving Holy Communion."

Beaming broadly, the priest reassured the boy, instructing him
to receive Holy Communion on the following morning. He called
the lad to him, patted his head, and gave him a nickel.

"God bless you, son!" the priest said as the boy left.

Slowly drinking his coffee, a glow of gratification spread through
the pastor. For had not this small incident been another demonstration of the power of God and the Church to enflame young
hearts with piety? And he and his assistants and the good sisters
teaching in the parish schools, they were all doing their work well
in the Master's vineyard. The seeds of faith planted in that lad's
heart would sprout forth a thousandfold in rich spiritual fruits

lovely to the sight of God Almighty. His name was Colahan, and
his father ran a drug store at Sixty-first and Vernon. A good family. Mr. Colahan was a good man and he had contributed fifty
dollars to last Sunday's Easter Collection. And the lad was just
the type that God would call to His holy altar. He was reminded,
too, that he should instruct the sisters to talk on vocations to the
graduating class until the end of the school term in June. And he
would deliver a sermon on the subject one of these Sundays. Also,
Father Doneggan and Father Marcel could go over to the classrooms. For one of his few disappointments at Saint Patrick's was
that not one of its sons from the parish school had yet been or-
dained. He believed that the parish school should be sending two
or three boys, at least, from each graduating class to Quigley
Seminary to start studying for the priesthood. This was an aim that
required cooperation and concentration.

After breakfast, he read his morning mail in his small office.
Several letters from needy parishioners requesting funds were
marked off for Father Doneggan's attention, and he would refer
them to a Catholic charity organization. He opened a vituperative
letter from an anti-Catholic, unsigned, and he cast it in his waste
basket with the word—*bigot*. He knew that he was a minister of
God's true church, and that Christ Himself had built the church
upon the rock of Peter, promising that the gates of Hell would
not prevail against it. Such missives could not shake him. His
face suddenly broke into a beaming smile, as he picked up several
letters containing delayed donations to the Easter Collection. But
two were five-dollar checks from families which could have well
afforded at least twenty-five. Another was from a politician giving
fifty dollars when twice that amount would not have hurt him. His
flock was made up of people who were good and generous, but
some of them required to be more strongly impressed with a sense
of their duty to contribute to the support of their pastor. And he
would have to remember that when he spoke on the next regular
collection. That reminded him that he ought again soon to be
delivering that sermon of his, *Mother Church: Why She Is the
Only True One*. It was one of his best sermons. And since he had
three shelves of the works of Longfellow, Shakespeare, and the
other great literary masters, he would have to be looking through
them to find a few apt quotations for his sermons. No harm in
making them more erudite.

His mail read, he seated himself in a deep and comfortable
chair, and discovered, as usual, that the morning paper was full
of dismaying items. Ah, the age was sinful and pagan. Prohibition
and bootleggers and gangsters, and the younger generation running

wild, promiscuous dances, assaults on women, people going blind
and dying in the streets from moonshine . . . ah, yes, a sinful and
pagan age. Still, he knew that the people of his flock were much
better Catholics than those in many a parish. And why? He was
not immodest, no, he was only recognizing a true fact when he
thought that it was his own example before them, his teaching and
guidance in sermons and the confessional. He knew too that he
was a much more conscientious shepherd than Kiley from Saint
Rose's church. And Kiley wouldn't be a Monsignor today if he
hadn't shown off and put on airs. Well, no one could accuse Father
Gilhooley of advancing himself by showing off and playing politics.

But that Collins girl? She still seemed determined to marry that
Protestant scamp after all his dissuasion, after he had talked to
her parents, explained to her, given counsel that was the fruit not
only of his own long experience, but also of the Church's ten
thousand years of wisdom. And she only a chit of a thing. Well,
they had come from Kiley's parish. What else could he expect?
And her whole family had only given five dollars to the Easter
Collection. If Kiley paid less attention to the Cathedral on the
north side, and more to his own people, and if her parents had
raised the girl properly, instilling in her respect for authority and
her elders, and a proper fear of the Almighty, she wouldn't be
crossing him now to the endangerment of her immortal soul. Well,
he had told her, and he would not permit the marriage. It was a
bad business. Ah, a bad business!

He read his office for the day, and then walked to look out the
window with a drifting glance. Below him was the large, rectangular-
shaped parish yard, to the right of the church building and ringed
with an iron picket fence—a half block of land alive with Spring
greenness. Soon the building on this ground would be started. Soon
men would be digging, preparing to lay the foundation for one of
the most beautiful churches in the whole city of Chicago. With
pride and gratification, he continued to stand by his window, his
hands in his trouser pockets beneath his cassock, his dream bursting like a rocket in his mind. When he had come to this parish in
1900, there had been nothing, only a handful of the faithful, and
he had celebrated his first mass on a Winter Sunday morning in a
vacant and chilly store on Sixty-first Street. This parish, it was
the work of his own hand, and his own heart, and his own mind,
and his own soul, and his own faith, the dedication of his life
which he had given to God. And he had been happy here in this
vineyard of the Master. Now, his greatest happiness and triumph
lay ahead of him. He prayed God to permit him to witness it. But
God would. God had preserved his health to this date. Ah yes, he

had built up the present parish and school, and now it was free of debt. Saint Patrick's was one of the few parishes in the city totally free of debt. Of that he was certain. And with the slowly accumulating sinking fund he had established for the new church, and the drive for funds that he was now almost ready to launch, he would build an edifying house of the Lord, a monument to stand in the Creator's honor long after, years and years after he would have returned to the dust from whence he had come. This dream and this hope, it was his life, his life's blood, and the mere contemplation of it intoxicated him with a sweet elation and pleasure. It would be a church second to none, the envy of pastors throughout the diocese, a temple and a house of beauty and worship that would make the Cardinal Archbishop take notice of him. Perhaps then and on the merits of his work, he would be made . . . Monsignor Gilhooley. He could visualize himself in this parish, in the new church which would draw rich and well-to-do people to the neighborhood. He could imagine himself in the rear of the church at late Sunday masses when the people would file out, inspired after the mass and by the beauty of the church, going home to happy dinners with the word and fear of God in their hearts, nodding and smiling to him as they left. Ah!

The thought of that chit of a Collins girl again broke upon him. She only eighteen years old, and to keep coming back to him, wasting his time with her begging and pleading after he had given her his final word. That chit of a girl! Well, he would not sanction the marriage to a Protestant. But now he had lost beyond recapturing that splendid vision he had just experienced. He turned from the window.

IV

"Gee Kid, you look fagged out. Why are you so sad?" Madge said to Peggy as they sat munching chicken salad sandwiches and sipping malted milks for lunch in a crowded and noisy Loop ice cream parlor.

"I'm terribly worried, Madge."

"I hope it's not your darling Graham again."

"It's serious. Graham's dear. I adore him. But it's the same awful trouble. It makes me feel just awful. I saw Father Gilhooley with my mother again last night, and he still refuses to let us get married. And my mother sides with him too, and we had such a terrible fight this morning. I left the house with the jitters, and cried half-way downtown on the elevated train."

"You're taking it too seriously, Collins. I'd like to see anybody pull that kind of a trick on me! I'd just like to see them! Come on,

kid, snap out of it. Tell them you've got your own life to live, and
if they don't like the way you live it, they can lump it."

"But Madge, dear, you know if you're not married in the
church, it's not marriage at all, and then it will be living in mortal
sin. He won't publish the banns and marry us, and my mother
keeps throwing fits. Gee, kid, I'm going nearly crazy."

"You poor kid! Now don't cry."

"I can't help it. I love Graham. And he's so sweet and kind to
me. If I had to give him up, I don't know what I'd do. I'd just
go and throw myself in the lake, I guess, because then I wouldn't
care about anything any more."

"Listen, kiddo, don't pay any attention to them. Take my advice, dearie, and you and Graham just step down to the City Hall,
and then let them jaw their ears off. God isn't a school teacher or
a fierce old giant, and he isn't going to go punishing people just
because they love each other and are honest about it. You and
Graham just go away and get married. It isn't hocus-pocus that
some old fool says that counts and makes you married. It's what
you and Graham feel inside your hearts."

"Madge, darling, you're not a Catholic, and you just don't
understand."

"Well, if that's what it means to be a Catholic, I'm glad I'm not
one."

"Madge, please don't say that!"

Madge shrugged her shoulders in a gesture of resignation.

"Of course, Peg, it isn't my business, but honestly, I can't understand why you let an old fossil of a priest who doesn't know
what it's all about, go sticking his nose in your business the way
you do."

"But if we're not married in the church, it'll be living in sin."

"Oh don't be a fool, Peg!"

V

The pastor partook of a sufficient luncheon with Father Doneggan, the wiry, thin, energetic, blond assistant pastor who was in
his early thirties. After suggesting to his assistant that they should
start a drive to turn the minds of boys and girls in the school to the
subject of vocations, Father Gilhooley mentioned the Collins girl.
Father Doneggan, speaking with careful reserve, suggested that the
only course of action, he feared, was to publish the banns and
marry the couple.

"Pat, I shall not!" Father Gilhooley said with stern stubborn-
ness, meaning "will" for "shall."

"Father, you know naturally that I agree with you *in toto* on the question of mixed marriages. But in this case, the girl being as set and as determined as she is, I think that marriage is the lesser of the two evils involved."

"Pat, it's a bad business. What she needs is for her mother to give her a hiding that will drive some sense into that flighty little head of hers," the pastor said, as a prelude to filling his mouth with steak until his cheeks bulged. Chewing, he added, "I shall not permit it!"

Father Doneggan knew the uselessness of reply. He recalled, with silent and frustrated anger, two fairly recent run-ins that he had had with Father Gilhooley. He had tried to persuade him that instead of preaching sermons and asking for contributions repeatedly, they might raise money for the new church by holding bazaars that would also have served the purpose of giving the parishioners a good time and welding them together socially. And Father Gilhooley had disapproved because the raffles held at bazaars constituted, in his mind, gambling, and he feared demoralizing the parish and setting a bad example for the young. Father Doneggan had tried, also, to convince the pastor that they should organize a parish young people's society and conduct clean dances in the parish auditorium. But the auditorium was on consecrated ground, so Father Gilhooley had refused.

Now, Father Doneggan continued eating. Father Gilhooley was in authority. And he was living in his own agony of doubts and temptations. He was beginning to see that the priesthood was the wrong place for him. The cancer of doubt, doubt even of the existence of the very God he served, was poisoning him almost to madness. He was drinking more and more, and he would not always be able to hide it. Sooner or later, he would face a showdown. He would even, possibly, have to face the choice of a future of hypocrisy, or else the road of an unfrocked priest, marked and scarred and defamed on every side, and almost totally unfitted for any worldly occupation. And the issue raised by the Collins girl only strengthened his doubts, adding one more instance to the contradictions between the raw life of emotions and passions and sins and waywardness poured into his ears in the confessional, and the dogmatization of life in the formal philosophy of the Church. He looked almost enviously at Father Gilhooley who was so corpulently contented, the fires of the flesh now dead embers, with gluttony and eating his only sin. Did the complacency on that blown ruddy face extend clean through to the man's soul? Was it sainthood or a barricade of fat around his spirit? Anyway he had not the energy to try convincing his pastor. He was drained from his own internal struggles. His will was paralyzed. Quickly finishing his luncheon, he left on the pretext of working over next Sunday's sermon.

VI

At three-thirty, Father Gilhooley left the parish house for his afternoon walk. Walking, he gazed at the fenced-in grounds where he would build his new church. In a few years now, when there would be a Eucharistic Congress in Chicago, his beautiful new house of worship would be an honor to God, a credit to himself, a tribute to the faith he served. It would be a mark of such beauty that thousands of visitors would come to behold its wonders. Visiting clergymen, bishops, perhaps even the Papal Delagate would view it, and after that, he would take a trip to the old country, and he might go, too, as a Monsignor. He stepped into his church, and thought, as if in fresh discovery, that it was very rapidly becoming increasingly inadequate for the needs of the parish. His new church would make the neighborhood grow, attracting to it the best types of well-to-do Catholics. It would be a rich parish. And Monsignor Gilhooley, wouldn't he then outshine Kiley?

As he stood thus in the rear of his church, his dreams and his visions alive within him, he saw a small boy leave a pew, hastily genuflect without touching his knee to the flooring, bless himself at the holy water fount with his left hand, and bound through the swinging doors. Father Gilhooley quickly followed and called the lad back.

"Good afternoon, Father," the boy timidly muttered, retracing his steps up the church stairs.

Answering the priest's question, the boy said that he was William Markham, in the sixth grade of the parish school. Father Gilhooley promptly recalled that the only contribution from a Markham to the Easter Collection had been two dollars.

"Did Sister ever teach you how to bless yourself?" the priest sternly asked.

"Yes, Father."

He ordered the boy to demonstrate. William slowly and correctly made the sign of the cross. Father Gilhooley told him that he should always bless himself with his right hand, and when he genuflected in the presence of the Blessed Sacrament, his knee should touch the floor.

The pastor stopped in at Strunsky's drug store for a cigar. The pinched druggist, aware that Father Gilhooley's displeasure could decrease his business, obsequiously nodded agreement to the priest's platitudes, and in parting, they agreed on the weather. Several passing laborers and school boys tipped their hats and caps to him, and he acknowledged the greeting with a dignified nod. Women parishioners greeted him with smiles and salutations which could have been no more humble had he been one of the Twelve Apostles. He paused to discuss the weather with the attractive and smartly dressed Mrs. Freeman. Her husband, a manufacturer of tennis rackets, had contributed a hundred dollars to the Easter Collection. Patting her youngster's head, he told her what a fine healthy child she had. She said she hoped it would grow up to be as good a man and a priest as the one who had baptized him. Beaming over the compliment, Father Gilhooley said that he knew with the good home influences in which the child was being reared, he was certain the baby would develop and one day be a tribute both to its parents and to Saint Patrick's parish. She thanked him, and they parted. A black-shawled, hunched little Irish woman with a shrivelled face almost bent her back in bowing to him. Superstitious admiration and reverence brought life, even freshness, into her small, suspicious eyes. She again humbly bowed, and mumbled a foreign phrase learned by rote:

"Ga lob Jasus Christe."

The homage paid to him as a man of God was warming, gratifying. This peasant woman, with her simple faith and humility, stirred in him memories of his own Irish mother. Ah, that she were alive to see her son today. He prided, in himself, his ascent from lowly origins, and his race. Had not the Irish preserved the faith in the face of oppression? And did not the Church owe a great credit to these simple Irish mothers who had been the backbone of Catholicism in Ireland, the women out of whose womb heroic and sainted priests had come? If only the young chits of girls these days would learn the great, simple lessons of truth from their Irish mothers and grandmothers! Chits of girls like the Collins one, with her powder, and her lipstick, and her thinking she loved a Protestant.

He called the woman "grandmother," said that it was a fine day, and told her how well and how young she looked. Passing on, his good humor lushly expanded, and again he grew proud in the dignity of his office. He walked like a great man. Once again, the recollection of that Collins girl threatening to cross him, bobbed annoyingly in his mind, and his cheeks flushed from anger.

I'll permit none of it! he vowed to himself.

Strolling back with an afternoon paper under his arm, he met

Father Georgiss, the pastor of Saint Sofia's, the Greek Catholic Church across from Saint Patrick's. Father Georgiss was a bearded, dark-browed man who always looked at Father Gilhooley with a roguish and enigmatic twinkle in his eyes. Scholarly, urbane, skeptical, even cosmopolitan alongside of the Roman Catholic priest, he usually managed to impress an uneasiness, even a sense of inferiority upon Father Gilhooley. Father Georgiss' church was larger and more impressive than Saint Patrick's, but seeing him, Father Gilhooley insisted to himself that it wasn't beautiful. Too oriental. Too sensuous. The two clergymen spoke to each other with excessive politeness, and Father Gilhooley assuaged his falling pride by casually remarking that very soon now he would let out the contracts and begin operations on his church. Father Georgiss congratulated him, but again there was that disconcerting look in his eyes. He accepted Father Gilhooley's invitation to drop over some evening for a chat. He said that he was busy these days pursuing his studies of Byzantine civilization. It was a great civilization, and it had saved Christianity for centuries from the Turks, and Father Gilhooley should read of it. Father Gilhooley said he would like to have Father Georgiss tell him of it, thinking silently that with all this Greek priest's reading of history, he could not see the truth and the simple necessity of the dogma of Papal Infallibility. They parted politely, agreeing that God had given them splendid weather.

VII

Peggy sat on the steps before the box-like yellow apartment building on Prairie Avenue, where the Collins family lived. She studiously looked into her purse mirror, and dabbed her face to mask the evidence that she had been crying. She hated her mother! That was an awful thought. But she didn't care. She didn't. She hated her! She did! And it was all so silly. This business of Catholics and Protestants. Graham's little finger was worth more than any number of Catholic boys she knew. And he was good and decent. Good to her. And she didn't care. She loved him. He had such nice eyes, and she dreamed about his eyes, and his lips, and she was always thinking she saw him on the street. She loved him. She wanted to love him with all of herself, forever, and her mother and Father Gilhooley were so silly about it. They must have never been in love. Because she knew that she couldn't help herself, and she would love Graham, even if her soul would burn for all eternity in Hell. And God! He couldn't be like Father Gilhooley, and want her to give up Graham. And the way her mother had cut up at the supper table! So silly. Oh, she just wanted to be away from it all, and to be alone with her Graham.

And she was going to see Father Gilhooley, and tell him he would just have to marry them. And again, tears came to her eyes. Because maybe it was too late now. Maybe religion had already been thrown between them like some terrible shadow, and, gee, she was afraid that they could never be happy together. She couldn't give him up, and she didn't want to, and. . . . She saw him swinging along the street, so tall, so handsome. She tried to dry her tears.

<h1 style="text-align:center">VIII</h1>

Father Gilhooley was contented, at peace with himself, at peace with the world, at peace with his God, after his hearty supper. His sense of almost somnolent well-being was disturbed by Mary who told him that that Collins girl was back again. He frowned. He said, sternly, that he wouldn't see her, and followed his housekeeper into the small reception room where Peggy and Graham waited.

"Good evening, Father!" Peggy said, meekly and with respect.

"Good evening, Father!" Graham said, restrained.

"Good evening, my girl! Good evening, sir! Be seated!" Father Gilhooley curtly said.

"Father . . ." Peggy began in a hesitant manner.

"I am a very busy man. I do not see, for the life of me, why you return here to waste my time after I have told you definitely and finally that I cannot permit such a marriage in my parish."

"But, Father, what can we do? We can't get married in another parish," Peggy said, despair creeping into her voice.

"I have already explained my reasons fully to both of you. I have nothing personally against this young man, ah—Mr. . . . ah. . . ."

"McIntosh," Peggy volunteered.

"Mr. McIntosh, my decision is not personal and directed against you. I am opposed to mixed marriages on principle, and on reflection after long years of experience as a clergyman. I have learned that oil and water do not mix. And this applies to the marriage of persons of different religions. I have witnessed the irreparable evil and ruination of souls that result from mixed marriages. This I have already explained to you young people. If I sanction this marriage, others will come, and you two will set a bad example for all the young people of my parish. I am not the kind of a person who waits to lock his stable door after the horse has been stolen."

"But Father, suppose I had been insincere and pretended to be converted. Then you could not have objected to our marriage. Because I have chosen not to be a hypocrite, you refuse to let us be married in your church," Graham said, controlling his voice, but the expression in his eyes was hard, as if they were knifing the priest.

"Sir, that is a matter for your own conscience. My action is impersonal, and I am thinking not simply of your temporal happiness, but of the soul of this girl which has been placed in my care, since I happen to be her pastor, and thus her spiritual guardian. And also, I am thinking of the souls of many more young people like her in my parish. I am older than you two people, and I am drawing on long experience, and the wisdom of my church through long years and centuries of history when I speak. You two are young, and you are letting yourselves be blinded by what you call love. I am older than you, and I see more. I see the danger to this girl's immortal soul, and to the soul of any offspring you might have."

"But Father, Graham—Mr. McIntosh—is perfectly willing to let our children be raised Catholic, and he will not interfere with my fulfilling my religious obligations," Peggy said, blushing.

"My dear girl, a house divided against itself will fall. A home cannot be built unless there is sympathy and understanding erected on the religion of God. There cannot be sympathy unless both parties see eye to eye on religion, because religion is the foundation stone of the Catholic home."

"But Father, we love each other!" Peggy exclaimed, impulsively, almost despairingly, and Graham glanced at her with raised eyebrows, pained.

"You young people take my advice. Forget this marriage, and stay away from each other for six months. Then come back to see me and see if I am not right. Mixed marriages are the principal cause of the pagan evil of divorce which spreads through the world these days like a cancer, and in so many cases it paves a sure road to Hell. I have given my decision, my dear girl, because I am your pastor, responsible to Almighty God for your soul."

"But Father . . ." Peggy exclaimed, startled, ready to cry.

"Father, you can't stop us!" Graham said, his face white, set.

"There is nothing further for me to say. Good evening!" Father Gilhooley said, arising and leaving the room with a swish of his cassock.

IX

From a window, he saw them pass slowly, arm in arm, under a lamplight, and move on, their figures growing vague in the spring dusk. His blood rose. He frowned, reassuring himself that he was right, and acting wisely for the best interests of both of them, and in accordance with the dictates and spirit of God and of God's true Church. And in his whole time as a pastor at Saint Patrick's, no one had ever crossed him as this chit of a girl had.

I'll have none of it! he told himself in rising fury.

His anger cooled. You could take a horse to water, but you couldn't make him drink. He had done his best to explain and guide the girl, and, under the circumstances, he was forced to recognize that marriage was the lesser evil. But he felt that, sure as the Summer followed the Spring, certain as the night succeeded the day, the girl was paving the road to her own perdition. He called Father Doneggan and instructed him to telephone the girl in the morning, and arrange all the details. But he would not perform the marriage, as the girl had requested when she had first come to him.

He returned to the window. They were gone somewhere with their love and their hugging and kissing. The Spring night now quilted and shadowed the yard, and he could hear voices and street sounds through the opened window. He thought again of how gray towers would rise above this quiet and darkened grass, piercing the blue heavens of God on nights like this one. The gray towers of his magnificent church, with vaulted nave, marble pillars, a grand organ, a marble altar imported from Italy, stained glass windows, handcarved woodwork, a marble pulpit from which he would deliver the first sermon to be preached in the new church, packed with faithful parishioners for the first mass. He could see how the edifice, in stone and steel and wood and marble, would stand in beauty and inspiration to goodness and the doing of God's holy Will amongst his flock . . . and perhaps, it would make him Monsignor Gilhooley.

But that chit of a girl! Suddenly he enjoyed the realization that she was making for herself a fiery bed in the eternal flames of Hell. A slip of a girl crossing him who might some day be Bishop Gilhooley.

He turned from the window, the excitement of his dream ebbing in his mind. And for the first time in his long pastorhood, he knew that he had been . . . defeated.

The Anvil Oct.-Nov. 1935

Aspirin

LEONARD FEINBERG

I am really sorry about those aspirins. If Miss Donovan had said anything about them before, I would never have taken them. There was no reason for her to act as indignant as she did.

Miss Donovan is the relief worker for my district—"case worker," we're supposed to call her. Whenever I go to the agency the first thing they ask is "Who is your case worker?" I used to be ashamed of going down to the agency and letting people see me there. But after a while I figured, "What the hell. I'm not going to be on relief all my life. It's a temporary inconvenience. That's all it is. So what have I got to be ashamed of?"

Miss Donovan was always very nice to me—until that aspirin business came up she never bawled me out or said a harsh word to me. I think maybe it was because we had both gone to the same college. Don't get me wrong—I never saw her on the campus. But when she first got my record she said, "Did you go to the State University?"

"Yes," I said. "I went there three years—1933 to 1935."

"Well," she said. "Isn't that a coincidence? I graduated in 1937. I never met you there, did I?"

Miss Donovan is a polite young woman.

"No," I said. "You never met me. It's a big campus."

"Weren't you in any university activities?" she asked.

I told her that I waited on tables for my meals. She said she ate her meals at the sorority. That may be why I never met her. Miss Donovan was very nice to me. Once she asked me to have a Coke with her, while she was resting from making her rounds. I was glad to sit with her, drinking a Coke, just as if we were equals. I even tried to pay for the Cokes, but she wouldn't let me. She said, "You don't have to try to impress me. I know how much money you've got." She was trying to be kind, I think.

When I couldn't raise tuition money for my last year at State I wasn't bothered very much. I figured I'd work a year, save up some money, then come back and finish up. I knew that if a man really wants to make a living he can do it. That's what my profs said at college. And I read that in one of the popular magazines. There was an article in that magazine which told how different people managed to make a living by using their initiative. One man arranged to shine all his neighbors' shoes; he built up a real business. Another man sold so many subscriptions to magazines that the circulation department gave him a steady job on straight salary. And there was another guy, just a young fellow, who invented a new kind of T-square; it sold like hotcakes.

I guess I don't have enough initiative. Somehow I never could make any money at these rackets. Maybe it's because I don't know the ropes. I read a book by a guy named Carnegie, which told you exactly how to get next to people and make them feel good so they'd buy anything. I tried it out on a guy. I said, "Say, fellow, isn't golf the finest game in the world?" The guy looked at my shiny suit and said, "How the hell would you know?"

But I knew that if a man really wanted to work there was a job for him. The big paper in my city had editorials every day proving that the unemployed that did all the hollering and caused all the trouble were all a bunch of lazy good-for-nothing foreigners who didn't want to work. My old man was born in Pennsylvania, so I know they didn't mean me. I started looking for work. Well, I know it's hard to believe, but I found only two jobs in three years. One lasted a week, distributing circulars. The other job I held on to for a couple of months. Working in a fruit store is no fun, but I liked it. I got there at six every morning, unpacked crates, set up window displays, and clerked. When the boss heard I'd gone to college he let me do some of the bookkeeping too, after hours. I was getting along pretty good, but I caught the flu. Of course they couldn't hold the job for me forever. I didn't really like working in a fruit store, anyway.

While I was waiting to get on WPA the relief agency began helping me out. That was when I acted so ungrateful to the government. I see now that no man on relief has any right to think about women. I should have known better, but I couldn't help getting mixed up with Betty. I guess she was pretty lonesome too. Her old man pushed a cart around the city all day, buying up old newspapers and junk. She didn't have to go to school after she was sixteen, so she'd quit three years ago. She'd never had a job in her life.

We got pretty friendly. I used to sit in her room and talk to her. She liked to hear about college and the big dances I'd gone to. It seemed a shame to disappoint her, so I made up some swell affairs for her. She got a big kick out of it, and it didn't hurt anybody.

Sometimes I got a little mixed up, like the time I was president of the sophomore class and chairman of the junior prom at the same time. But she wasn't very bright. She never caught on.

We played around a little, I'll admit. But I sure didn't know we were as wicked as the newspaper said. Lurid love life on relief, the tabloid called it. Betty's old man knocked hell out of her and cursed me. "You gonna marry her?" he wanted to know. "Sure," I said. "I like her. But I ain't worked in two years. You want to support me till I find a job?" He swore some more and Betty went away with him. I don't know where they live now.

Miss Donovan was very shocked. She gave me a real pep talk. "Mr. Crane," she said, "you're losing your self-respect. I understand how you felt—I took psychology—but you must get a grip on yourself. You have everything to live for—don't spoil your future now." I was plenty ashamed of myself. Miss Donovan forgave me, and got me back on the relief rolls.

I've still got a lot of hopes. I know that things are going to get better—they have to. And when prosperity's back they're going to need men like me, with three years of college education. I've got a future. But this winter they cut the relief. I'm not griping. Hell, I'm thankful for what I get. I can live on fourteen bucks a month. Who can't? It's just that when the relief money ran out in December, and they gave us apples and potatoes instead of cash, I started getting headaches. Not stomach aches. Hell, my stomach'll take anything. It's toughened up. But my head used to buzz after I'd had potatoes and apples, potatoes and apples, day after day. I'm not griping. I'm plenty grateful. But I couldn't help getting headaches. I couldn't sleep at night, and I felt sick all day.

So I began to take aspirins. Whatever money I got I spent for aspirins. They seemed to help a little. Honestly, I didn't know the facts about aspirins. I just took them to stop my headaches. If I knew the truth about them I'd never have taken one. I can see why Miss Donovan was so angry. She sure gave me hell. I promised never to take another aspirin. Miss Donovan says that every time you take an aspirin you cut ten whole seconds off your life.

The New Anvil July-Aug. 1940

Mussolini's Nightmare

MICHAEL GOLD

Like most bluffers, super-salesmen and murderers, Mussolini doesn't sleep so well. Lately, though the days have been filled with glory and glitter, the nights have been awful. For instance, after a historic day on which he had told England to go to hell, and sent another 50,000 boys to the deserts of Africa, and invented a magnificent new uniform for himself, and had been freer than usual from his chronic indigestion, there was this particularly bad dream.

Benito had sat up late, writing another insulting note to Ethiopia. He took his stomach pills, removed his military corset, and the flunkey provided him with his imperial hot water bag. His favorite young masseur rubbed his aging body, that carcass which found it harder every day to maintain the Peter Pan role of flaming youth that fascist dictators must play. Well, Musso was comfortable enough and was dozing off pleasantly, when bang! back he was in the whole six-day bicycle grind of being a great dictator!

He had been dreaming, it seems, of spaghetti, war, and beautiful blackshirt virgins, when suddenly Napoleon butted in.

"Greetings, Benito," muttered the little Corsican dictator, a sneer on his pale face.

"Greetings, Bonaparte," said Busy Ben, irritably. "Why do you visit me at this hour? I must rest now. And why that jealous mien?"

Napoleon would have laughed except that dictators are maniacs who cannot laugh.

"Jealous?" he sneered. "Of you? You for whom the hangman waits only six months or a year away?"

"Bah!" said Mussolini, bravely. "I've done well enough up till now; my luck and brains will again carry me through."

"Bah!" said Napoleon in turn. "I had a luckier star and a better brain than yours, and I landed on Elba."

"I refuse to argue with a failure!" said Mussolini, turning his back, and hugging his hot water bag. "Avaunt!"

Napoleon grew larger and larger, and suddenly floated to the ceiling, medals, boots, cocked hat and all. Then he settled with a loud clunk on Mussolini's chest.

"Little Ben," he whispered, "every dictator has been a failure. Do you know of one who succeeded? Go on yelling; you can't bluff me or history, you poor stuffed imitation of myself. Where are the dictators of yesterday? They died in exile, or of the daggers of assassins. And their systems cracked with them."

"No, no!" shrieked boisterous Ben. "I will last forever! Fascism will be here for a thousand years!"

The ghost of Napoleon did a strange thing. It let out an enormous belch that filled the room with stifling poison.

"Gas!" said Napoleon. "We are things of gas, we dictators! I thought I could stop a people's revolution, Benito. But I died on Elba, and the revolution went on. You have betrayed a people's revolution, too. But they will win in the end; they always do."

"They, they?" shouted Musso defiantly. "Who's they?"

"The people," whispered Napoleon coyly. "As Abe Lincoln said, God must have loved the common people, since he made so many of them! As Voltaire said, erase the infamy! And as Hoyle has said, a full house beats a pair of kings! Look before you leap! A bird in the hand is worth two in the bush! The paths of glory lead but to the grave!"

He would have rattled on with this nonsense, but Mussolini, infuriated, leaped up, threw his hot water bottle at Napoleon. The little Corsican vanished, chuckling grimly, and trailing a noisome odor of poison-gas and death.

Mad Musso sweated nervously after this encounter. He tried to compose himself for sleep, and to think only about pleasant things, about his medals, his uniforms, his speeches. But then a tall figure appeared, a pale man with a high, pure forehead and mournful eyes. He was entirely nude, and from forehead to ankles he was crossed with ghastly wounds.

"Go away!" Benito shrieked, his pop-eyes bursting out of their head. "Who are you?"

"Matteoti," said the tall figure, quietly, "Matteoti, whom you had your gangsters murder. Like the thousands of your former Socialist and trade union comrades whom you murdered. Do you think we are forgotten? Can even you forget us?" He loomed larger and larger over the frightened dictator. "Traitor, we will be with you to the end. We will march beside you in Ethiopia and in Austria. We will be in the factories where your munitions are made. We are on the little farms, and in the hearts of mothers. We will escort you to the gallows when they hang you."

"You are dead and done with!" Mussolini shrieked. "You are only a bad dream! The trains run on time in Italy! The heroic age has begun!"

Matteoti answered nothing, but his silence was worse than any words he might have spoken.

"Who will hang me? Who will dare hang me?" Mussolini shrieked.

"The people," said Matteoti, blood pouring from all his wounds. He vanished.

A little wrinkled old peasant woman took his place before Mussolini. "Mother, what are you doing here?" stammered the dictator. "Go away, mother, you have nothing to do with politics."

The little old woman wept over Mussolini. "My son," she quavered, "why have you been so bad to your own people? Is it Christian? The peasants are hungry, and here you take their sons for another war."

"Mother, mother, go away, or I'll have you arrested as a rebel!" shouted the desperate dictator.

But the mother continued sadly: "Your father was a worker and a Socialist. Now he is very angry at you. He would not come with me to warn you."

"Warn me? Against whom? Whom do I fear?" Mussolini shouted.

"The people," said his mother, quietly, and she too disappeared, while Benito, out of sheer habit, shouted, "Arrest her! Give her the castor oil!"

But it was not the end of the night. Red flags filled the room, and the strains of the *Internationale*. He pulled out his automatic and shot the full clip. A great black stallion cantered into the bedroom. It snickered at him, again and again, maddeningly. Napoleon returned with Empress Josephine. They danced a can-can on Mussolini's bed, dripping blood. Somebody dumped a barrel of medals on Mussolini, and he could not breathe. He was flying in an aeroplane next, and the sky rained lemons, leaflets and spaghetti and broke his wings. He was falling, falling—

Would it never end? The Czar of Russia marched in, at the head of an army of naked princesses. They sneered and pooh-poohed Mussolini. It was sickening. A young Italian peasant boy, playing a shepherd's flute, suddenly turned into a machine-gun that shot into Mussolini. He fancied next that he was in a great hall, where all the glittering kings and rulers of earth were assembled. Mussolini was making one of his tremendous speeches to them, but they seemed not to hear. They were pointing at him, and laughing. He looked down; horrors, he had no pants on!

And again red flags and the *Internationale* of his youth filled the room. His big blacksmith father appeared and with a hammer banged him on the head to the beat of the *Internationale*. A million hens, with faces like Russian dukes, flew around the room, clucking and cackling, and covered Mussolini with their droppings and other Freudian symbols. Suddenly he began to strangle; he was being hanged!

"Mamma," he screamed and woke up. "Help, help, lights!" The flunkies rushed in; they were used to his nightmares, and they clicked on the lights.

Shivering, Mussolini sat down at his writing table, and drew up a set of new and more terrible instructions. . . . Every Socialist, Communist and liberal in Italy must immediately be hunted down and shot, once and for all. After years of absolute power, Mussolini still feared his chief enemy, the people of Italy; they still brought him bad dreams.

The Anvil Oct.-Nov. 1935

Dr. Brown's Decision

LANGSTON HUGHES

Promptly at seven a big car drew up in front of the Booker T. Washington Hotel, and a white chauffeur in uniform got out and went toward the door, intending to ask at the desk for a colored professor named T. Walton Brown. But the professor was already there, sitting in the lobby, a white scarf around his neck and his black overcoat ready to button over his dinner clothes.

As soon as the chauffeur entered, the professor approached. "Mr. Chandler's car?" he asked hesitantly.

"Yes, sir," said the white chauffeur to the clean little Negro. "Are you Dr. Walton Brown?"

"I am," said the professor, smiling and bowing a little.

The chauffeur opened the street door for Dr. Brown, then ran to the car and held the door open there too. Inside the big car the lights came on, and on the long black running-board as well. The professor stepped in among the soft cushions, the deep rug and the cut glass vases holding flowers. With the greatest of deference the chauffeur quickly tucked a covering of fur about the professor's knees, closed the door, entered his own seat in front, beyond the glass partition, and the big car purred away. Within the lobby of the cheap hotel, a few ill-clad Negroes watched the whole procedure in amazement.

"A big shot!" somebody said.

At the corner as the car passed, two or three ash-colored children ran across the street in front of the wheels, their skinny legs and cheap clothes plain in the glare of the headlights as the chauffeur slowed down to let them pass. Then the car turned and ran the whole length of a Negro street that was lined with pawn shops, beer joints, pig's-knuckle stands, ten-cent movies, hairdressing parlors and other ramshackle places of business patronized by the poor blacks of the district. Inside the big car the professor, Dr. Walton Brown, regretted that in all the large cities where he had lectured on his present tour in behalf of his college, the main Negro streets presented this same sleazy and disagreeable appearance: pig's-knuckle joints, pawn shops, beer parlors—

and houses of vice, no doubt—save that these latter, at least, did not hang out their signs.

The professor looked away from the unpleasant sight of this typical Negro street, poor and unkempt. He looked ahead through the glass at the dignified white neck of the uniformed chauffeur in front of him. The professor in his dinner clothes, his brown face even browner above the white silk scarf at his neck, felt warm and comfortable under the fur rug—but he felt, too, a little unsafe at being driven through the streets of this city on the edge of the South in an expensive car, by a white chauffeur.

"But then," he thought, "this is the wealthy Mr. Ralph P. Chandler's car, and surely no harm can come to me here. The Chandlers are a power in the Middle West, and in the South as well. Theirs is one of the great fortunes of America. In philanthropy, nobody exceeds them in well-planned generosity on a large and highly publicized scale. They are a power in Negro education, too, and that is why I am visiting them tonight, at their invitation."

Just now, the Chandlers were interested in the little Negro college at which the professor taught. They wanted to make it one of the major Negro colleges of America. And in particular the Chandlers were interested in his Department of Sociology. They were thinking of endowing a chair of research there, and employing a man of ability for it. A Ph.D. and a scholar. A man of some prestige, too, like the professor. For his *The Sociology of Prejudice* (that restrained and conservative study of Dr. T. Walton Brown's) had recently come to the attention of the Chandler Committee, and a representative of their philanthropies, visiting the campus, had conversed with the professor at some length about his book and his views. This representative of the Committee found Dr. Brown highly gratifying, because in almost every case the professor's views agreed with the white man's own.

"A fine, sane, dependable young Negro," was the description that came to the Chandler Committee from their traveling representative.

So now the power himself, Mr. Ralph P. Chandler, and Mrs. Chandler, learning that he was lecturing at the colored churches of the town, had invited him to dinner at their mansion in this city on the edge of the South. Their car had come to call for him at the colored Booker T. Washington Hotel—where the hot water was always cold, the dresser drawers stuck and the professor shivered as he got into his dinner clothes; and the bellboys, anxious for a tip, had asked him twice if he needed a half pint or a woman.

But now he was in a big warm car and they were moving

swiftly down a wide boulevard, the black slums far behind them. The professor was glad. He had been very much distressed at having the white chauffeur call for him at this cheap Negro hotel in what really amounted to the red light district of the town. But then none of the white hotels in this American city would keep Negroes, no matter how cultured they might be. Roland Hayes himself had been unable to find decent accommodations there, so the colored papers said, on the day of his concert.

Sighing, the professor looked out of the car at the wide lawns and fine homes that lined the beautiful and well-lighted boulevard where white people lived. After a time the car turned into a fashionable suburban road, and one saw no more houses, but only ivy-hung walls and shrubs and boxwoods that indicated not merely homes beyond, but vast estates. Shortly the car whirled into a paved driveway, past a small lodge, through a park full of fountains and trees and up to a private house as large as a hotel. From a tall portico a great hanging lantern cast a soft glow on the black and nickel of the body of the big car. The white chauffeur jumped out and deferentially opened the door for the colored professor. An English butler welcomed him at the entrance, and took his coat and hat and scarf. Then he led the professor into a large drawing room where two men and a woman were standing chatting near the fireplace.

The professor hesitated, not knowing who was who; but Mr. and Mrs. Chandler came forward, introduced themselves, shook hands and in turn presented their other guest of the evening, Dr. Bulwick of the Municipal College—a college that Dr. Brown recalled did *not* admit Negroes.

"I am happy to know you," said Dr. Bulwick. "I am also a sociologist."

"I have heard of you," said Dr. Brown graciously.

The butler came with sherry in a silver pitcher. They sat down, and the whites began to talk politely, to ask Dr. Brown about his lecture tour, if his audiences were good, if they were mostly Negro or mixed, and if there was much interest in his college, much money being given.

Then Dr. Bulwick began to ask about his book, *The Sociology of Prejudice,* where he got his material, under whom he had studied, and if he thought the Negro Problem would ever be solved.

Dr. Brown said genially, "We are making progress," which was what he always said, though he often felt as if he were lying.

"Yes," said Dr. Bulwick, "that is very true. Why, at our city

college here we have been conducting some fine inter-racial experiments. I have had several colored ministers and high school
teachers visit my classes. We found them most intelligent people."

In spite of himself Dr. Brown had to say, "But you have no
colored students at your college, have you?"

"No," said Dr. Bulwick, "and that is too bad! But that is one
of our difficulties here. There is no Municipal College for Negroes
—although nearly forty percent of our population is colored.
Some of us have thought it might be wise to establish a separate
junior college for our Negroes, but the politicians opposed it on
the score of no funds. And we cannot take them as students on
our campus. That, at present, is impossible. It's too bad."

"But do you not think, Dr. Brown," interposed Mrs. Chandler,
who wore diamonds on her wrists and smiled every time she
spoke, "do you not think *your* people are happier in schools of
their own—that it is really better for both groups not to mix
them?"

In spite of himself Dr. Brown replied, "That depends, Mrs.
Chandler. I could not have gotten my degree in any schools of
our own."

"True, true," said Mr. Chandler. "Advanced studies, of course,
cannot be gotten. But when your colleges are developed—as we
hope they will be, and as our Committee plans to aid in their
development—when their departments are headed by men like
yourself, for instance, then you can no longer say, 'That depends'."

"You are right," Dr. Brown agreed diplomatically, coming to
himself and thinking of his mission in that house. "You are right,"
Dr. Brown said, thinking too of that endowed chair of sociology
and himself in the chair, the six thousand dollars a year that he
would probably be paid, the surveys he might make and the books
he could publish. "You are right," said Dr. Brown diplomatically
to Mr. Ralph P. Chandler—but in the back of his head was that
ghetto street full of sleazy misery he had just driven through, and
the segregated hotel where his hot water was always cold, and
the colored churches where he lectured to masses of simple folks
exploited by money-grabbing ministers he dared not warn them
against, and the Jimcrow schools where Negroes always got the
worst of it—less equipment and far less money than the white
institutions; and that separate justice of the South where his people sat on trial but the whites were judge and jury forever—like
Scottsboro; and all the segregated Jimcrow things that America

gave Negroes and that were never better, or even equal to the things she gave the whites. But Dr. Brown said, "You are right, Mr. Chandler," for, after all, Mr. Chandler had the money!

So he began to talk earnestly to the Chandlers there in the warm drawing room about the need for bigger and better black colleges, for more and more surveys of Negro life, and a well-developed department of sociology at his own little institution.

"Dinner is served," said the butler.

They rose and went into a dining room where there were flowers on the table, and candles, and much white linen and silver, and where Dr. Brown was seated at the right of the hostess, and the talk was light over the soup, but serious and sociological again by the time the meat was served.

"The American Negro must not be taken in by Communism," Dr. Bulwick was saying with great positiveness as the butler passed the peas.

"He won't," agreed Dr. Brown. "I assure you, our leadership stands squarely against it." He looked at the Chandlers and bowed. "Dr. Kelly Miller stands against it, and Dr. DuBois, Dr. Hope and Dr. Morton. All the best people stand against it."

"America has done too much for the Negro," said Mr. Chandler, "for him to seek to destroy it."

Dr. Brown bobbed and bowed.

"In your Sociology of Prejudice," said Dr. Bulwick, "I highly approve of the closing note, your magnificent appeal to the old standards of Christian morality and the simple concept of justice on which America was founded."

"Yes," said Dr. Brown, nodding his dark head and thinking suddenly how on six thousand dollars a year, he might take his family to Paris in the summer, where for three months they wouldn't feel like Negroes. "Yes, Dr. Bulwick," he nodded, "I firmly believe as you do that if the best elements of both races came together in Christian fellowship, we would solve this problem of ours."

"How beautiful," said Mrs. Chandler.

"And practical, too," said her husband. "But now to come back to your college—university, I believe you call it—to bring that institution up to really first-class standards you would need. . .?"

"We would need . . . ," said Dr. Brown, speaking as a mouthpiece of the administration, and speaking, too, as mouthpiece for the Negro students of his section of the South, and speaking for himself as a once ragged youth who had attended the college when its rating was lower than that of a Northern high school and when he had to study two years in Boston before he could enter a white college, when he had worked nights as red cap in the station and then as a waiter for seven years until he got his Ph.D. and couldn't get a job in the North but had to go back down South to the work he had now—but which might develop into a glorious opportunity at six thousand dollars a year to make surveys and put down figures that other scholars might study to get their Ph.D.'s, and that would bring him in enough to just once take his family to Europe where they wouldn't feel that they were Negroes. "We would need, Mr. Chandler. . . ."

And the things Dr. Brown's little college needed were small enough in the eyes of the Chandlers. And the sane and conservative way in which Dr. Brown presented his case delighted the philanthropic heart of the Chandlers. And Mr. Chandler and Dr. Bulwick both felt that instead of building a junior college for Negroes in their own town they could rightfully advise colored students from now on to go down South to that fine little campus where they had a man of their own race like Dr. Brown.

Over the coffee, in the drawing room, they talked about the coming theatrical season and *Four Saints In Three Acts*. And Mrs. Chandler spoke of how she loved Negro singers, and smiled and smiled.

In due time, the professor rose to go. The car was called, and he shook hands with Dr. Bulwick and the Chandlers. The white people were delighted with Dr. Brown. He could see it in their faces, just as in the past he could always tell as a waiter when he had pleased a table full of whites by tender steaks and good service.

"Tell the president of your college he shall hear from us shortly," said the Chandlers. "We'll probably send a man down again soon to talk to him about his expansion program." And they bowed farewell.

A few moments later in the car as it sped him back toward town, Dr. Brown sat under the soft fur rug among the deep cushions and thought how with six thousand dollars a year earned by jigging properly to the tune of Jimcrow education, he could carry his whole family to Europe where just once for a summer they wouldn't need to feel like Negroes.

The Anvil May-June 1935

We Are Nurtured

BORIS ISRAEL

So it is that in hate we are nurtured. Today life streams through the streets, through the golden air mucky like hot butter churning in a soft, sweltered world. The heat flows quietly over the disgusted fields into the long and short canyons of our city, over the cobbles with scarcely an eddy, out over the water of the great, slow river. How I should like to love you. What can we do, then, but hate?

Margaret was unknown. She lied to me. I could not reproach her, it was her right. One night we walked to the park and sat there on a bench, looking across the railroad tracks and the dark river beyond. After a while an empty freight rattled past and I looked into my own face white against the black depths of the box car, my legs dangling over the edge, the lips dropping restfully, turned slightly by hate, the eyes excited, searching the flashing, limited horizon with hate. I saw the eyes, rimmed in black, above the smooth, dusty throat, for but a moment, then only the empty faces of the box cars, fluttering torn bills of lading, the caboose, a red lantern, the dying click and the fading rattle.

Then there were the riding lights of a fishing tug anchored in the river, and still there was myself who had passed on northward through the hills, the rolling grasslands, the corn plains, the loudening clang of the factory towns and the fire blazing against the sky of the steel mills. I dangled my legs and sat tense and hunched in the doorway of the empty box car, going on.

Margaret I had left there, Margaret whom I had never known, to settle into the hot, yellow days softly, allowing her tight, small breasts to melt and grow flabby, her solid thighs to spread, her eyes to grow misty, her thoughts to lose their compact, secret, haunting quality and sprawl listlessly about. It was for all this that I hated Margaret.

She touched my arm, then, that night in the park looking out across the great turgid water, but I didn't answer her. She spoke, quietly, for we were not alone. "What if I should marry you?" she

84

said. Her words startled me, although it was not a new idea. I watched a slender girl in a white dress, and a tall boy in a white shirt wander into the bushes of the river's edge, hand in hand, Marry. Forever and ever, do you accept this Margaret, unknown, inviting now, here tonight, hard tomorrow, gone again out past the riding lights of the tug, riding at bay in the river carrying itself southward. Always, always?

"Let's don't talk about that now," I said, and wanted to lay my head on her lap, but looked about us instead. What I saw made me ask against the hurt, exposed look I knew rested in her eyes, "Did you ever sleep in the park?"

"No," she said. "Please—," I waited, "don't misunderstand." I looked straight at her then in the dim light and her lips were turning, her jaw tightening, her eyes barricading the hate for what she had said.

I tried to smile, but it was too difficult. "I never misunderstand. That's a fault of mine. I like you," I told her and the last part of it was true. "Let's just be together," I said, and she moved closer and put her face close to mine. The sleeping man on the bench ten yards away had his back to us and did not move.

Pretty soon the young girl came out of the bushes and her dress was still white and so was her throat. She was followed by the boy who stopped to light a cigaret, the match flaring a moment in the darkness.

Margaret picked up the book I had laid on the bench. She read the title aloud. It was not a very big book, "Prepare for Power," she read. "The international situation and the tasks of the sections of the Communist International."

"May I read this?" she asked me, and she was a bit excited. Her cheeks flushed through the freckles and the dimness. I laughed, but that was wrong. I didn't mean it that way. I knew she would not be interested in this book. But Margaret had never been able to finish high school, and this made her sentimental about books. The pressure of hunger was not sentimental, though. I thought then of her salary and of her desire for me and for the book.

I remembered the marriage idea, then dismissed it. Let's not be sentimental. "Why do you want to read that?"

"I just want to read some books like that," she said. "I'm sick of novels. Really," she tried to convince me, she put her hand on my arm and held the book to her.

"Not that," I said, knowing she would be disappointed. "I'll bring something around," and I really intended to, but never did. For the first time I kissed her. I wanted her to know that I understood. She knew.

We moved away from each other, and she strained to read passages from the book by the fly-specked half light. I watched the street beyond, where a few cars stopped for the red light. One was a very big car and its black metal shone in the sundry light of the city evening. In the stream of its headlights something jerked from curb to curb. The legs were twisted violently, one feebly pulling, the other roughly shoving in stops and jerks. It reached the curb but did not stop, the sides of its deformed feet scraping the concrete raucously with each move. The huge automobile pulled strongly away without a sound.

I couldn't see who was in the automobile. It was too far away. It was another world being drawn before our eyes by silent, strong gears, behind dark, shined metal, polished glass, brushed upholstery.

The cripple had a long, dead face, cut jagged from black bone, the lips closed and bitter, the eyes not to be viewed. His clothes hung from his shoulders, his hips, what must have been a knee sticking out before him.

The man on the bench turned over and his arm fell from his chest. He slept on, on, his unshaven jaw to the sky, the sweat furrows clear on his dusty forehead, his wrist bound with a rag where a dark spot was his dried, black blood.

"Did you go to college?" Margaret asked me.

I didn't know how to answer. I never finished. It wasn't worth it. "It wasn't worth it," I said, and she didn't ask me more.

I looked up at a tall building and there were lights in three windows where the scrubwomen made their rounds on hands and knees. In the early morning they waited on corners for early street cars, grey and gnarled in shapes which repulsed investigation.

"I want to know these things," Margaret said and I waited a moment before I answered, searching for the proper words. I wanted to tell her as sharply as possible.

"Hate!" and I tried to punctuate it, to spit it out as an unavoidable command.

She waited, looking at me, never before nor since looking so tender and she touched my hand.

"Did you see that black cripple drag down the street a while ago, and he's still dragging," I said. "He didn't twist himself." Nor that weary sleeper, I thought, the scrubwomen deformed on hands and knees, you at a five-dollar-a-week job, the boy and girl snatch-

ing soggy pleasure in the grass of a river bank, wanting to love
and be at peace, but finding only bitterness certain, undisappoint-
ing. "We are not to blame."

I spoke quietly but felt as if I were screaming. Margaret listened,
one hand touching my arm, the other fidgeting her handkerchief.
I think she understood only too well. I looked far out toward the
eastern shore of the ever-flowing river, lost in darkness. The
strong, steady water quieted me.

"We're sick, Margaret. We're all of us, and our world, sick.
It's down inside of us." I turned to her, wanting her help to go on.
She was there. "We've wanted to love people, wanted the world
to be lovely, have wanted to be good, simple persons, enjoying
each other. We did not want hate festering inside."

She might have asked me, or I her, why we could not be this
way? Why we could not find our separate, peaceful path, could
not work by day and love in the evenings. Neither of us put the
useless question.

We do not live in that sort of a world. Ours is twisted and
crippled and all separate paths must, somehow, conform. I try
sometimes to dream in a clean life, sometimes to clear my bitterness in this, to harden my hate, to understand our own malady
and prepare to cut sharply into it.

"I hate you because you will get flabby, will spread your hips
bearing children under cramped multitudes of other lives, will
sicken into the soft, unbitter base for an aimless, dying world.
I cannot love this."

It left me breathless, that speech. Margaret had taken her fingers from my arm and she stared at them in her lap.

So it is that in hate Margaret lied to me, promised she would
never give in. I did not exact a promise from her, and I cannot
reproach her now. It is given to some of us to sharpen our hate,
to prepare for power, to build our bitterness, on that great ca-
pacity for love which we, ordinary folk, have by nature.

How long is it since that night by the river? Long. I have been
to the steel mills and back again, have fed on the leavings of a
world I disdained, have in fact spent myself and have been constantly replenished, have asked no quarter and hope I shall never
be so weak as to give it. We are nurtured, unwanted children of
this world, in preparation for power.

The Anvil Sept.-Oct. 1934

In Season

EUGENE JOFFE

As I came out of the subway I thought mildly that since I'd been fool enough to try for a job *again,* there was really no good reason why I shouldn't see Laura for awhile before I went home; so I went up to her office.

"Hello there," she said. She had stopped typing. "What happened?"

"Not a thing," I said. "How are you?"

"Where were you?"

"No place."

"Looking for a job?"

I nodded seriously, "I just can't seem to learn," I said severely. "I still go around looking."

"What was it this time?"

"Oh—" I told her.

She nodded offering me a pack of cigarets; I took one.

"Oh well," I said mildly.—"How's the boyfriend?"

She shrugged her shoulders. "Why don't you go around and see?"

"Hell, he's *your* boyfriend."

"Much to my regret," she said.

"Oh yes? When are you getting married—this month or the next?"

"Married? Not me."

"Not even for the baby's sake?"

"Be good, now," she said.

"To whom—you? How—kiss you?"

She said, "Oh, this is so sudden," and put down her cigaret and started typing again. Her boss had gone home half an hour ago and she'd be leaving soon herself. I didn't have a boss: I had a mother and father; there was no comparison.

"Stepping out much?" I said.

She shook her head no.

"What's the matter with Phil?" I asked.

"Not a thing."

88

"Well—?"

"—Except that he isn't working."

"Not yet?"

She went on typing. It would be a damn long time before she got married. Was Phil her lover or were they waiting for Christmas, or what?

"Hell," I said, "do you know anybody except yourself who *is* working?"

"Oh yes. I came across someone last week, only I didn't get a chance to ask his name."

We laughed a little. "For God's sake," I said, "stop that damn typing." She quit, and leaned back.

"How's everybody at home?" she asked.

"Living."

"Really."

"Do you know what it's like to stay with your family and not have a job?" I said. "Not a damn thing to do all day, having to ask for every damn cent, and my old man moaning about the rent and the light and his business and the money he wasted on my college, and all of them just goading me and goading me—"

"Why don't you go out and become one of these homeless boys?"

"That isn't half as ridiculous as you're trying to make it."

We sat there.

"Oh yes," Laura said. "Three girls across the hall were laid off this week."

"How do *you* keep working so long?—Oh, the hell with it— Say something, do something, will you? No job, no dough, no fun, no point in any damn thing—Jesus, I'm sick of it. If I could just get up the guts enough to lie down and not get up anymore. Jesus Christ!"

"Ah, poor thing," she said. "Want my shoulder to cry on?"

"Sure." I went over to her. "Boy, am I crude."

I sat on the desk beside her and put my arm around her shoulders. She was a few years older than I was and I didn't feel awkward. As she was lifting her cigaret to her mouth I held her wrist away and kissed her. Suddenly I wanted to stay like that a long time, with my face next to hers and my arm around her . . . I sat up.

"Just to show you," I said.

"You're not showing me a thing."

"I'm not your boyfriend." I got off the desk.

"Why don't you get married to somebody?"

"Why don't you talk about something interesting?" I lit a second cigaret from the butt of the first.

"For instance?"

"Just —finding me a job, little one," I said. "Let's start right there."

The Anvil Nov.-Dec. 1933

Collar

JOSEPH KALAR

Lying in bed, frowning, Mister Crawford stared sourly at the ceiling, on which, like fat grey flies, beads of moisture had gathered clammily.

"Oh Jesus!" he yawned, turning limply, burrowing his nose deep into a stained pillow. "Oh sweet, sweet Jesus Christ!"

The sun poured a flood of yellow light through the window, inundating the small room with a deceptive brilliance that smarted in the eyes. It was nearly noon. With a despairing anguish, Mister Crawford found that it was impossible to sleep all the day away; with the sun prying underneath his eyelids, Mister Crawford discovered again that Time was a wound in the mind, distilling a sweat of misery that soaked deep into one's being. He had awakened with a smile that was sleepy but confident. For a moment or two he grinned at the ceiling as if trying to gather the loose scattered ends of his dreams together, then with an intolerable pain he remembered suddenly that really he was no longer Mister Crawford, the assistant time-clerk, walking stonily isolated and impervious among the workers, but merely and weakly a tired little man, with grey wandering eyes and a sharp nose always snotty, who now had nothing to do but lie in bed until his back ached against the springs under the mattress, and stare at the ceiling with veiled unhappy eyes, while at the back of his mind, heavy and leaden, forlornly played the hope that he would yet be put back to work and thus again become Mister Crawford. For a brief instant, this fragile hope cheered him; the moment the hope left him, it seemed as though his head was caught between two hands as rigid as a vise, thumbs pressing deep and powerfully upon a spot right above his eyebrows, until his mind was filled with a terrifying shuffling of darkness and he seemed to tread over a deep pit that sucked at him horribly with a black mouth. For a short while longer he lay in bed, then he could stand it no longer. Leaping in frenzied desperation from the bed he walked feverishly up and down the floor of his small, distasteful room.

From under his bed, the little dog bounded and began to bark loudly, its little eyes bright and immobile as glass, like two shiny black buttons. It frisked at his feet, tugged at his trousers, leaped on the bed and growled. Mister Crawford grinned looking at it and his hand patted softly the little brown head. "Only my dog . . . nothing but my dog . . ." he muttered vacantly. "Jesus, but you are a crazy son of a bitch!" he laughed. "Lay off now, you tyke, lay off, or I'll put the boots to you." The dog fell back on his rump, cocking his head, his short tail wagging fiercely and adoringly.

Every morning the dog jumping like that was a tonic to Mister Crawford. The room seemed less drab and even the sunshine seemed less deceptive. His mind seemed for a few moments to be cleansed of cobwebs that clung suffocatingly in the far reaches of his head, and standing before a mirror, he could square back his rounded shoulders and adjust the personality of a Mister Crawford as adeptly as he adjusted his frayed and shabby tie. Walking up and down the room he regained that attitude of inviolate immobility that was like a cold wind to the workers in the shop. "You there, you, what is your number?" he said crisply to the mirror. "You, Mr. Jacobinski, you, is it not understood that no smoking is permitted under any circumstances?" he said sternly to the chair, elaborately writing in the palm of his hand with a cigaret-stained forefinger. "A little less insolence, Mr. Swanson, after all . . ." suggestively firm to the combinet, the rounded contour of which gleamed white and cold near the green foot of the bed.

After a few moments, Mister Crawford sat suddenly on the bed, which sagged and creaked raspingly, his shoulders collapsing into limp symbols of despair. Staring into the mirror he saw with distaste a small colorless face turning yellowish with faint tints of blue under eyes small and expressionless. He made a wry grimace and blew his nose noisily between his fingers, while with the back of his hand he wiped his eyes that had suddenly become filled with tears.

"Oh sweet, sweet lovely Jesus!" he wheezed, running his hands through his hair fiercely as though to pull every last strand of it out by the roots.

For a moment or two his eyes contemplated the oil stove, his mind, gingerly and with a faint touch of nausea, thinking of food. His stomach lay heavily within him, like a distended bladder, remote and heavy as a stone pulling at his belly. He belched sourly. "Christ!" he said, wrathfully. "God damn these biscuits and stale rolls! Just like clay in my guts." He walked around the room and kicked viciously at the chair. "Just like chewing clay, by Jesus!" he repeated, sitting on the bed again. For a long time Mister

Crawford sat impassively, staring into the mirror with eyes that saw nothing, an absurd little creature, suddenly all limp and soft collapsing into his clothing. The little dog whined nervously, its short tail jerking uneasily. Turning his head so heavily that the cords in his neck almost seemed painfully to creak, Mister Crawford looked for a long time at his dog, his eyes vacant and cold.

"Oh Lord!" he sighed finally, kicking with half-hearted viciousness at the dog, who growled mildly and backed uneasily under the bed. "Let's get to hell out of here before I get the shakes, sitting here thinking about it."

When they got into the street, the sun was pouring blistering heat upon the pavement. People were crawling like chilled flies, slowly and torpidly, from the shade of one awning to the next. By the Brunswick pool hall several men in shabby overalls lounged indolently, chewing plug and squirting brown streams of juice into the gutter. Mister Crawford winced with a small limp fear as he caught sight of Swanson, Jacobinski, Reilly and Satero looking at him with cold sneering eyes. From force of habit, he could not rid himself of an authoritative air, and though he now felt his entire being turning into the consistency of mush under the compulsion of a nameless fear and embarrassment, he strove to walk briskly, tried desperately to look unconcerned, chill, distant, and immaculate. And yet, as he walked toward them, his legs seemed to turn, inexorably, into the stiffness of wooden stilts, jerking at his buttocks.

"For Christ's sake!" bawled Swanson so loudly that the cop leaning sleepily on the lamppost looked up suddenly alert. "For the holy love of Jesus, look at this louse, collar and all!"

Mister Crawford jerked onward, his feet falling stiffly and woodenly on the pavement. The men roared loudly, their laughter releasing a rich spring of scorn that made Mister Crawford wriggle weakly in his clothes.

"Say, Mister Crawford," Jacobinski simpered, his voice round and fat with a caricatured obsequiousness, "Jesus, I'm sorry. I forgot to punch my damn card this morning. Be a sport, Mister Crawford, and O. K. it for me, won't you?"

Reilly spat a brown liquid stream that just missed splattering over Mister Crawford's left shoe, which, though the leather was cracked and brittle, was elegantly polished. With mock gravity and severity, he walked beside Mister Crawford, wriggling his buttocks with female deftness. Mister Crawford looked at him out of the corner of his eye, inwardly raging. He said nothing. He saw, finally, with considerable satisfaction, that he had passed the pool hall, and that Reilly was no longer within range of his eye. Just as he began to feel at ease again, and felt his legs being resolved into plastic flesh, Reilly shouted "BOOOO!" right beside his ear, so suddenly and loudly that Mister Crawford involuntarily threw up his hands. Loud scornful laughter beat upon him, in which even the policeman by the lamppost joined. Mister Crawford felt suddenly terribly alone, a dry bitterness tugged at his ribs, and his eyes became moist. "The bastards!" he muttered, "the dirty bastards. . . ."

He walked rapidly toward the railroad tracks. The rails thrust themselves into the distance brilliant in the sunshine, two shining parallels of steel. Beside him the little dog trotted, its tail perpendicular and quivering. Mister Crawford stared unseeingly at the brown wrinkled button of the dog's rump. His feet, he thought distantly, tired very quickly these days. He stumbled over the ties several times, and once he sprawled heavily to his knees, his hands skidding painfully over sharp flinty cinders. "Jesus," he said, rising weakly, shaking his head, a flood of bitterness threatening to deluge his eyes with tears.

He picked his way more carefully over the ties. "Just eleven months ago today," he muttered absently. Eleven months ago, he thought now bitterly. Mister Crawford walked coldly about the shop, magnificent and serene in his power. How beautifully the workers had quickened their pace, glancing at him furtively out of shadowed eyes as he came by. And how beautiful it had been when he came into the office and crept softly to a far corner, hugging his grandeur behind a high stack of timecards, whispering tenderly over and over, "Mister Crawford, Mister Crawford, Mister Crawford. . . ." Eleven months ago. . . . "By God! it ain't fair!" he shouted loudly, sudden anger surging in his blood. Now he had to walk by the men of his department in fear and shame. They, though unemployed, had grown in boldness and clung more and more to each other, common needs creating a bond that pierced the fog of color and nationality, while he, Mister Crawford, had nothing but his dog and this dry bitterness for the scornful men whose timecards had been placed away in dusty archives which grew dustier with the months.

He fell again, skinning his knees. For a moment or two he did not move, his hands burrowing into the cinders weakly, a sudden inertia rendering his muscles powerless. The little dog jumped upon him barking, its shiny black eyes flickering with excitement. With a moist warm tongue it licked at Mister Crawford's ear. Mister Crawford became incongruously furious. "Give over, you

little bastard!" he shouted, "or I'll bust your back for you." With
his hand he reached for the little dog's throat. The dog backed
away in fear. "Come here, you tyke," Mister Crawford growled.
The dog, apology in its eyes, backed farther away. "Aw, come on,
come on, tyke," Mister Crawford wheedled, but his voice was so
unpleasantly rasping in its hypocritical tenderness, that the little
dog budged not an inch. It sat on its haunches in stony immobility
and whined.

Slowly Mister Crawford rose to his knees, tenderly and cautiously picking cinders out of his skin. His eyes were malignant
now and his thin small lips had curved into a tense line. With one
hand he brushed as though completely absorbed, but his eyes
watched the dog vigilantly. Softly and cautiously, his feet moved
inch by inch, and with every movement forward, his hand increased its brushing. With a sudden bound, Mister Crawford fell
upon the dog, his hand clutching its throat. He lifted it and held
it up before him, shaking it viciously. The little dog could whine
no longer, its little eyes, now filmed as with smoke, bulged
perceptibly, while its feet pawed spasmodically at Mister Crawford's chest.

Mister Crawford panted. Sweat gathered into beads on his forehead and rolled into his eyes, blinding him. His eyes were as
vacant as glass. His dry tongue licked at lips suddenly all parched
and cracked. Beside the track a small ditch, full of a brown, filthy
water, covered with splotches of oil and grease, caught his eye.
Shaking the dog, now slowly becoming more limp, he stared at
the ditch as though trying to remember something, then suddenly
he jumped to the edge of the ditch and fell to his knees. He thrust
the dog deep into the brown liquid until only the rump pro-
truded. For a long time the dog kicked, at first with considerable
strength, then convulsively and with increasing weakness, its struggles generating small whirlpools in the water which sucked at the
lily-pads of grease and broke them into whirling pieces glinting
with purple and silver and gold.

Mister Crawford's frenzy left him as suddenly as it had come.
Now he realized dully that the little dog was gone. The water in
the ditch became calm, the pieces of oil rushed gladly together,
forming huge living splotches growing like a strange, sinister water
flower. Sitting on the edge of the ditch, his chin in his hands, Mister Crawford looked at the water for a long time. His mind became
vacant of thought, felt like an alien aching weight within his
head.

When Mister Crawford started to walk toward town, the sun was still high in the sky. Sweat continued to form into oil beads on his forehead. His neck was hot and damp. Running a finger around his neck underneath the collar, Mister Crawford felt sweat smearing his skin like butter. The collar, frayed into sharp ends of thread that pricked his neck, had become so wilted and tight that it felt like a noose around his neck.

The Anvil May-June 1934

Wake to the Hunting

I. L. KISSEN

"C'mon out, boy," said the sheriff, grinning friendly. "I got good news for you."

I was scared. Sheriffs never have no good news for black folks, especially when they're in jail.

"How'd you like to get turned loose, ten bucks, and all the bar-becued ribs you can eat?"

I'd been scared ever since they put me in that jail house, and now I was even more scared.

"I ain't done nothing, mister Law," I said. "I was just looking for a job of work."

"Why, I know you ain't done nothing, sonny," he said, nailing a-hold of my arm and drawing me out of the bull pen. "You gonna thank me the longest day God lets you live. You gonna have more fun than a barrel of monkeys, and you gonna get ten bucks for having that fun, besides all the barbecued spareribs your black belly can hold."

Then he taken me outside the jail and there was a big bunch of people waiting there. I knew some of them. They were all the plantation folks and riding bosses from miles around, along with their women folks and young ones. All of them was dressed up like circus day. Miss Jenny Patterson from Tulip Tree Plantation raised a little gold horn and blowed: "ta ra! ta ta ta ra! ta ra!"

"Here comes our fox!" she squealed. "Hello, you sly old fox, you better tuck your tail between your legs and run."

"I ain't done nothing," I said again, sort of looking for a rope among the crowd. I knew they was up to no good.

"Well, folks," said the sheriff, "how's he stack up? Them long legs of his look like they could git up and go, don't they?"

They all got to looking at my legs, and I felt like they would buckle right in under me. I didn't care whether I run or not, be-cause like as not a rope or something else would be waiting for me when I got through running.

"Listen, folks, and you, too, boy, so's we'll all understand the rules. This boy's gonna have a good half hour's start before we

turn the dogs loose. They're tied to the bandstand up at the
square. After the headstart we're all going after him with the dogs
and lassoes. The idea is for him not to get caught, and for you
to catch him before five o'clock. If he don't get caught, he gets
a twenty dollar bill. If he does get caught, he still gets a ten dollar
bill and all the barbecued ribs he can hold. Now all you folks rally
back around the bandstand when I fire five shots. That'll tell you
he's caught. If I don't fire any shots, come back at five o'clock
for the square dance and the eats. Everybody understand?"

They was all grinning at me and sort of fidgeting and tapping
their legs with riding whips.

"We're doing them hi-falutin English folks one better," the
sheriff said. "We'll have a real human fox hunt. They only got a
puny little animal fox.

"Please, sir," I said to the sheriff. "I can't do it. I know you
ain't aim me no dirt, but soon's I get in the bresh them dogs or
some of the young hotheads will hurt me, sure as shooting."

Then the sheriff come up close to me and talked so low nobody else could hear.

"I want to give you a break and you ain't got no thanks for
me. I got all this planned up and the folks all waiting. You aim
to disappoint them? You'll either run or I'll hit you one that will
jar your old grandmother's black ass back in Africa."

I had to run for it, that was all.

"Don't let them dogs maul me, please, sir," I asked the sheriff.
"Some of them's mighty mean, especially to colored folks."

"Hell, boy, they won't have time to muss you up none. Somebody'll be right on hand to take 'em off of you. You don't run
no more risk than a babe in arms. It's as easy as falling off a log,
and you're bound to snag a ten dollar bill and enough spareribs
to make the grease run out of your ears. Now give me your hat
so's the dogs can get your scent."

He jerked off my hat and started away with it. The crowd broke
up and moved toward the square. I knew I didn't have no more
chance than a rabbit. But what could I do? They could take me
back to that jail house and throw away the key and forget about
me. They could beat me to a jelly, too, and nobody would know
nothing about it except the Laws themselves.

"When I holler 'go' you git up and skedaddle," the sheriff
called back to me. "And when I say 'go' I mean it. You'd better
make them feet stir up the dust."

I felt kind of weak and sick inside. I sure didn't feel like walking, let alone running. But I knew he meant it.

"All right! Go!" the sheriff hollered, and I made a start. I was so flustered I fell flat on my face. He come running up and fetched me a kick on my behind. I got up, a little wobbly, and he give me a push.

"Come on, come on," he said. "Don't spoil the fun and make it harder on yourself. Take out. You're just stiff from sleeping in the jail. You'll get suppled up, all right."

I made a start, but not a very fast one. In a minute or two, I heard the dogs baying and I knew they had smelled my hat and wanted to be after me. The people was all yelling and blowing their little horns.

The woods was only a couple of blocks away, and I was tickled to get in them. Anything for some cover. I run till I had pains in my side, and my stomach kept climbing up inside my frame. I guess it was a good thing I hadn't had much grub that morning.

I made a lot of noise at first, bumping into bushes and falling around. I just couldn't help it, I was that scared of the dogs and the people. For all I could tell somebody would take a pot shot at me and it would just be a sad accident nobody could help. I only wanted to put some space between me and them faces and most of all between me and them dogs. Nothing sounds more scarey than a hound when he's on a human scent.

I was soon scratched all up and my side hurt worse. I wished then I had had something to eat. Once I thought of climbing a tree. But that's no good. Ain't no escape from the dogs on top of a tree. They got you right where they want you. I tried to remember if there was swamp land thereabout, so's I could wade through it and put them off the track. But my head ached so and felt so whirly that I just couldn't recall.

I tried to keep my ears cocked for all sorts of sounds, but all I could hear was dogs. Every time a bird cheeped or a wind rattled the leaves, it sounded like a dog to me. I been in the woods many's the time, but never before did all the different noises sound exactly like a dog on the scent.

I kept jog-trotting away and wishing I knew where there was water. Being thirsty didn't help none, either. I got so crazy in the head I banged into tree trunks and like to have knocked out my fool brains.

"Why don't you wait and rest yourself?" my mind told me. "It ain't no use. You can't get away, nohow." But my feet never paid no attention, just kept moving along. Lord, but I was spitting cotton. My tongue was hanging out a foot. Then I had some luck.

I run smack dab into a swamp. It was full of mud, and little bubbles kept oozing to the top and busting with a bad smell. But the dogs couldn't track me through it. Only thing was that I might mire down in it. There was a lot of big logs, and I'd best chance jumping from one to the other till I reached the other side. When I tried, though, I slipped off and got a lot of stinking goo all over me. No use. I'd rather face the dogs and lassoes. I run along the edge, wishing to see a clear stream I could wade down for a spell.

I fell across rocks a couple of times and skinned my shins, but I got up quick enough. I wondered what time it was and if they would really quit when it got to be five o'clock. I wondered how I could tell when it was five o'clock and whether I could sit down and blow a little. I could tell when it got dark, anyways, and then I'd go back to the square and get my twenty dollar bill. That is, if they'd been telling the truth. I didn't trust them any too far.

The dogs began to sound like they was right at my heels. I knew they must be quite a ways off, but I hurried up a little all the same. I was slowing down, though, in spite of all I could do. My side was full of stitches.

I tried to stay in the bushes. My heart was beating so hard it shook me from head to foot. One dog seemed to pull out ahead of the rest. He'd be socking his teeth into me any minute, and nobody knows how long it might have been before somebody came up to take him loose. Only thing now was a tree, and I went up like a monkey after a cocoanut. Soon's I was safe in the top branch, I began to feel stiff and sore and I saw that I was bleeding in a lot of places. The branches and thorns did it.

The dog was barking treed at me and scratching at the trunk.

A big fat lady came puffing through the branches and throwed her lasso up at me. But it would catch in the limbs.

She got mad. "Loosen that lasso and git down here so's I can claim you," she ordered. "Be quick, now. I don't want no argument about who caught you. I ain't gonna hurt you, and I'll keep the dog off you."

I slid down. The dog nipped me a couple of times, but she beat him off. I could hear the other dogs getting near, and worried about whether she could shoo them all away. She'd have her hands full, and maybe she'd just give up and let them worry me to death.

"Bend down!" she hollered. She was sweating all over, but mostly under her arms and around her waist. She would have looked funny if I had felt like laughing. I bent down and let her slip the lasso over my shoulder. She pulled it tight, and stood holding the end of it, watching for the others to come through the bushes. The sheriff was the first to break through. He started kicking the dogs around. They was excited and seemed bound to have a piece of my meat whether or no.

"I got him! I win!" the fat lady hollered.

The sheriff raised his gun and fired five times.

"You win, sure enough, fair lady," he said, bowing low to the woman with the rope around my shoulders. "Now everybody back to the bandstand for the eats and the dancing. You come along, too, boy, and git your ten dollar bill and all the barbecued spareribs your black hide can hold. This thing is all on the level, and you're gonna be treated fair and square just like I promised."

Old Daddy Blackwell from our town was doing the barbecuing, and I felt so ashamed when I saw him that I wanted to sink in the ground. He peeked up at me and shook his head when he handed me a big juicy rib smeared all over with that good old hot sauce that only Daddy knows how to mix up. Somehow I didn't feel much appetite now. I only wanted to get away from the music and the laughing white folks and lay down in a spot where it was dark and still. I didn't like Daddy Blackwell to be pitying me. I hadn't done nothing wrong to be in jail in the first place, and I run through the woods like a fox because I was afraid not to. I reckon worse things than scratches and bruises and being ashamed of myself might have happened to me if I'd balked at playing fox when the sheriff told me to and meant it when he said it. I'll bet you any man would have done the same in my place.

I finished the ribs and stood around, forgetting for a while where I was. The sheriff and some of the others didn't like me hanging around, I guess, because the sheriff said after a while:

"Well, boy, you got your ten dollar bill and your ribs. Now maybe you want to dance, too. Want me to get a partner for you?"

This spelled as plain as plain that he was getting mad. My feet bore me away from there before my mind caught up with them. With everything in such a hullabaloo I'd forgot how tired and sore I was, and before I reached the city limits I began to feel sick again and wished I hadn't took the spareribs after all.

The New Anvil May-June 1940

Reunion

ARKADY LEOKUM

As I crossed the street and walked toward him, I remembered. Our college lunchroom, a noisy, nervous place in the basement. Sid was squeezing toward me between the tables, pushing through knots of students in a careless, familiar way. Our lunchroom had long white tables and you didn't sit at them to eat—you stood. It was always so tightly packed with students that if you bought soup or a plate of vegetables or coffee, half of it would be gone— upset or jostled out of your hand—by the time you found a dirty corner of the table to put it on.

So most of us just brought sandwiches from home. Most of us couldn't afford more.

But Sid seldom brought anything. He'd ease his way from one end of that noisy cellar to another, his coat open, his hat planked down on his head as if someone had thrust it on him, saying, "There! Now wear it!"; and if he had even the slightest acquaintance with you and you were there he was sure to get to you.

"Hi," he'd say, and the food stuck in your throat while he watched you. You gossiped idly about some teacher. He stood awhile, smiling uneasily, putting his hands in and out of his pockets awkwardly, and then finally he'd venture: "You couldn't spare half that sandwich, could you?"

He said that very quickly.

Sometimes we gave him a sandwich—but most of us got tired of feeding him. It was easy to refuse him. He was so damned inefficient. So hopeless. Futile. Why should a fellow bring his own lunch? It was easier to pick it up here and there, get a bite from this one, an apple there, a cup of coffee from the fellow who sat next to you in Psych.

I always said, "It's all I've got, Sid."

He did the same thing in his work. Sponged on all of us, shirked a lot of unpleasant work we all wanted to shirk—but didn't. That Art Appreciation course, for instance. It was "culture"—required for the degree—so it roped in a lot of fellows who cared more about Joe Louis' style than about Picasso's. Yet everyone who took that course had to hand in an Art Notebook, with a set of pictures and commentary.

Sid didn't. He talked a fellow into giving him his old notebook, patched it up here and there, re-wrote a page or two, and passed it in.

I really had nothing against Sid; I don't think anybody did. But he gave that impression of why-work-when-you-can-get-away-with-it that made you feel like an ass for grinding away, for tackling the hard jobs. It's not a feeling that gives you an affection for a fellow.

Now he stood there across the street, slouching on his feet, half turned toward me as I crossed—and it all came back. The unfriendliness probably crept into my voice, but I couldn't help it.

"Hello, Sid," I said.

He looked at me with that amused stare that made me feel like a sap for no reason at all. "Hello, Bob," he said, his hand in his pocket. I dropped mine.

"Well, well!" I said, sounding cheerful and meaningless, while I tried to think of what to do with him.

We were both class of June '36, and I hadn't seen him since Commencement, yet I felt at once that here was the same old help-less Sid. His coat was greenish, heavy and dank—as if it had absorbed torrents of rain and never been dried properly, his shoes misshapen and unshined. If we were back in that college lunch-room, I thought, he'd ask me for a sandwich in a moment. It was very difficult for me to talk without getting that into my voice.

"What are *you* doing in Radio City?" I asked.

"Watching the skating," he said. "Very pretty."

"I work here, you know," I said. He raised his eyebrows.

"This is my lunch-hour," I said. "How about grabbing a bite—on me?" I added.

"Sure," he said. "Thanks."

We turned toward Sixth Avenue. "I'm in advertising now," I said. I buttoned my gloves. "Write copy and all that."

He thrust out his lips in that way that means "Really?" "Sure," he said, "I remember. You edited the literary magazine in college."

"This is lots more fun."

We walked along a while.

"Working?" I asked.

He shook his head. The last time I had heard of Sid he was wrapping packages in a department store basement.

"How about WPA?" That was postgraduate work for most of the class of '36.

"For a while. They found out my mother was feeding me—so they canned me."

We walked into the cafeteria, pulling the tongue-like tickets from the machine. He didn't want to take his coat off, but I hung mine up, and my scarf and hat on top of it.

He put ketchup all over his vegetables and took big bites.

"Nice little racket—advertising."

"Oh, yes," I said. "Lots of fun, though."

"What did Mike Gold call it?"

"I don't know. Why?"

" 'The most parasitic, most venal of all professions—' "

"I don't read him any more. But he would.—You know, I've been able to get married on it."

"Swell," he said.

"Six months ago."

He nodded, balanced a forkful of string beans, and swallowed them.

"I've got a swell little apartment."

"In the Village?"

"How did you know?"

"Oh—I don't know. Just a guess."

Sid never starched his collars. He still didn't.

"What sort of work you looking for?" I asked. I knew he'd still take a job wrapping packages if he could get it. He looked at me, smiling.

"One commensurate with my abilities."

"Of course," I said. We understood each other.

I suddenly noticed he was eating with his left hand. God knows why, I thought. After the coffee I reached over and took his check. There was a heart-shape punch through 40.

"I gotta be going," I said.

"Sure. Thanks for the grub."

I put on my hat, scarf and coat while he waited. At the corner of 50th we stopped. "Here's the people I'm with," I said, giving him a card. It said: "George Baker—9 Rockefeller Plaza." He glanced at it and stuck it in his pocket.

"Well—goodbye."

He held out his left hand. "Closer to the heart," he said.

I pointed to his right arm questioningly. It had been in his pocket all the time. He shuffled around clumsily.

"Oh—" he said, "some Italian fascist bastard had punk aim."

"What do you mean?"

"In Spain. Ebro. Not much—but it nixed me for the army. Anyway, that was a flop, too."

He pulled his collar up with his left hand, his eyes on the ground. He turned, and the crowd swallowed him up.

It was three to one. I hurried to work.

The New Anvil June-July 1939   ·

Sequel to Love

MERIDEL LE SUEUR

I am in the place where they keep the feeble-minded at Faribault. This place is full of girls moanen' and moanen' all night so I can't get no sleep in to speak of.

They won't let me out of here if I don't get sterilized. I been cryin' for about three weeks. I'd rather stay here in this hole with the cracked ones than have that done to me that's a sin and a crime. I can't be sleepin' hardly ever any night yet I'd stay right here than have that sin done to me because then I won't be in any pleasure with a man and that's all the pleasure I ever had. Workers ain't supposed to have any pleasure and now they're takin' that away because it ain't supposed to be doin' anybody any good and they're afraid I'll have another baby.

I had one baby and I named her Margaret after myself because I was the only one had her. I had her at the Salvation Army home.

Pete and me had her but Pete never married me. He was always at the library after he lost his job.

Pete said he had a place on a farm. I guess he had a farm then and he said he would take me out there and give me red cheeks and we would have a cute kid.

I been workin' in the five and ten since I was twelve because I was big and full for my age. Before the New Deal we got eight dollars dependin' on if a girl was an old girl or a new one and extra girls got $6.25 a week for fifty-hour hours work, but if you only worked fifty hours you got thirteen cents an hour. I hear from my girl friends it's different now and they cut down the girls a lot and a girl there now has got to do the work of two. That's what I hear. I ain't worked there now for a year and a half.

Peter used to meet me after work on Seventh there, and we used to go to a show or walkin' or to the park, and he used to tell me these things. He was a good talker and I guess he meant it. He never made the depression, although you'd think it the way people talk about him.

Gee, the baby Pete and me had was pretty! Red cheeks and

kind of curly hair. I would like to of kept her right good. I hated havin' her and was sure I was going to die off, but after I seen her I would have liked to of kept her good.

When I had her I was missen' all the shows in town and I was mad. They had to strap me down to nurse her and I had to stay there so long that I was even missen' them when they come to the fifteen centers and after that you have to go a long ways out to see them.

But where I got mixed up with the charities was about havin' this baby. One month I missed and got nervous and went to a doctor and he wouldn't do nothin' because I didn't have no money. I went to three like that, and then one give me some pills and I took one and it made my ears ring so I was afraid to take any more. I cried for about two days but I didn't take no more pills.

I went to another doctor and he told me I was goin' to have a baby and I come out and went up to a corner of the hall and began to cry right there with everybody goin' by and a crowd come around. I thought you got to be quiet or you'll get arrested now so I was quiet and went on downstairs but I was shakin' and the sweat was comin' off me.

My girl friend tooken me home with her and told me I better go on and have it because to get rid of it would cost about one hundred dollars.

My father is a garbage collector and he wouldn't be ever makin' that much.

I swan that summer I don't know where I was goin' all the time. I kept lookin' in all the parks for him because I thought he was goin' to skip town and when I see him he hollered at me that he didn't have no money to skip.

I went to the clinic and they told me to eat lots of oranges and milk for my baby. My girl friend didn't have no work and her and me went out lookin' for food all the time because she kept tellin' me I had to eat for two now.

I kept lookin' and lookin' for Pete and lookin' for somethin' to eat. When I could see Pete seems like I could rest. I would follow him to the library and sit in the park until he come out and I would feel alright.

We kept lookin' for food. We walked miles and miles askin' at restaurants for food. I got an awful hankerin' for spice cakes. Seems like I would putnear die without spice cakes. Sometime we would walk clean over town lookin' and lookin' for spice cakes.

I thought I was goin' to die when I had my baby . . . I was took to the Salvation Home and had it there but I didn't like it none there and they had to strap me down to make me nurse the baby. Seems like there is a law a mother's got to nurse her baby.

I wanted to keep the baby but they wouldn't let me. My dad wanted to keep it, even, and my sister's got twelve kids and she wanted it. Even then it was such a cute kid. Kind of curly hair. But they rented it out to a woman and now they got me here.

My dad spent about fifty dollars with lawyers to keep me out but it ain't no good. They got me here until I have that operation.

I got a letter from Pete and he says you got no business to be there; you ain't dumb. Miss Smith that comes here to talk me into havin' an operation says I like men too much, that they can't let me get out at all.

I like men. I ain't got any other pleasure but with men. I never had none. I got to lay here every night, listenin' to the moanen' and thinkin' are they crazy, and my dad keeps saying to have it done it will be alright, that I won't get old or anything too soon. It ain't a natural thing that it should be done to a young girl.

I might know a man sometime with a job and getting along pretty, and why shouldn't I have a baby if it was alright so the Salvation Army wouldn't take care of me or anything and I wouldn't bother them? Like before, which wasn't our fault because I believe what Pete said to me about the farm and all.

We had a cute kid, an awful bright kid, Miss Smith says it sure is a cute kid, an awful bright kid alright.

They keep sayin' I like men but why shouldn't I like men, why shouldn't a girl like a man? But for us girls that work for our livin' we ain't got no right to it and I was gettin' seven dollars at the five and ten and that seems to be all I got a right to, my measly seven dollars, and they're firin' girls all the time now so I wouldn't get that back, even.

They don't want us to have nothin'.

Now they want to sterilize us so we won't have that.

They do it all the time and the police follow a girl around and the police women follow you around to see if you're doin' anything and then they nab you up and give you a lot of tests and send you here and do this to you.

They don't want us to have nothin', alright.

Pete and me sure had a cute kid, but we'll never see it any more. Now I'm locked up here with the feeble-minded.

The Anvil Jan. 1935

They Follow Us Girls

MERIDEL LE SUEUR

She was comin' up behind me with her shoulders scootched up and walkin' kind of soft. I saw her before and every time I saw her the cold shivers went down me. Since I saw her and she followed me I have lost my happiness. Here I've always been workin' since I came from Wisconsin and lost my ear-hearin' from hangin' out wash in the cold wind, and I never did anything but work and here they are followin' me around like I was a criminal, and I don't know what I did except now I haven't got a job at all for three years and I've been workin' hard to try not to starve and I got a front tooth that needs fixen' and I have to work weeks and weeks to get the clinic doctor to be fixen' it up so's I can sleep nights without the pain shootin' into me like a dagger in my face. It only costs one dollar all told to be fixen' it but they won't have it done with all the money they got and all the work I been doin' since I was a girl.

Mr. Hess tells me that's the way it is if you are a worker. Nobody is caren' but your own folks how you come out. And now what Mr. Hess has been tellen' me how it comes out that we haven't any jobs and these people followin' us like we was criminals, and he's been tellen' me this for a long time but I had no ear for it and now it gets clearer and clearer, yes clearer.

Anyway, the way it is that they think that all the girls and women on relief is bad, that's the way they figures it. Low grade intelligence, they says. And I been runnin' women's houses that can't run it themselves and nursin' their babies for 'em.

The way it is that the dicks follow you and the police matrons follow you tryin' to get some dirt on you so they can cut off the food from your mouth. And this woman, I found out later her name was Bradley, would be followin' me like a shadow. I would go to the market, wherever I would go, I would be buyin' a bunch of carrots and kind of turn my head to look at another truck and my blood would stop right in my skin, there she would be standin' right over there by a truck, lookin' at me kind of scootched up

with a black dress on and her face as bright as a clown's. She's a
stool, I know that, and why should she be followin' me around
so I can't be happy?

The dicks hate me, too; they follow me around. I went down to
the five-and-ten to buy myself a little bowl and there she was
standin' with a dick right by the hot-dog stand, kind of lookin'
above my head but she didn't fool me. She kind of waited there
and I fooled around as if I was lookin' at bracelets and then I beat
it out and turned my head around and there she come right behind
me and there was the dick on the other side of the street walkin'
along kind of fast. They must be knowin' when I go to the store
and they are watchin' me. Maybe they don't want me to pay five
cents for a blue bowl. Maybe I shouldn't have a blue bowl. I've
lost my happiness. I can't go down town. I have to sneak along
and look around the corners.

I can't go anywhere. I'm scared. I wouldn't get married now
and have a baby. I would be scared. If they see you so much as
look at a boy they say you are immoral and shouldn't be havin'
any relief. If I had a baby at home with all the curtains drawn
down tight and never went out maybe they wouldn't know anything about it. But that's the way I would have to do it. I've lost
my happiness. I can't be goin' around anymore at all.

I can't even be goin' to Mr. Hess'. Mr. Hess is a very old man.
He comes from Virginia. Oncet he worked on a chain gang in Virginia and oncet he was in prison for a year and it tell on him.
He's an old worker. A worker gets old quick. I will get old pretty
quick. But he never offered to do anything with me. He's too
old. He's forgotten anything about what's between his legs, I
guess. That's why I like to have talk with him. He makes things
so they go together with some sense.

For instance, he told me about this Anna Bradley. I says to him,
Why should she be followin' me around? And Mr. Hess says to
me that he knowed her for a long time and she was a well-known
whore, she ran a house, you know, a regular house on the north
side, and her name was Bradley. I says, She's an old woman and
don't look to me no good for a man, but Mr. Hess says, Well you
see even them, even Anna Bradley, they was only usin' them, he
says, they're workers, too, he says and kind of smiles. He's a pretty
thin man and all his teeth are out of his head. And his eyes are
fallin' back into his head and the bones of his nose is the only
thing that comes sharper and sharper out of his face. They're
right sorry womens, he says, even if they are in with the dicks and
get a few dollars a day for followin' up girls, he says, they're right
tragic womens. And I believe it after he says it although I was mad

as hops at her for always bein' there with her rouged-up mug and her tight black dress always followin' and followin' me.

She give me the willies followin' me around, yes, everywhere I turn walkin' along feelin' right good in me and the mornin's real good, thinkin' to buy me a bunch of carrots or a head of green cabbage. And there I see her and my blood freezes right in my body and the sweat comes in my hands and feet because I am scared and there she is lookin' right above my head and I'm scared of what I see. And Hess says to me, you know she wants you to run that house, she thinks you're a whore, with your good fat arms, he says, and your rosy cheeks, she thinks you would be a good plump cherry to run her house.

But I says, I ain't no whore and she ought to know that. I ain't never done it. I always worked all my life. Sure, he says, but now you ain't workin' for three years, ain't it? Sure, I says, three years in August, so what? Well they're kind of tired, he says, havin' you on relief I guess, what with about twelve hundred more girls goin' on every month. They ain't so particular about what kind of work you're doin'. I got mad then, I says that Mrs. Black on the relief never would want a girl to go into a house or on the streets, that she was very particular, that they followed me around maybe just to see I wasn't a bad girl. At that Mr. Hess kind of laughed. He says, you better come with your own people, he says, you better come down to the Council with me, he says, with your own people, they're the only ones that care a tinker's damn about you, girl, your own people.

But I don't pay him no mind.

The next day I went to the relief and there was Anna Bradley sittin' right behind me. I don't know if she came in after me. I didn't see her till I been sittin' there about ten minutes and then someone was kind of kickin' the bottom of my chair and I turn around and sure as shootin' there it was, Anna Bradley large as life and twice as bright. And kept kickin' my seat with her high-falutin' high-heeled shoe and her old face made up for the kill and she sat there and went in right ahead of me to see Mrs. Black and I knew she was maybe goin' to tell her something. Maybe she was goin' to lie and tell her I went to that house when I didn't. Or maybe she was goin' to tell her about my goin' to Mr. Hess some time at night, though we always pulled down the blinds and I always went into the toilet when anybody rapped on the door. I could feel my skin shrivel and I sweated thinkin' now she'll take the food right outen' my mouth.

I went in next and I says the minute I sat down at Mrs. Black's desk, I said, what did that woman say about me, you know what she is, I says, and my face got so hot like fire was burnin' within an inch of it. And she says, well, we don't pay no attention to any gossip or what one person says about another in here, she says, but I think I will have to give you only four-eighty this month for food. Jesus Christ, who can keep their skin alive on four-eighty a month for food? You can't buy chicken feed, you couldn't fatten a chicken on it. Then Mrs. Black says, holdin' up a paper like she was readin' something very serious, and her tight little mug gets very serious, you know. She says, as if readin' from the paper, that if you live with a man you ain't married to then you won't get relief, we can't have any immorality around, she says, still studyin' the piece of paper.

Honest, I shook and my thighs stuck together and I could feel the water run out of my arm pits just like I was squeezed together and I said, Jesus, you don't think I live with that stinkin' old man, I says, I just go there to be talkin' with him. He smells old, I said. Pshaw, I wouldn't be livin' with him, he's the only friend I got to talk to. I got to talk to somebody, I says, and I talk to him, he's real educated. He's a gentleman, I says, he wouldn't do any harm to a girl. Oh, she says, as if she just ate a plum, so it's that old Mr. Hess, so it's him? And I bit my mouth together. I knew she caught me in a trap.

Well, she says, all right, but that's what I hear. You'll have to be mighty careful, she says, and I says, well I will, does that mean I can't talk to him none? Well, no, she says kind of slow, I wouldn't say that but still it might not be a bad idea, you know, girls like you got to be mighty careful, she says, men will take an advantage over you, she says.

I felt like bustin' out in a big laugh. I was really almost cryin', too, but I wasn't goin' to let her see it, so I got up to go and just then the telephone rang and the paper she had fell down on the floor and I picked it up for her and it was a blank sheet of paper. There was nothing on it at all. I looked at her and she looked at me and I knew we were enemies.

I always thought Mrs. Black was a friend of mine and I felt bad. I went to Mr. Hess and he was tellen' me, he says, yes, it's because you is workers, that's what he says, and I began to see it; yes, it's because you is workers, you and Anna Bradley too, and that's why they hound you—you ain't no good to them. They got enough workers, they got too many; that's why they don't want you to have no babies. Look at you, he says, you are good, he says, and he kept looking at my body so I felt bad and good at the same time. You got a warm good body, he says, for a hungry man but there ain't a man can take you. The man for you he ain't got a job either, so he can't be askin' you. Mr. Hess gets pretty sad sometime. We just sat there and Mr. Hess' cat came up and jumped on my lap and kind of curled around my neck and I put up my hand and stroked his body and it gave him a pleasure and he rubbed against my breast and arms and I began to cry, I don't know why. And Mr. Hess patted my hand and let his hand stay there and I saw how there was knots on it at every joint like an old tree and we just sat there.

After a while he said, you'll have to come down with me now, he says, where they is all together.

Who is? I said.

Why, the workers, he says.

We sat there.

I'm good, I says, I wouldn't be no whore. Of course you wouldn't says Mr. Hess. They're just forcin' me on the streets, I says, and I felt like my throat was swellin' up like a man I saw choke once. Not them, says Mr. Hess, it ain't them. It's something else, he says.

We sat there and outside the sun was shinin' very bright and everything looked very clear. And my girl friend, I says, she died havin' a baby, that's what happened. She died and they didn't care.

No, says Mr. Hess as if waitin' for me.

I used to go around with her, I says, and now where is she? Who cares if she had a name even, who cares about her bones, the blood in her, the way she walked?

I care, says Mr. Hess.

Who else? I cried out at him.

All, he says, all that knew what she knew. All that feel the same, they are together. All, says Mr. Hess, with hands like that —and he lifted up his arms like the branches of a tree that has been struck by lightnin'. All, says Mr. Hess, that are followed and worked to the bone and hounded and bled and murdered, says Mr. Hess.

And I knew I was one of them.

We sat there and I knew now what he was goin' to say and that I was goin' to do it.

All right, finally says Mr. Hess, why don't you come to the meetin' with me now, he says, the Unemployment Council, he says, meets tonight. You better come down.

My God, I says, I'm goin'.

Don't dress up none, he says.

I says, yes I'm going to dress up because if this is a meetin' of workers like you say, if this is where they all come together, why I want to be there, I says. I want to dress up for it.

The Anvil July-Aug. 1935

Below the Belt

SAUL LEVITT

I have been going up to this place near Lincoln Square every Saturday night for about a year now. The American Railway Express fellow on Thirty-sixth Street goes up too. But I never met the boss up there before.

At first, when I got out and I walked on the street, I kept saying so that people looked at me: "How the hell did Mr. Josephs find out about that place?" It couldn't have been the expressman, because the boss isn't the kind of a guy to get chummy with expressmen. I couldn't figure it out, and I kept wondering how it was, because even in times like these a man like Mr. Josephs has money. He's simply got to have money.

The way I felt when I finally reached the park and sat down! It was dark and down below on Fifty-ninth Street there were a lot of lights running along from East to West. I sat there awhile, and then went home, and today is Sunday, and I keep thinking of tomorrow. What's going to happen tomorrow?

Mr. Josephs is a pretty dignified man, except when he gets a little soused with the mill men. He wears a nifty brand of suit. You can tell it's expensive, the way it fits him around the shoulders and down the back. He is always dignified except when the mill men come in, which is about once a month. He takes them up to the little office on the balcony, and you can hear the bottles, and then they're talking loud. First they talk about silks, and then go on to talk about the silk market and the stock market, flinging thousands of dollars around.

The day after, though, Mr. Josephs is just the way he was before he got soused. He'll get on the wire and talk to salesmen away out in Chicago, fast and sharp. He'll talk smoothly and easily to the buyers from the big dress houses, and he looks pretty spiffy and he's smiling and puffing on a cigar when he talks to them.

He looks like the goods, a real big shot in every way, the way he talks, the way he dresses and keeps his hair. He must take a haircut every day for sure to keep that gray pompadour so neat and clean around the edges, and so shiny. He's got a sort of square face, and when he's busy it's all locked up tight and his brows wrinkle. You can't talk to him because he won't listen. The dyers once started loading us up all of a sudden with more than a dozen trunks, and I ran upstairs to see Mr. Josephs about it, and began to talk to him. "Get the hell out of here, for God's sakes," he said. He was dumping a load of old satin as a job lot on some dumb buyer, and when he got rid of them why he was all right again. He relaxes after a trick like that and says hello when he sees you, but otherwise he doesn't.

He was relaxed yesterday all right, and when the mill men came they all went into the private office on the balcony and they began to talk silks, and then they got soused and started flinging the thousands around.

We were working late yesterday. Leonia calls up at 12 o'clock to say they want to send over half a dozen trunks. Leonia always sticks us with a load of fresh-dyed stuff on Saturday and we have to wait for them until late in the afternoon and then unload them, as the stuff spoils in the trunks. I went up to the floor and called up to Mr. Josephs that the trunks were coming over. He said let them come, as he wanted to see the new fall colors they were going to handle this season.

The two fellows on the floor had thought they were going to make a break about 1, and they felt pretty bad when they heard what the boss said. They were sitting on the long tables where the silk is spread for the dress house buyers, and smoking, and now their jaws fell down, which didn't make me feel so bad, the way I love floor men.

At 3 o'clock the shipment came in and the floor men came down to help me. They're both pretty ordinary guys, though they think they're a hell of a lot because they're on the floor and handling silk. Some day, though, they'll be out selling, but a shipping clerk in a silk house never gets a chance to handle silk and so he never gets on the floor. These floor men are just kids, cousins to salesmen or the boss, and usually they're graduates of commercial high schools. They dress well, but the shipping clerk just craps around a cellar in an old pair of pants with the trunks and the bins of silk and the out-going shipments.

The two of them were down there helping me. They opened up the first package of silk and then one of them went up and got Mr. Josephs down to look at this new dark blue shade. The three of them admired it and fingered it, and the two floor men were licking the boss's pants the way they squinted and rubbed the silk. It made me feel lousy because I knew there was nothing to it but just fingering the stuff and looking wise and holding it up to the light and palming it off on the dress house silk buyers who don't know anything either.

While they were tossing the packages to me to put away in the bins, I thought of how I'd wanted to work in a bank when I left high school, but I couldn't land a job, so finally I had to go to work for a contractor on Twenty-fourth Street. I never wanted to work for a dress contractor, but there I was. Before I got this job, though, I'd hunt around in the mornings answering ads which about a million other kids answered with me. After running around and getting nothing all morning I'd go down to the docks with a half idea of landing a job on a boat, but I never got up enough courage, so I went to work for this contractor on Twenty-fourth Street.

You know what Seventh Avenue is like below Thirty-third Street. In the summer time the sun gets into that ground until it begins to get soft, because there aren't so many tall buildings. I used to deliver dresses to the houses uptown in a hand-truck. I'd wheel that truck in traffic just like a horse or a coolie, and stop at the lights—for fifteen bucks a week! I was working there awhile when a fellow from a silk house who came into the place told me I ought to get into a silk house, as they don't work you so hard, the hours are better, and there's a chance for advancement. I didn't quit this contractor immediately, but every time I went uptown I'd stop in at one of these silk houses on Thirty-fifth and Thirty-sixth Streets and ask for a job.

That's how I got in here. There are four brothers, but Mr. O. Josephs is the only one who actually runs the store. The others come in once in a while, but they don't do much except peek into the books and go out. Mr. O. Josephs is the real boss.

And I was up there on the ladder, thinking about this job, how lousy it was, and how lousy the times are. These two chorus boy floor men from Flatbush kept tossing up the silk and looking bored. Every once in awhile one of them took out a handkerchief and blew into it to get the dust out of his sweet nose.

Finally we were through, and it was about 5 o'clock. We went up to the floor. Mr. Josephs was in the little office upstairs and the bottles were clinking. He looked out and told us it was all right to go home.

I went down again, put out the lights, shut the door which leads from the store cellar to the building basement, and then I washed up. I took off the old pants and put on my good suit, and then I went out.

It was a sunny day, and the girls who work in the dress houses were going home. Everybody feels good to be out on Saturday after work, and the girls were walking fast along the streets, going home or going over to the department stores. You know what girls look like when they walk fast. Everything just bobs up and down. Gee!

I lit a cigarette and got on Seventh Avenue. Then I walked up to Forty-second Street and stood on a corner for awhile, looking at the crowds. There were a lot of fellows in uniform with girls. They were pretty dumb-looking guys from West Point, as straight as sticks and otherwise like sticks too, down on Broadway after the Notre Dame game and looking for a swell time.

I went up to a Chinese-American restaurant near Forty-third Street, and got a seat near a window from which I could look down on the crowds. The chow-mein was good, there were a bunch of fresh-looking high school girls down from the Bronx for an evening on Broadway, maybe for a Shakespeare show. I sat there awhile and I couldn't help laughing with some of the girls, just as if I was in the conversation. They were mighty sweet-looking girls.

By this time it was dark and I put on my hat and went down. I hopped into the State and saw a show. A lousy picture about how a banker weathered the crash, and a good vaudeville bill without any Japanese acrobats. Then I went out on Broadway. It was about 9 o'clock and I walked north. The crowd was pretty thick and I couldn't move fast until I got up to Fifty-third Street. Then it petered out and I was able to walk faster.

I always like this walk after the show. Above Fifty-third Street it's a little darker than it is below. There aren't any theatres, just those big buildings, and maybe a hotel sign or two up in the darkness. I walked along feeling comfortable and smoking and looking at the automobile show windows between Fifty-third and Sixty-fifth Streets, and particularly at the roadsters which always remind me of Pelham Parkway, hot janes and a roadhouse. Oh, boy, for a roadster!

I was above Fifty-ninth Street and I walked on until I was a few blocks before Lincoln Square. Then I turned west, went down to the street, stopped at the house and went up the way I always do.

Inside they had a radio going. It was nice and cozy. I said hello to everybody, including Mamie. I sat down and waited, and pretty soon the blonde girl came in. I didn't want to go in yet. I wanted to sit there for awhile and look at Mary because she's pretty nice.

So I sat there and looked at her awhile. After a few minutes the other girls went inside and she and I were sitting there alone.

She asked me whether I wanted to go in, but I just wanted to sit there because I'm getting wise to this game. If you just sit still for awhile you get keyed up and since you're paying good money you might as well be keyed up. But besides this I just wanted to talk to her the way any fellow wants to talk to a girl, and I sat there and kept thinking of what I wanted to say.

I was looking at the floor and thinking of how I was when I first came up here, and the way I must have looked, before and after. Before I was shivering, and afterwards I was standing in the room, holding my pants and garters in my hands, and Mary was saying: "God, the way some of you kids act the first time you come up to a house, you'd think you're gonna die. And you're all so god-damn grateful you want to cry."

And that's what I was thinking about when a man came in. I saw his legs in gray with spats and I looked up and it was Mr. Josephs. He got red when he saw me and I just sat there and didn't say anything. Mr. Josephs flopped down into a chair and didn't say anything either. The two of us were sitting in chairs, like kids in front of the whole class. There was that radio going and Mary sitting on a sofa and looking at us. She was scratching a shoulder and her breasts jiggled undernearth her thin dress. She began to giggle and we just sat there and we must have been looking pretty dumb. There was just one thing running through my mind, about that lousy bitch of an expressman who had this idea of a joke.

Mr. Josephs took off his hat, and he wasn't looking like a boss at all, but just like any fat old man. His face was all flabby and he scratched his head and I saw that he didn't have so much hair after all, but that it was just combed carefully.

He wanted to say something and at first he couldn't. His eyes were working like a dog's and after awhile he said: "We're all human, aren't we?" Then he sat still for a few more minutes and said finally: "Well, everybody's got to live once in awhile," and then after that dumb remark he took off his coat.

He began to look at Mary and gradually his mouth opened a little and he kept putting his finger to his upper lip. He forgot about me pretty completely, except that once or twice he reminded himself that I was there and looked around at me apologetically and tried to wink. Then he got up and Mary got up, and they walked to a door. I was looking at the floor and I could see Mary's legs and the boss's legs in spats, and then they got inside the door and I kept sitting there.

Mamie came in and some of the other girls and she said to me: "Gee, are you still here, kid?"

I got up and I put on my hat and coat and yelled: "What a god-damn dirty joint this is!"

She got sore as hell because she's pretty proud of her joint, and she yelled back: "What's the matter with you? You can't sit around here like this. This ain't a restroom. You'd better try the Library."

"It's just a plain dirty whorehouse," I said, and I walked out to the street.

I was turned inside out and I didn't know what to do. I couldn't figure out how Mr. Josephs had found out about this place, and I kept saying it out loud, so that people looked at me. "How did the boss find out about this place?" I couldn't see Mr. Josephs getting on friendly terms with the American Railway Express man.

I walked on into Central Park. I looked up and saw I was in the middle of the park. All around it was black, the sky was high and cloudy, there were buildings on Fifty-ninth Street, all lighted up and way up in the air. Everything looked big and lonely, and I was just a cheap little shipping clerk sitting on a bench. My new lid fell off on the ground, and I didn't pick it up. How could I pick up a hat when I was seeing the boss's legs in spats and Mary's legs when I was looking at the floor and they went inside?

I had to think of Monday and of how we would both feel when I came in and when I spoke to him, and when he put in those snappy long distance calls to Chicago.

I had to think of people in general until my head got dizzy. I couldn't stop thinking—until I had it figured out that everybody is the same below the belt, and that everything else don't mean a damn, and that the King of Spain and Morgan and the President of the United States are no better than the shipping clerk in the Quality Silk Corporation on West Thirty-sixth Street, New York, N.Y.

I sat there in the park figuring out these surprising things while it was raining down on my new hat, and it made me feel good, but at the same time I felt bad because of Monday and I might lose my job.

But what the hell! Even though I lose my job, nobody can tell me anything about big shots any more, because I saw one of them who flings around thousands and guzzles high class whisky with the men from the silk mills, and he was sitting on a chair with his mouth open, looking at a whore's legs.

Down the Skidway

H. H. LEWIS

Hunger—like the police dick who stalks by banks, luxurious hotels, jewelry stores, elite cafes, shadowing a *starved* American to catch him mooching,—the hunger beast had stalked me many times before. But merely as a threat from which I had always escaped by darting aside *into jobs*. Then in the autumn of 1929 the stock market crashed like all Heaven itself crashing to Hades, and jobs became scarce. Then two confidence men slid mesmeric fingers around the rest of my savings, thus left me "on the spot" there in a Southwestern city. . . . The hunger beast pounced upon me, chewed me up, digested the sweet juices of my egotism, and dumped me *down and out,* phew, to reek on the social veldt. In other words, when I slumped down to brood on the *slickness* of those confidence men, I began to slip. Suddenly I was "shooting the chute" in a most dazed downward fashion, being knocked from side to side, becoming shabby and unclean, wearing out the seat of my britches and scooping up the lice of downwardness. . . . And I haven't struck bottom yet. Society seems to have no bottom. From the way respectable babbitts turn up their noses at a scootling in their social gutter, it seems that I'm bound for some yawning sewer and Hell.

All aboard, then, vermin o' mine! Phewp, phewp, goddam, here we go, talking about it again.

At Fort Worthless of the unbearable recollection, oh, that's where it began. That taking of my money by the confidence sharks. Unable to find work in my good clothes, I had to enter a pawnshop and reappear metamorphosed for work of a different generality. The farther down the work-seeking scale I went, the fiercer the competition became. I was soon panhandling strangers: "Mister, how's chances for the price of a feed?" That's how to say it, what I heard said. There was a horde of us panhandling, and sleeping in scratchhouses, brooding and cursing and going down. . . .

Away down there, darkly hunkered over a serving of beans in a slummy restaurant, I jerked up to a raving rumpus back in the kitchen. "You goddamn poky, triflin', clock-watchin' deadbeat

you, ye won't WORK! Hyer's what je've 'earned' sence mornin'.
Now git!" The cook was firing the pearldiver. "GIT, I said, you
rotten-lazy dingbat, you fly-blowed—Well, by God, that's good rid-
dance. Charley, see if they's another bastard out thar fer the job.
En if they ain't, stick yer damn sign up at the winder."

I immediately lunged for the job, procured it, flung on the div-
ing-suit of a greasy apron and dived desperately—for one dollar
per ten hours, meals included. (Should that be called butting bottom in America? No. For some dishwashers in hard times work
all day for their meals only.) Weakened by the long hunger, I all
but drowned in the sudsy sea before the first day ended. I was
afraid of coming up too frequently for air, was feeling those eyes
upon me. . . .

That "stove-devil," heat-blanched and heat-crazed, gaunt and
flagrantly dirty, up against it for twelve hours daily, received $60
per month. The waiters got $1.25 per day.

The restaurant belonged to a chain of such for dime-gripping
bums and lowpaid working-stiffs. Came gringoes and greasers for
coffee-and, stew, hash, beans—a large bowl of brown beans for
a dime. Came Negroes, humblest of all. Came "mouthmen" and
"wolves," proletarian beasts of the ghastliest ilk. From the poverty
of America, in this bottomless hell, came these contorted and
condemned souls.

When, partly by cheating the garbage can of the best that returned, I became "sloffed up," as the boes grate about undoing
a protracted starve, my broken spirit mended somewhat. I began
to work less hang-doggedly. During my third week there I ventured to parry one of the stove-devil's insults. Bingo, he canned
me. Just outside the screendoor, I peered back and snarled, "Hey,
fool, take this!" as I vigorously thumbed my nose. He hurled the
kindling-hatchet, which cut through the screen and clattered
bloodlessly upon the alley stones. I retreated to a safe distance.
When he came for the hatchet I horselaughed raucously, gave
him a nasal wigwag with both hands and then a brainward whirl
of finger such as indicates daftness in the other fellow.

I went straightaway to an employment shark and handed him
two days of potscrub's earnings for a floorscrub's job in a sanitarium.

"Well, guy, how do you like your *janitorial position?*" asked
another roustabout, grinning wryly, when the day's work was over
and we were down in our stuffy basement quarters.

"Not much position to it: *all motion*," I retorted. "They sure
keep a fellow jiggin' around here."

"Do they! It's the doggonedest dancin' school I ever struck, and I've had all kinds of jobs. Had a whirl at just about every kind of common labor in the country, it seems. Did a stretch in a Northern hospital—but that was nothing like this, brother."

"En sich pay, sich pay!" griped the third exploitee. " 'Nine dollars a week with room en board.' Hell, that's turned smackdab around: it's room en board with the nine bucks jis' sorta throwed in extra-like!"

Only three janitors in a hospital that should have employed at least two more, we were lying on our cots and fanning with pasteboards, trying to get cool enough for sleep in our dungeon. The mattresses beneath us fumed with a delousing dope. And the walls around were, like in a crapcan, no less pungent with the scratchings, the *verbal* scratchings, of many a come-and-gone Curse. While there above the door was a convenient bell for jangling even our slumbers whenever the night doctors and night nurses, *professionals,* could use a "day" menial.

After its nocturnal irregularities, however deplorable, that gong would redeem itself by sounding regularly at dawn. Routine thus restored, my fellow-scrubs would climb with pails and mops to the upper story while I used a hose on the twilighted veranda and sidewalks. Then, after breakfast at 6 o'clock, our day would commence in earnest.

We were everybody's flunkies. Nurses', doctors', the wakeful superintendent's, the sanitarium-owner's and his concerned wife's. At the mercy of about seventy bosses dinning, "No, do it *right now,"* their each anarchical request the most important, we were trotted from this to that and then bawled out for what remained undone. Busy nurses proceeded to apprentice three roustabouts; performing their own professional duties, we carried trays of food and lifted patients about, we emptied phewpots and escorted week-kneed convalescents to the toilet door. Versatile janitors! I and another of the three once hurried outside with a stretcher and back with a patient, we unclothed him and applied hot towels—and feared that the doctors might order *us* to do the surgery. I washed dishes, I bathed the madam's poodle, I belabored a Pulmotor, I—was called a janitor.

After such a jig we would have supper at 6 o'clock. But we often had to resume work—for not a cent added to the nine dollars—to scrub and sweep for hours in order to "get ready for tomorrow," as the night superintendent fancied. These extra grinds came so frequently that I declared them not extra: that getting off at 6 was a special favor. At any rate, we would eventually be at liberty to lie down under that gong. . . .

The sanitarium was full of white-enameled refuse-pails with tops that niftily opened and shut by footlever. There must have been about thirty of those things. Twice daily I had to fetch all of them to the basement for incinerating their polluted contents in the furnace. Then I had to scald and scrub their interiors. Gee, what lowdown work for a feller with lofty ambitions, I brooded.

Somebody had carelessly dropped something explosive into a refuse-pail,—probably a small can not entirely emptied of its ether. Among surgical dressings and wads of bloody absorbent, into the fire it went. Stooped aface to unshut furnace, I was repeating the act. . . . Boom, I got singed—and only seven dollars at the end of that not incapacitated week, two going for slight medical treatment; because I had previously been told to separate the metal or glass objects, all unburnables of any considerable size, from the rest of the refuse and to dispose of it elsewhere, not to choke up the furnace with it.—Furthermore, one of the menials warned me to "be keerful from now on en pick out a nurse, too, if one happens to fall in."

A scabbiness came over my scorched mug.

It hurt me to laugh.

I was in a quitting mood anyway, so, when bawled out for sleeping on the back lawn rather than in that hot hole where the gong had sounded in vain, I demanded a summary payoff.

After the seven-day weeks of burial in that job,—O liberty awhile! Now I understood what liberty could mean. I went downtown and bought a new pair of overalls and a ten-cent cigar. Then I just strolled about, strolled about in tremendous relief.

With fifteen dollars left I preferred to loaf a few days, till the scab sluffed off, before seeking another job. I floated about in a trance, tenderly dreaming of the Day . . . when I could somehow get back to moneyed respectability. I thought about my soul: if it were tangible and worth money in this objective world, and if I could just get a hold on it, I'd jerk the goddamned thing out and sell it for so much per square inch. But good clothes, a "fine front," ye haloing externals, that's soul nowadays, and I had already hocked mine. . . . So I watched the chain gang going out to build roads, I saw the Ku Klux Klan parade. Finally a bull got after me for sitting too long in one place.

Then I went to the slavetrader and bought a job. He phoned; and the third member of this deal, who had been waiting in the

cool of his downtown office, got into his car and came over to the
slavemarket. My new master: a hang-jowled and potbellied boomer
of real estate bargains. He took me out into a suburb to a cheap
little three-room house, vacant. I should jack up the swayed floors
and put pillars under them, renail warped weatherboarding, then
clean the inside and paint the outside of the bargain. The job ought
not to require more than a week, said the boomer.

I brought eats from the neighborhood grocery-store and slept
at my working-place, on newspapers and towsacks.

Disturbed one night by a banging about, I discovered an Afro-
American behind the privy. He claimed to have an agreement with
the boomer; and I believed, for the loot in this case certainly was
not tempting. Lonesome, I swapped talk. My grumbling bitterly
about late experiences—and my Northern-ness, too, maybe—
loosened his tongue. Sewers were coming, then he would have to
go begging for different work. But meantime, at 25¢ per privy,
he was earning from $3 to $4 per night, had more work than he
could get done—for the lot-and-house men were booming this
neighborhood—and *some* additional person would soon have a
night job—till the sewers came. So *hinted* the scavenger, smearing a shovelful into the pushcart. . . .

Ach, as if backwardly quailing in horror from the very idea—
such lowdown work, done only in darkness!—I returned to my
pallet.

But, the housework over, I was not able to buy, beg nor steal
a relatively decent job. Grown penniless and panic-stricken, I returned to the neighborhood at night and slunk abysmally about
behind the privy-rows, ready to take that hint, seeking my black
brother. I couldn't find him. After a night of it I went to the
grocery-store and pretended: where could I get a nigger to clean
out my backhouse? So I learned where the scavenger lived. Late
in the afternoon I went to his hut. His woman fed me. Another
pushcart and shovel were procured. And the essential shade
deepened. . . .

Ew, the shade deepened around my young ambitions,—hell, I
would never amount to Something this way! . . . Down, down,
down the skidway!

The Anvil May 1933

Not Without Propaganda

LOUIS MAMET

He is a writer on special assignment for the *Standard's* Sunday Magazine—his task each week to bring within the confines of two thousand words or less a figure preeminent in contemporary life.

On this occasion he is to weigh a banker, who has to his esthetic credit a personally designed, architecturally respectable office building.

The writer, Sidney Rosen, discusses the interview with the Sunday editor.

You'll find him a pretty affable fellow, Sid. No fuss . . . ready to oblige. . . .

A veritable pollyanna, eh?

No, no, Sid, just a regular guy. He contributes to a raft of charities, can *take* it, and is a swell fellow all around. You'll enjoy *this* interview.

Tuesday, December 5.

The writer is in a hurry. The interview is scheduled for ten, and it is close to that now. He hails a taxi.

Step on it, will you, buddy?

Where to?

Across the bridge . . . Wall and Broad.

Say! Ain't you Sidney Rosen?

That's my name, all right.

Standard?

Right.

A buddy pointed you out to me. Like your articles. Who you gonna write up this time?

A banker.

Goin' to interview him now?

Right.

I like the one you done on the mayor. Say! Does he really smoke nickel nails?

So he says.

Funny, ain't it? A guy with his dough, too! When you got to make this appointment?

Ten.

Maybe I'd better take you down the side streets . . . make better time.

OK with me, as long as you get me there without a ticket.

Leave it to me, Mr. Rosen. Say, when'll this story appear?

Week from Sunday.

What's this Sunday?

Lawyer.

Big?

Biggest . . . Liebner.

Boy! I won't miss that one.

A sudden shift of the car to avoid hitting some respectably dressed individuals listening to a soap-box orator, vexes the writer.

You almost sent me through the window!

Sorry! I had to, if I wasn't gonna hit the crowd, Mr. Rosen.

What's the meeting about, do you know?

You asking *me?*

Why not? You know more about the front page news than I do.

Dispossess! The whole block!

Who's doing it?

Search me. Maybe bank! Maybe mortgage company!

The banker rises to greet the writer, hand outstretched.

Delighted to make your acquaintance, Rosen.

How are you, Mr. Ames?

Make yourself comfortable, will you? Cigar? Cigarette? How about a cocktail?

Cigar.

Read your interview with the mayor. I think you'll find these just a bit easier on the throat.

I'm taking that for granted.

(the banker laughs appreciatively)

How do you work, Rosen? I want to make it as easy for you as I can.

I'm working now.

How's that?

Get impressions as I go along. Got some on the main floor. Your handiwork?

Like it?

It seems restful. That's all I know about it. I know damn little about architecture.

I designed the entire building.

Study architecture seriously at one time?

In France . . . on a scholarship.

Banking more interesting?

A heritage . . . in the family.

How about this room? Your work, too?

Furniture and all.

Victorian?

Elizabethan.

Well, give me credit for knowing it to be English (the writer grins): (the banker laughs in agreement).

Mr. Ames, one of the questions I have on my list is your opinion on business, ethics, practice, the whole works . . . from any and every angle.

Want me to lecture, or ramble?

Impressions will do.

I see banking as a profession, then; a profession like medicine, the psychologies, science. So far it's been a pretty open profession, except in the highest circles.

Keep pretty close together, there?

Only because it's easier to do business with one of our own kind, that's all.

Hold for all business, or just banking?

Quote me only on banking.

By the way, one of the questions is: Do you favor the government regulation of banks?

Heavens no, Rosen! The phrase 'individual liberty' is no idle one in this country. Too much government in business as it is.

What if a banker betrays his trust?

The group to which he belongs can handle him.

Suppose the betrayal were indicative of the profession?

Impossible, Rosen. Banking is a necessity in modern civilization, despite the fact that it doesn't produce.

. . . the strong argument of the opposition, isn't it?

Yes; but so silly. What kind of civilization would we have if all the people were tillers of the soil . . . or fishermen . . . or hunters?

The conversation, earnest and sharp, is interrupted by the flashing of a little light in a rectangular box on the banker's desk.

This will be the only interruption, Rosen, I promise you. These papers must be signed today.

Why not?

(reflectively) No, Rosen, we can't all be laborers. Civilization must have thinkers, scientists to broaden and prolong life. We must have humans to transact the complexities of modern civilization on its basic terms. . . .

A well-dressed man in his thirties, well-proportioned, English cut clothes draped smoothly about his body, comes in with some papers which he places before the banker.

Riggins, Rosen of the *Standard*. Rosen, my secretary.

Your stuff's interesting, Rosen.

Thanks. But as a writer, I resent the word 'stuff'. (The writer grins. The secretary laughs appreciatively.)

Sorry. I think it's interesting anyway. (Three laugh.)

Here you are, Riggins.

Thank you, Mr. Ames. Glad to have met you, Rosen.

Same here.

And now, where were we, Rosen?

On banking, and its noble deeds.

All kidding aside, Rosen, I really think banking to be a necessity in modern civilization. And if some people blame us for keeping it a closed corporation, well, they may be justified from their point of view; but we have our own angle: we like people around us we can understand, people with whom we can reminisce, people who are interested in the same things we are, had the same upbringing we did. . . .

Suppose we let that slide for a moment. How about this tough one? Did banking ever exact any action for which you might personally feel repugnance? I mean. . . .

I get it, Rosen. A fair enough question. Banking has a code of ethics, just as every other profession. Being a banker, I'm partial to that code. It doesn't mean that it's the sort of code which you as a writer would give us. And perhaps the man in the street won't agree with us; but it's the best we know at the moment. I've never broken with the code, myself.

It doesn't answer the question entirely, Mr. Ames.

I said you wouldn't be in harmony with it.

My Sunday editor says something about charity. Mind telling me *why* you give? I know that you *do* give. And if I need the names of the charities, I can get it from the morgue.

Morgue?

File for past news, that's all.

Why I give to charity? Well, it's not so difficult. First of all because I'm a Christian, and Christians are supposed to alleviate the sufferings of their fellow men. The Old Testament has something about that, too (the banker smiles).

Yes, I know (the writer smiles in return). Jews are quite familiar with it.

Quite right. When I said 'Christian'. . . .

. . . it was not a judgment of the Jew.

Right. No wonder you write so lucidly.

One . . . because you're a Christian? (prompts the writer).

And two . . . is 'family'. We have a tradition in ours that has a certain proportion of our incomes going to charity. And three . . . is 'society'. It is so constituted that I couldn't avoid giving even if I wanted to. Society expects the wife of a banker to head some charity. Quite naturally, mine does. She also has her fingers in a number of others. She asks for checks, and, of course, gets them.

Pretty frank statement on your part. Hope it doesn't boomerang.

I've found frankness to pay dividends. Of course, there are times and places.

How about this, Mr. Ames? Do you believe charity unethical?

Unethical?

I mean from the angle of the economist who has no irons in the fire for capitalism or labor . . . individualism or collectivism?

I still don't get it.

Do you believe the present system of distribution of the world's goods, the best possible? Or, do you think that a more equable proportioning of the world's income would be better . . . for the world?

Socialism? Communism?

Any form of government that would exclude charity!

Of course not. It may be that I'm steeped in the old tradition. Yet, I think that I would object to a change quite objectively.

I understand your feeling.

But you don't think I'm correct?

Frankly, no, Mr. Ames.

Puzzle it out for me.

Not part of the assignment. Get into too much hot water. (The writer smiles enigmatically.)

Writer and banker parry for two hours. They discuss religion: "religion" in business, "religion" as ethics, "religion" as a philosophy. They discuss Spinoza, Schopenhauer, Nietzsche and the Greek trio. The banker is enthusiastic about music and architecture, his hobbies. They discuss sport: polo, tennis, and the past season of Harvard football. They debate the value of current fiction, and find a surprising similarity in taste.

Now, past twelve, the banker invites the writer to lunch. A writer attached to a newspaper never refuses a meal—whether it be in Jack's Busy Bee or the Ritz Carlton grill. Rosen nods. And the discussion centers on old-time downtown restaurants and theatres—the contemporary stars, their starts, zeniths, disappearances.

When they complete luncheon, the writer is inwardly enthusiastic about the banker. The Sunday editor was right—a gentleman. Rosen might not be a welcome guest in the Ames' Long Island home; but on business, Rosen can speak to the banker with ease and confidence.

The writer is not left at the grill. The banker wants to know his destination. When he discovers that it is a matinee show of a current Broadway hit, the banker is genuinely sorry that he cannot go along. But even a banker must put in a certain number of hours.

When the writer comes into the street, the door of a taxicab is held open for him by the doorman. The banker has issued orders.

It pleases the writer. When he sits down to write the story of the banker for his "million" readers, it is done with smiling features and an ease of mind. In the story he touches upon the banker's humanitarian qualities, air of gentility, natural courtesy, grace as a conversationalist, host. . . .

The Sunday editor smiles as he looks over the proofs. "I was right, wasn't I?" he comments to the writer. The writer nods, reflectively. They then discuss the next human to be interviewed.

Wednesday, December 6.

Many in the living room of Joseph Muller. They breathe on each other's necks. Standing in a chair is a chunky, black-eyed, flushed male. Hands gesticulate. Mouth hurls words fast, almost indistinguishable to the silent, unmoving many.

Who is responsible? Who is responsible? We all know who's responsible! *The bankers!* The depression forced us to mortgage our homes. For which we slaved! Our gardens! Flowers! Lawns! Our homes! All go to a non-human bank. Why? Because the law is so manipulated that they can foreclose. Foreclose on something to which we have given our lifetime. I tell you, neighbors, December 5th, the day Ames signed the order to foreclose on our homes, is a black day in our civilization. It indicates just how much we actually mean to our country. We're just about as important as a drop in the ocean. The Constitution gives us the right to "liberty, life, and the pursuit of happiness." That's the only reason why I called you all here. Let's see if that phrase means anything. We cannot be a liberty-loving people without homes. And we cannot live unless we have self-respect. And we cannot pursue happiness when we have to pursue a chance to work. Let's get together and send a petition to the President of the country. He should be interested. . . .

The Anvil May-June 1935

Fingers

ROBERT RAMSEY

Between the two men in the poor room there was only the difference of perhaps five years, and a little difference in the clothes they wore, as though one were dressed for some occasion, and the other dressed for work. The elder wore a tie and a white shirt with a wilted collar and crumpled, sweat-stained sleeves; the other wore overalls, faded by the sun and much washing. About the necks and hands and faces of both of them was that glared, fierce stain of the skin from many hours in the sun.

Beside them on the table there was a stiff new bag of the kind carried by doctors. The man in the white shirt reached out his hand and took the bag.

He said, "It ain't like you had the money coming, Harper. It ain't like you had a crop to draw against until fall. I just ain't got no chance to get my money back, this way."

Harper said, "But Dr. Bean, I. . . ."

"I already put out more on credit than I can afford. Medicine and gasoline, coming out here. It counts up. Maybe you don't know how much it costs, practicing medicine. Maybe you wouldn't believe it, but I still owe on that two years at the school in Kansas City."

"Yessir, I know that. I know it takes money. And I aim to pay—"

"And then on top of that finding out that the law wouldn't let me practice in but one state, and that they ain't none too glad about it here—"

"Yessir, I know that, Dr. Bean. Ever'body's got to have their money."

"So I just can't afford to be putting out medicine on credit, and gasoline coming out here. Not when I'm taking such a chance on getting it back."

"But I aim to pay you, Dr. Bean. Hit ain't like—"

"Look. Do you know how much it took to go to that place two years?"

"No, sir. Plenty, I reckon."

"Well, I still owe them two hundred dollars. That'll just give you an idea. And maybe you'll understand why I can't keep coming out here on credit when I got all that to pay back—"

From the next room the woman wailed softly. It was a patient, muted sound.

"Anyway, what did you leave your crop for to go to work in a sawmill?" the doctor asked.

"I wanted to make me some money, Dr. Bean. Some steady wages—"

"If you'd of kept your crop you'd have a little credit for things like this."

"I wanted me some steady wages. I thought hit might be better'n what I been gitting ever' year. So when them fellers come and put up that new sawmill. . . ."

"I reckon I can understand that. It's little enough a man ever gets out of working another man's crop."

"But I didn't know then them fellers in town was going to come out and garnishee me on my paycheck, as soon as they knowed about hit. To git back a grocery bill I owed two year ago. I didn't know about that. And as soon as I git hit paid I'll. . . ."

"Yes. Well, that's the trouble. And I can't come any more unless you've got the money in your hand."

"Yessir—"

"I'm sorry, but it won't do any good unless you've got the cash money."

The doctor left, and Harper from the door watched the old Ford wheel slowly out of the yard and bounce over the unpaved street and disappear in the direction of the town.

He went back into the room with his wife.

He sat down by the bed, touching his wife's face, stroking it.

She said, "Harper."

"Is hit bad now?"

"I felt hit right smart a while back, but that shot he give me eased me some. Hit pains right smart without that . . . I reckon the chap's beginning to move around now."

She smiled weakly and he touched her hair, feeling its softness flowing out over the pillow.

"Honey," he said. "Are you sorry we left Mr. Rick's?"

"No, Harper," she said. "Hit's like you said. We done come up in the world right smart, I reckon."

"Yes," he said. He tried to make it sound like when he had said it before. "Do you want anything, honey?"

"My head's hot," she said. "I would sho like to have me some ice. . . ."

"I can't git you no ice, honey. I'll git some cool water."

He went out in the back yard, in the still hot air left baking by the afternoon sun, and pumped furiously and steadily until the flow of water ran cool. He caught a bucket of the water and took it in by his wife and soaked a rag in the water to place on her forehead.

"Mrs. Harper Dorman," she said softly. "Hit's a purty name. Even after being married seven months hit still sounds purty. . . ."

He awakened before daylight the next morning and crept softly from the bed and stood looking down at his wife's swollen face.

He cooked his breakfast of side meat and corn pone and molasses, and before he left put a bucket of cold water with the breakfast on the chair beside the bed.

He was so worried when he got to the sawmill that the foreman spoke to him twice. He was the off-bearer, one of several men who stand before the whirling saw to take the clean planks from the saw as it rips them out from the moving log. He was so worried that before he had been there an hour he reached too far in for the plank and the saw flicked off his index finger at the second joint. He hardly felt it, and he looked down curiously at the stub of his finger, pink, a faint blue where the end of the severed bone showed. Then the blood began showing in faint pricks at first; then it flowed out bright and red and fell to the ground.

The foreman came up and cursed. He took a bit of resin from the log on the saw carriage and stuck it on the end of Harper's finger and hurried him, stumbling, out of the mill and into a car.

"Where do you aim to take—"

"To the doctor, you bastard; where do you think?"

"But I can't pay; I ain't—"

"You ought to pay for it, anybody that would be dumb enough to stick their hand in front of a saw. But you don't have to; the insurance company'll pay for it."

On the way back from the doctor, Harper said, "I'm right beholden to you for the doctor. For—"

"Hell, it ain't us; it's the insurance company," the foreman said. "They'll pay for it; not us."

When they got to the mill the foreman went into his office shed and brought out a typed sheet of paper.

"This is so everything will be all right," he said.

He spread the paper out on a plank and gave Harper a fountain pen. Harper made a cross on the paper where the foreman showed him, and the foreman and another man signed the paper underneath Harper's cross.

At Harper's house that night there was a man waiting in a car. The man was a lawyer. Harper had seen him a few times, standing on the steps of the courthouse, and on the streets.

"Hello, Harper," the lawyer said pleasantly. "I hear you had a little accident."

"Not much of a one, I reckon," Harper said, standing impatiently and without interest, wanting furiously to go into the house.

"Anybody say anything to you about it?" the lawyer said. "Anybody ask anything?" He looked at Harper sharply, in his face a kind of questioning more intent than in his words.

"I don't recall nobody," Harper said slowly. "The foreman seen it, the doctor seen it—"

"What doctor?"

"I don't rightly know his name. Some doctor for the sawmill people—"

"Who else?"

"Nobody. That's all, I reckon." Harper's face was pained with the effort of remembering.

"I see," the lawyer said. "And nobody gave you any money?"

"No, sir," Harper smiled, as though he thought the man expected him to respond in that way, as to a joke. "No, sir. I'd like to see somebody come handing me some money. Yessir, I'd be right proud to see that."

"Just a minute. Nobody offered you any money. And you didn't sign anything, any kind of paper?"

"Yes," Harper said. "A kind of paper—"

The lawyer cursed. "All right! You signed it, and they didn't even give you anything for signing it. Is that it?"

"Yessir. Why? You mean I done wrong?"

"Listen, you poor bastard," the lawyer said. "Don't you know that in this state the law doesn't protect a man who works for a company and gets hurt? That he's got to go to the law himself for protection?"

"I don't know about that. But I figger that courts are mostly for fellers with money; that a poor man ain't got no business going into court—"

Harper was already withdrawn, his mind and attention withdrawn and closed behind suspicion and a kind of visionless independence.

"All right," the lawyer said. "All right. That's enough." He clamped his mouth down, and Harper heard his foot kick the starter into the whirring sound. Then the car was veering out in a wide arc through the yard and back into the street again and Harper went into the house, the man and his ideas already forgotten now in his urgent haste.

His wife's face was hot. She moaned a little when he bent over the bed, and then she looked up at him and he saw that she meant to smile.

"Hit ain't too much for you, honey?" he said.

"Hit hurt right smart today."

Harper kept his hand behind him, or in his pocket.

Then his wife said, "Ain't they something wrong, Harper?"

"No. Nothing's wrong. Don't fret."

"Harper, you ain't lost your job, have you?"

"No. They ain't nothing wrong."

He brought in another bucket of cold water and sat by the edge of the bed, laying the cool cloths on her forehead.

It was three days later before the stranger came out from the insurance office in Memphis.

He got out of his car and went first to the foreman, talking a little while, looking at Harper where he stood by the saw carriage. Then they came up to Harper and the stranger said, "Let's see that finger."

Harper stuck out the finger, timidly, a little worried.

"Well, it's not so bad. Hell, you're right lucky. What if it was your whole hand?"

"I don't know, sir," Harper said, "I reckon hit—"

"What do you think it's worth?"

Harper said, "Worth?"

"What about twenty-five dollars?" the stranger said. "That's a lot of money, twenty-five dollars cash."

"Yes," Harper said suspiciously.

The stranger took out a billfold and put five five-dollar bills on the saw carriage by Harper, very close to him. "Now," he said. "Just sign this paper for me now. Just to show everything's all right."

He took out a typed sheet of paper and showed Harper where to make the mark, and then the foreman and another man signed the paper.

"Now, you want to take good care of that hand," the stranger said. "Maybe you ought to take the rest of the day off."

"Why, hit's all right—" Harper said.

"Sure," the foreman said. "It's a good idea."

"But I. . . ."

"Go ahead on home," the foreman said. "Go on home and rest. You'll get a full day's pay. Hell, we want to take good care of our men." He looked at the stranger, and then both of them looked away from Harper slightly.

"That's right. He's right," the stranger said. "You go on and do like he says."

Harper walked into town first. It was only a little over a mile and a half. It was a little more than a mile to his house and then a half mile into town. He wanted to see about his wife but he hurried on into town first.

He went to the grocer's who had turned over his account to the courthouse for collection and gave them fifteen dollars. The man looked at the money suspiciously and then gave Harper a receipt. Harper had only owed them for eight dollars' worth of groceries, but by the time the grocer had added on his interest, and after he had taken it to the courthouse and they had added on a collection fee and their interest the bill was eighteen dollars.

"Hit ain't but three dollars now, is it?" Harper said.

The man looked into a ledger. "Three dollars," he said finally, closing the ledger and looking at Harper coldly. "Maybe you'll learn to pay your bills a little better next time."

"Yessir," Harper said. "I aimed to pay it, in the first place, only I had a little trouble."

Then he went to the doctor's office. He gave the doctor the other ten dollars. "Will you come now, Dr. Bean?" he said.

"No," the doctor said. "You still owe me five dollars more. You got to have that, and the money to pay me with for the next call, in advance, before I'll come again. I can't afford—"

"Yessir," Harper said, a little wearily now. "I reckon you know your business; it looks to me though like it's hard on a poor man."

When Harper got home there was a quietness about the house. He stopped in the doorway of the room and looked at the bed, feeling the thunder of his heart in the stillness.

His wife moved her head weakly and he went to the bed, stumbling, his feet sounding heavy in the room.

"Praise God," he said.

"Harper," she said. "I want the doctor again. I think hit's might nigh time now."

"Can't you wait a little for him?" Harper said. "Maybe till the end of the week? Can't you wait that long?"

"I can't make hit wait, Harper. Hit's going to be time afore then, tomorrow, tonight, maybe."

Harper looked through the window dully. Then he stroked her head above the eyes. "You get a good night's rest; I'll see about him for you tomorrow."

"Yes, Harper."

He sat by the bed quietly and stroked her head until she closed her eyes finally and went to sleep. Then he got up softly and went out of the house. It was three o'clock in the afternoon then, and in the glaring sun he walked the five miles out to the plantation.

He stood before the screened porch of Rick Lofton's house and called. After a while a man came out on the porch and stood looking through the screen.

Harper said, "Mr. Rick, please, I need some help.

"Well, what do you want me to do?"

"Mr. Rick, I . . . I want to come back on your place. I done my best for you afore when I was here, and I reckon I made a mistake when I left, thinking—"

"I can't take you now. I haven't got a place for you now."

"But please, Mr. Rick, I want to come back. And I'll work hard—"

"Sorry. It's too late in the season anyway. Crops are almost laid by. I couldn't make a deal with you this time of year. I'm sorry."

He turned and walked back into the house and left Harper alone in the sun again.

Harper walked back home. It was seven o'clock and his wife was still asleep. He cooked the same meal he had eaten at breakfast. Then he went into the bedroom and slipped into the bed. He reached out his hand timidly once to touch his wife's face; then he turned on his side and slept.

He had already cooked his breakfast in the morning and was eating it when he heard his wife scream the first time. His face went white all over and the piece of cornbread hung in his throat as though it were going to be vomited even before it had time to reach his stomach.

He fled from the kitchen in a cold frenzy and stood open-mouthed above his wife. She smiled up at him with a trusting, placid look.

"Will you get him now, Harper?" she said. "The doctor?"

"Yes," he said. "Yes."

He left his breakfast unfinished in the kitchen and walked to work, although it was yet a half hour ahead of time.

It was ten o'clock before he could get to the insurance agent's office. It took him nearly an hour of the time to find the man's office, to find out who he was by describing him to men on the street and asking if they knew him and where his office was.

He stood in the man's office then, holding the rag-bound finger in his hand. Then he laid it on the desk, unaware of the man's revulsion and disbelief, standing with a patient courtesy by the desk, his hat held in his unmaimed hand, holding out the hand with two fingers gone now.

"You ain't the same man," Harper said, "the one that paid me afore. But being as you are with the same company I reckon hit's all the same. And I brung hit this time. The finger. I brung hit to make sure there wouldn't be no mistake."

"Good God," the man said softly, looking at Harper's face. "You carried that finger all the way in here to show—"

"Give me the paper now and I'll sign hit," Harper said. "If'n—"

"What paper? Sign what paper?" the man said.

"Please," Harper said. "I got to get the money quick. If hit ain't too much trouble. I mean—"

"Wait. What paper are you talking about, and what money?"

"I don't know what hit said, the paper. But hit was for the money, when the man for the insurance company give me the money the time I cut the other finger off."

Now the man's eyes swerved down from Harper's face, turning to the desk and the aimless still papers on it. "I see," he said. "Yes. You cut your finger off. Then the adjuster came out to see you. He settled—"

"Yessir, that's hit. He gave me the money as soon as he come."

"And now you've cut off another finger and you expect me to pay you for it."

"Yessir. If'n hit ain't too much trouble. I would like to sign the paper and git the money now, this morning, without you or him having to come to the sawmill to give hit to me."

"I see." The man picked up a pencil and held it, looking at it.

"Or if'n hit's too much trouble, or if'n you ain't got the money with you, if'n you would just give me a piece of paper saying I got hit coming, that would be all right. Hit would do just as good."

"Goddam," the man said suddenly. "You poor bastard. What do you think I am?"

Harper moved back a little, his eyes pained, uncomprehending.

"Sir? You mean— Ain't I going to git hit . . .?"

"Look. All I do is sell insurance policies and try to collect for them. I can't pay you for cutting off a finger."

"Yessir. But I figgered you worked for the company, and—"

"If anybody's going to give you any money for it, it'll be out of the claim department, where it came the other time. All I could do is write them about it for you, but I guess your foreman's already done that, and maybe got you to sign a release, too. I don't guess he wasted much time doing that, before some jakeleg lawyer got hold of you—"

"Yessir. I done signed hit, the paper—"

"Well, that's all. I'll write the claim department. That's all I can do."

Harper stood looking at the man with his wide, bewildered eyes.

"Well, what are you waiting for?" the man said. "I can't do anything else, I said."

"Well, sir. Couldn't you give me a piece of paper saying I had hit coming?"

"No. Goddam it!" the man almost shouted.

"You got to. I got to have the money," Harper said. He stepped forward, raising his hand a little with a mute gesture of half-violence, already restricted and dead before the thought was fully expressed in the lifting hand.

The man moved back in the chair, watching what he thought to be the beginning of a threat.

"Go on," the man said. "Go on and get out. Making trouble won't get you anywhere."

Harper's hand fell down slowly. Holding the shapeless hat, it came to rest along his leg. After a moment he said, "I don't aim to make no trouble. I reckon that's the last thing I want: any more trouble."

He turned away, moving slowly, leaving the office.

Walking in the morning sunlight, along the streets, and then beyond the houses, on the edge of town, he gradually became aware of words moving up in his mouth. He heard them, the words addressed to the air before his face; and they sounded hopeless and foolish and without meaning as he heard his mouth framing the sound of them. "Oh, God, don't let her die now. Not yet, anyway. There ain't no call for her to die now."

When he reached his wife her lips were already clawed back

over her teeth in the still face, and there was a bad odor, a stench, all through the room.

He began waiting then in the room. He sat in a chair and all time and the motion of his life waited, arrested and unstirring in the still room about him, unrecognized by him and not believed. Like a long wind that blew him back from the beginning and then died in its own inertia and dropped him in the still room the mute fury of his waiting hung about him in the air. It was not a period of time that he was aware of; it was perhaps four hours.

Then he stirred and looked out placidly. He saw the empty hands across his legs; then he saw the people in the room with him, the men and women of the houses beyond him on the street. They looked at him with a kind of awe and fear as he stirred. Then they came to him and began to lead him from the room; he went with them into the other room and sat in another chair. He sat for a little while looking at them gratefully. He became aware of the lifting voices of the women in the bedroom; then he began to hear the sound of carpentry from behind the house.

He said, "I done right. Can't no man say I ain't done all air man could do."

"No, Harper," one of the men said. "No man could of done more than you done. You put your mind at ease."

He sat with them, the sound of talking men and women around him, the sounds of the working men and the carpentry coming in from the yard. He sat with them, and the long wind began to brush his memory again; and his breath stirred with it and began to go fast.

It was a beautiful day.

The New Anvil May-June 1940

Jesus Saves

YASHA ROBANOFF

I am trying to catch a ride, and I wave to a fellow in a brand new Ford, and he stops and picks me up.

Take me to Berkeley?

Sure, I'll take you there. I'm going there. I have been up here on a job. I am foreman up here. Sheet metal work. I get ten dollars a day.

My wife had a baby last night. This is our second. My wife is a good woman. I married her six years ago. And what a bum I was. A gambler I was, and a boozer, a tobacco fiend, a sinner. The worst sinner you ever saw. Well, after I got married I went to hear this good woman, this good Christian woman, Aimee Mc-Pherson, this woman that was kidnapped by the enemies of Jesus and God. After hearing this good woman I opened my heart and Christ came into my soul and I got myself a job right away. I was a bum before that, a sinner and a bum, but after that I was no longer a sinner and I got a job right away.

I got converted on a Sunday night. I remember just how it happened, just like it happened yesterday. After I got converted I stayed up until the early edition of the *Examiner* got out and right away when I took a look, right before my eyes I read: "Men wanted, experience unnecessary. Good pay. Chance for advancement." There it was right before my eyes, a miracle from God. I went to bed and got up bright and early.

I went over to San Francisco and went where the ad said, and I saw lines of men, one on one side of the street the shop was on, and some in the street. What a commotion it was. I paid no attention to it. I was out to obey the voice of Jesus. I had promised my wife never to leave the straight and narrow path of Jesus. So I got in line.

Soon I heard the men in the street shouting "Scab! Scab!" One of them Unions had gone on strike, and they didn't want us to take the jobs. At first the devil began to torment me. Ah, brother, I know the old devil. I began chewing tobacco when I was six. There is not a house in the red light district in the Bay Cities that

I haven't been in. I know more whores than any man my age in these here Bay Cities, and they are plenty. I could take you to 'em right now.

As I say, I know the old devil. This same devil was at my elbow and began giving me sugar talk. I saw the old bastard right in front of me just as real as you are now sitting on my right. And he let his vile tongue go, "Now, you shouldn't take this job. This job you are after is a scab job. These men on the other side have families and babies. (I didn't have any babies then.) These men are your brothers. You shouldn't take a job like that." I didn't move on. I tried not to listen. Ear muffs for mine when the old devil talks. Still he wasn't conquered. No, sir!

Then he began on a different line altogether and, believe you me, never did I battle with the old devil like I did that morning. He began quoting Scripture—"Take not the bread from the mouths"—something like that, then something about the lilies of the field. I kept swinging back at the old devil's jaw. The old hypocrite was at his best, and I knew I had to fight to keep him from ruining my chances with Jesus.

Just as he was about to overcome me, it's pretty hard to tell what happened—but everything got pitch dark, just like a fellow goes blind all of a sudden. It was Jesus who was on my side then, boy, as you can tell by what followed. You see I was no match for the old devil in argument. He had ten clever arguments to my one, and I felt like I felt when I got kissed on the chin in boxing.

But Jesus saved me. My knees gave way and I was kneeling on the sidewalk and I began to pray. A fellow standing beside me began to kick me, "Get up, you! You look funny down there. Get up!" But I kept on praying. There was a commotion. Pretty soon somebody come out of the office. I heard them say he was the boss, and I took a look at him. He came over and asked me what was the matter, and I told him to take me into the office and I would tell him there. I went in with him and he give me a job.

And do you know from that day to this I have never been out of a job? Oh, Jesus saves! Once or twice I did fall off the wagon but I come back. My boss likes me. The strike lasted two months. Some of the strikers were pretty rough. The boss found out that I could handle my mitts in great shape. Many an evening when he went home I saved his skin. And he is thankful to me to this day. There is nothing I can't have in the shop. I am foreman now, getting ten berries a day, and I expect to get a raise.

I know some of the strikers still there getting less than six. They have been there twelve years, some of them, and I have been only three. They have paid dues in the union all those years and I haven't paid a cent. I'm my own boss. Nobody tells me nothing. I do my work and I sure work. I'm no slacker when it comes to work.

And now I'm buying myself a home. I got this Ford paid for. And I am happy in Jesus, the Savior of my soul.

The Anvil May-June 1934

Beyond the Mountain

JOHN C. ROGERS

Upon the wall lies the checkered shadow of the cell. I hear the sound of voices, indistinct and far away. My body stretches upon the thin mattress that covers a narrow, uncomfortable cot. A train whistles shrilly somewhere between the eastern and western hills; a door slams, and trucks go sputtering down the street. The cool floor feels good to my blistered feet as I walk two cells down and find a wandering farmer, who was convinced the bugs would carry his carcass off in the night, is snoring quite contentedly; his lean frame curled into the uneven hollows of the cot and his toes stretched fanwise through ragged, woolen hose.

"George, hey George," I say, and the sound of my voice echoes around the narrow room. "I'm going over the mountain, George," I tell him; but he only talks incoherently, as in a dream. I remember that he said there was nothing over the mountain—only small farms growing weeds, and family plots with only board headstones, taking the men and children of men back into the barren soil.

"Let him sleep," says Jim, "he must be tired. This is the end of his journey."

We go out of the jail, and down a street that is yellow-grey in the rising light of morning. The mountain is so close to the town you cannot see the top; only a road that crosses a stream and loses itself in the valley shows the height and the way we must go.

"He knew my grandfather," I says to Jim.

"He knew your grandfather?"

"George, the farmer, knew him."

"Oh, yes," says Jim, "so I heard him say last night."

We walk silently towards the mountain that had been scarred on the north by a quarry from whose chalk face we hear no noise, but whose even sides destroy the beautiful contours of a green hill that lies in solid shadow with white blooms of laurel showing at the wood's edge. An old woman wearing an assortment of ragged clothes stops her heavy body and smiles at a worker, who drags his feet heavily along the railroad-track path towards the

144

woman. Like a mass of kneaded dough is the woman's face, and though she faces the sun, her pallor is like a weak blue-black shadow of a watercolor.

"You done got a job at last?" she asks the worker.

"No," he says wearily, "there ain't no jobs to be got."

"Jes a-carryin your lunch-box to keep in practice, I spose?" The woman laughs, and from her puffy face there slowly fades a smile of one who has worked too long and hard. The worker continues his aimless journey beside the rails, toward a town that has no jobs for men who helped to build it, or whose good fortune gave them life in a country of anemic slaves.

Smoke floats in a thin spiral from a large building labeled DUPONT SILK MILL, as near as we can make out from a distance. We pass another single-story building, with a shady lawn that is clean, and filled with benches under low trees that border a large fish-pond. It is a rayon-mill, but we see only about five persons in the long room that is filled with machines. There is only an empty park and a silent mill. A few workers pass us, with their lean shadows dancing before them; each a standardized product of a well-organized system of exploitation that uses enough of the mental and physical strength of a worker to make him (or her) an unconscious victim of the system he supports.

A small roadster stops beside us, and we sit on an already crowded seat with a white-collar worker and his young brother. He will be glad to take us across the mountain as far as he goes, and leave us only eight miles from our destination. I learn that the Dupont mill is not running full-time; only TEN hours a day, with a small force, and possibility of a shut-down anytime. The girls make a higher wage than the boys after they become capable robots, and may attain the munificent sum of 45c an hour, as compared to the boys' 20c and 35c an hour; beyond that the unorganized mountaineer cannot ascend without the sanction of the Baptist church and the House of Dupont.

"I don't believe nobody could buy a job here-abouts," says our host and tells us about a hobo hitting his head on the tunnel, and riding into town with a fractured skull, holding his head with his hands and staring dumbly, vacantly into space until taken to the hospital where he lingers on the edge of death. "For a short-cut," he tells us, "take the first dirt road to your right beyond the second orchard on that hill," and he points out a thin ribbon of road that stretches far below us, where the valley goes fanwise eastward, between a range that is cut up into a lot of mountains

of various shapes and heights on the south, and bordered on the
north by a solid range that terminates into a low haze of blue.
"So long, good luck," he says, leaving us at the base of a mountain with blistered feet and eight miles to go.

We find the dirt road, and head into the hills; their contours
of uneven beauty showing dark masses of shadow and brilliant
sunlight that roll in silent swells against the skyline. We feel small
and insignificant, like the persons in a Rousseau painting. There
is a long lane of honeysuckle-covered banks, and the air is warm
and sweet, like wind across a hayfield after rain. The estates of
the rich are far back from the road, in groves of oak bordered
by boxwood; and the fields are filled with horsejumps painted
white, and we smell the breath of cows with an odor of garlic.

Along the road are the homes of the tenants and other classes
of workers; their homes are sometimes very neat, and often very
old and bare, with mud falling out of the cabin chinks and many
children staring pop-eyed as we pass.

"In Mississippi the people what never work don't associate with
those what do. Only the poor whites and negroes work in that
state. I wouldn't want to work there or live there less'n I wuz a
worker," says Jim. "I think workers have a better time of it than
them what is always after money." Jim has worked in a steel-mill,
at country clubs, and mostly on farms; he likes the farming,
because he can always leave for a hitch-hike home to the family
acres when things are slack and there's no butchering or planting
to be done. I gave up trying to classify him as anything but a
passive proletarian, whose interests are confined to playing the
guitar, cooking, and hiking over the mountains to some remote
village where the people play checkers and make rugs.

"I got another blister under my toe," says Jim.

"One of mine broke," I says, "but I feel better now."

Yes, I feel better, for we have gone beyond the mountain.

The Rebel Poet Oct.-Nov.-Dec. 1931

The Gaffer

MARTIN SAVELA

The Gaffer and I were working on the sand-pile, putting the lumpy sand through the riddling machine, he going through the motions in a mechanical way, digging the shovel in and lifting, not once stopping to catch breath or to wipe the sweat out of his eyes, though when I'd straighten to ease my back he'd break the rhythm slightly to leer at me—then he'd go on working while I'd stand leaning on my shovel and watch him hatefully.

"Don't kill yourself, Gaffer," I said.

"I . . . won't. . . ."

Then I turned and looked at the valley and sky. The foundry was outside of town, almost in the country, and in the morning, with the sliding doors open at the rear of the building, the wind blew in and when you looked up from work you could just see the sky there beyond the shoulder of the valley. You could see the scarred brown earth, disfigured by heaps of greyish slag and cinder, with here and there a hardy clump of grass and some of those blue flowers, johnny-jump-ups we used to call them, that we found in the dunes during the earliest time of spring. The patch of earth looked far away when you looked at it through the smoke-haze inside of the foundry, like some kind of dream-land.

"Don't kill yourself, either," the Gaffer said.

I kept looking at the valley and the sky and didn't say anything.

It was just before the pouring of the morning heat, the furnaces were roaring, and the sandblasters and grinders were all going full speed. Then the super came in and Casimir, the foreman on our floor, went over to talk to him. The super yelled, "How's the new guy on the floor?" pointing at me, and Casimir shrugged, smiled and spread out his hands, saying nothing. "How's the Gaffer getting along with him?" Casimir just shrugged. The super grinned. "Say, Cass, maybe we'll fire both of them and get a couple big black niggers, what say?"

I bent down to work again and the Gaffer paused, shovel in mid-air, and for a split-second looked at me with his dull, smokey, bluish-grey eyes. Then we began to work hard, as if we were competing, our arms going in unison and the sweat dropping off of us into the green sand. . . .

Harry, the furnace-man, twisted the valves and yelled at the top of his lungs, "Heat! Heat!" The blasting of the furnaces died off with a long sigh, you could hear the metal burbling in the sudden stillness, and the molders stopped working, relaxing at their benches.

The Gaffer and I put down our shovels, drew on thick gloves, and went into the furnace-room. The metal was fluxed and ready for the pouring. I walked around and behind the furnaces to attach the big grappling-hooks to the neck of the crucible, and stepping between a furnace and a nearby wall like that is like stepping into fire, but after it has seared you through it is not painful. The Gaffer didn't seem to mind the heat at all but leaned over to peer straight into the crucible where molten iron shimmered like quicksilver, and shook his head, his seamed little face frowning. "Don't worry about it, Gaffer," Harry laughed. "That's my job."

We grasped hold of the chains and lifted the crucible free of the furnace-mouth, then we moved the crane out of the room and along the aisle to the first row of molds and began to pour. The Gaffer held the pronged end of the rod and did the pouring while I just held onto the other end and moved when he did. The metal flowed smoothly as thick cream down the ingates, the way it does when it's at just the correct temperature and the sand is just right in dampness and texture and a skillful man is pouring. When we reached the end of the first row the Gaffer glanced at me inquiringly because there it was usual to rest, but though my throat was puckered up with fumes so that it was hard to swallow or breathe, his vacant eyes angered me and I said, "Go ahead," and muttered, "god damn you!" We poured the next row without resting, and the next, until at last the first crucible was empty. Walking back to the furnace-room, gulping air into scorched lungs, I wondered which way the molten iron would run if I were to drop the crucible—would it spill toward the Gaffer or flow back around my own ankles?

In the furnace-room we hooked the grapples onto a new crucible and began all over again. . . .

I leaned down over the sink, turned the faucet all the way, and cupping my hands under it began to drink. I let it bubble up cold over my face, held it in my mouth, spat it out and then allowed a thin trickle of the good water to slip down my throat

into my dry hollow stomach. Right away the sweat burst from
the pores and my body began to cool off. I wiped my face and
went back to the floor. A new heat was being started. The Gaffer
was breaking up molds and taking the castings into the shipping
room on the truck. His face looked old and tired.

"Tired, Gaffer?" I said.

He didn't say anything. All right, I thought, see if you can do
this—see if you can keep up with this. Feeling fresh and strong,
I began lifting two molds at a time and carrying them to the sand-
pile and dumping them. The Gaffer began to do the same. He
barely was able to lift the two molds, his thin back trembled
with the effort and he staggered when he carried them, but he
did it. And when we had shaken out all of the molds and took
up our shovels again, his rhythmic pace was the same, mechanical and unbroken, so that only his strained, hoarse breathing
showed that he was tired, that his body was all bruised and sick
with tiredness.

We had worked so hard that the floor was cleared and the
sand all riddled a full hour before it would be time to pour another heat, so there was nothing for us to do after we had loaded
the junk onto the wheelbarrows and dumped it. Coming out from
the heat and clattering din of the foundry into the open air and
seeing the quiet sky, anger vanished. It wasn't important any
more. There was a soggy cigarette tucked behind my ear and I lit
it, inhaled deep, and sat down on the wheelbarrow. The sunlight
danced over the dunes in silky yellow and amber waves and the
wind blew in cool gusts off the lake, smelling of fresh water,
sedge grass and clover. Above the land the whole sky was diluted
to dull blue by the smoke from the furnaces of the Calumet
region, but it stretched out to a clean, fragile blue above the lake
and near the horizon it was streaked with wispy white like spun
cotton. During the pouring of the metal and afterward I had forgotten to look out of the door and had become unaware of anything except the work—but now the sun, wind and sky made it
seem unimportant, the noise of the shop diminished and faded
away, I even forgot to hate the Gaffer. But then, turning around
suddenly, I saw him kneeling down in front of the junk-pile shaking
a sieve back and forth and I said, "Christ, Gaffer, what's that for?"
He muttered something about metal in the junk and went on shaking the sieve. When all the junk was sifted he dumped the tiny
scraps of metal that remained into a bucket and re-filled the sieve
with burnt-out sand, slag and cinders from the pile.

"You sure are killing this job, Gaffer," I said.

Then he turned and looked at me in a strange way. Often when we were working I'd notice him looking at me this way. His eyes had a vague, expressionless stare but there were depths in them where the remnants of a long-dead fire seemed occasionally to glow, flare, in momentary angers the way a spark will leap out of grey ash when you breathe on it, and die down again. Slowly he turned away and began to rattle the sieve. "Listen, Gaffer," I said bitterly, "I can out-work you and you know it and Casimir knows it. That kind of stuff isn't going to do you any good when the lay-offs come. What counts is work."

I got up and threw away the cigarette stub and went inside.

"Honest to Christ?"

"Yeah, going through the junk-pile with a sieve. . . ."

The men laughed and Farrera, a molder, said, "Oho, that Gaffer, he is a good company man all right."

"He's a home guard all right," Harry, the furnace-man, said. "The other day I come back from lunch and what did I catch him doing but breaking ingots. I took the sledge away from him and told him off, told him to keep his nose out of my furnace-room."

We were sitting outside in the shadow of the wall of the building eating lunch. Some of the apprentices had finished eating and were throwing a baseball back and forth in the bright noon sunlight. The Gaffer was not there. He never observed the lunch-hour. At twelve o'clock he would sit briefly on a sand-pile to chew at some dry sandwiches, washing them down with water, and then get up and go to work again in the deserted, quiet shop.

"What's the matter with him, Harry?" I said.

"He's like a punchdrunk fighter. All he knows is work, work, work. He's got to beat everybody else but he doesn't know why any more. See, he was always a little guy and he had to work like that to keep a job until he got the way he is. Hell, the guy ain't human."

Pederson, the lanky Swede core-maker, came out and yelled across the yard to Charley, the mechanic: "Hey, Charley, is Gaffer working for you now?"

"Like hell," Charley said.

"Well, he's going around oiling up the shafts."

"Son of a bitch!"

But in spite of all that I didn't know why I hated the Gaffer the way I did. It was not only him that I hated—it was something more than that. The Gaffer himself was only an old man, work-broken and mean, and you could pity him or despise him but he was not strong and important enough to hate the way I hated him. He was short and thin with skinny hairless arms and Slavic features, and he walked stooped over, always staring at the ground, chin against his chest. It was not his ugliness, not the way he worked, not what he said that enraged me, but the lusterless and impersonal way that he stared about him with those long-dead eyes, as if he were blind, or as if all that he saw, heard, felt and responded with had died long ago and an outer husk, impotent and hateful even to himself, had gone on living. Even when I had become more accustomed to working with him and was able to ignore the rest of it, I would suddenly look up to catch him staring at me in that unfathomable way and then I'd burst loose with a wildly crazy effort to out-work him—but he had a desperate kind of strength and courage that made him able to match everything that I could do in these spurts and keep on going after I was winded and spent. Then I realized that it was useless to compete with him--there was nothing left inside him that could be hurt enough to make him admit defeat if he had been beaten. He seemed to enjoy the pain of exhaustion and to grow stronger on it. Nothing could touch him any more.

By the time spring ended I had given up trying to out-work the Gaffer, and when the long hot days of summer came it was all I could do to keep up with him.

In mid-July we were casting brass. It was a large rush order, and four extra molders were put on in our section, but no extra laborers. The Gaffer and I were working overtime every night to clear the floor for a fresh start in the morning but no matter how hard we worked we could not keep pace with the molders—they were yelling for new sand before we had shaken out the castings from a previous heat. From dawn till sunset the temperature was in the nineties. The lake wind did not allay it. Inside the shop the furnaces were going all the time, their *harff harff* sounding like a crazy laugh.

Asleep and awake my forearms, shoulders and back ached painfully. It was like working in your sleep or being asleep at work; the only thing that divided the two was that walk in the morning and evening coolness from home to the foundry and home again. The rest of the time was spent working in sleep and sleeping in work.

At the shop I followed the Gaffer, watching him through heavy-lidded eyes and doing what he did, duplicating every move. Then it passed. All my weariness was gone suddenly, the stiff muscles became very lax and pliant, my mind seemed more lucid than it

ever had been, and a new strength flowed all through me so that I
didn't notice the heat at all and the work became ridiculously
easy, like playing with toys. And I saw everything with a new
clarity, all of a sudden I saw it, and it was so obvious that I swore
at myself for not realizing it before. It was a trap, and the Gaffer
was part of it. That was why he looked at me in that secret way,
wondering if I'd found him out. Ah, Gaffer, Gaffer, I thought,
you're not as dumb as you pretend to be. You're smart—but you're
not smart enough. . . .

I threw away my shovel. It fell with a clatter on the concrete
floor. The Gaffer stopped working, straightened up, and looked at
me with a long unwavering stare.

"What's the matter, Gaffer?" I said. My voice sounded brittle.

"What?" he said stupidly.

"What?" I mocked him. "Thought you had me, didn't you;
thought I wasn't onto your game, didn't you? Well, I'm not so
dumb. . . ."

I looked around me carefully. You had to be careful. I saw a
sledge hammer leaning against the wall and began to edge sideways toward it, keeping my eyes on the Gaffer all the time.

He kept watching me intently. Moving slowly I reached the
wall and curled my fingers around the sledge handle. But just
then it all became quiet in the foundry; the furnaces stopped
blasting, sighed; the molders stopped working and turned around
and looked at me, and Harry came out of the furnace-room and
yelled, "Heat! Heat!" Then I let go of the sledge, drew on my
gloves, and walked calmly toward the furnaces. I didn't trust anybody, I had to be careful about it. When I entered the furnace-
room I looked straight at Harry and winked.

"What's the matter, kid?" Harry said.

"Nothing."

I winked again slowly and pointed at the Gaffer.

"Want me to pour this one off with the Gaffer?" Harry said.

"No, I can do it," I said. "Just watch me."

"You look pretty bad."

"I just got my second wind. I'll fix the bastard."

The Gaffer had gone behind the furnaces and attached the
grapples to the crucible. We lifted it out slowly and moved it
out to the floor, then I grasped hold of the worn, smooth shaft
and we went slowly down the first row of molds, pouring the slug-
gish metal. It poured too slowly—it was too thick. Inside the mold
it bubbled and hissed. But I never took my eyes off the Gaffer to

look at it, and when he glanced up at me I said to him, "Keep going, keep going, god damn you!" The crucible did not seem to be
getting any lighter as we poured and when we had passed the
third row I finally looked down and saw that it was still full to
the brim.

"Well, that suits me," I said.

"What?" the Gaffer said, looking up, his face haggard.

"Tired, Gaffer?" I said. "Well, keep going, keep going, now
we'll find out about this, once and for all."

I kept getting stronger and stronger, until the brimming crucible
felt light as a teacup to my arms, and we kept going down an
endless row of molds, pouring the unending metal. I was waiting
for the Gaffer to tire because I knew that he was too old to have a
second wind and had to break some time, had to—no man could
keep up a pace like that forever. It seemed to me that the only
way I could escape from the trap was to beat the Gaffer. Then the
shaft began to wobble, became steady, shook again violently, and
I knew that he was weakening. Then I saw that the Gaffer was
trembling all over as if with ague, and I thought to myself tri-
umphantly: There he goes! Hurray, he's through! Pretty soon
he'll set it down and everybody will know that I beat him!

Suddenly the Gaffer stumbled, the crucible fell and shattered,
the molten brass flowed out over the floor and encased our legs
like glue, and the strange thing was that it didn't hurt, didn't
even feel bad—instead it felt rather pleasant. But I could not move
my legs. "Oh, Gaffer," I moaned, "look what you did." He looked
down at the brass, puzzled. It kept mounting higher. "Oh, you
crazy old son of a b—," I said. "I had you beat but you wouldn't
admit it and now look what you did. Why did you do it, Gaffer?"

There was a great distance between us. We were standing at
the opposite ends of the long corridor-like aisle between the
benches. But when he raised his head and looked at me across
that distance, his eyes seemed very near and I could look right
down into their clouded, obscure depths.

I turned my head away. It was terrible to look into those eyes.
He spoke to me across the distance in a dull voice:

"Let me out."

"I can't."

"Let me out. Please let me out."

"I can't, Gaffer. I'm caught, too."

I looked around and tried to call for help but the *harff harff*
of the furnaces drowned out my voice. The rest of the men were

too busy finishing up the rush order to notice what had happened but Harry was standing idly in the furnace-room door and I motioned to him with my hands. He came over.

"Help, for Christ's sake!" I yelled.

"Sure, kid, you'll be all right," Harry said. He leaned over and pushed me deeper into the brass.

Then the super came in and yelled at Casimir, the foreman, "Hey, Cass, fire those two and hire a couple big black niggers."

"Let me out! Let me out!" the Gaffer screamed, and he began to thresh and churn his legs about in the congealing metal. I yelled across to him, "It's no use, Gaffer! They've got us in a trap!" I relaxed, fell backward limply, and the brass swallowed me up, encased me, soft and warm.

The sunlight was warm on my eyelids, then I opened them and there was the sky. I was lying on my back in the grass of the yard. The Gaffer and Harry were standing over me. At first I couldn't remember a thing and I said, "What's the matter?"

"You passed out," Harry said. "Brass fumes. But you'll be all right. Lucky for both of you the crucible was empty when you keeled over—"

"—But I thought he did. . . ."

"What?"

"Never mind," I said. "It's all right."

After that I didn't try to keep up with the Gaffer any more. I was beaten. But he went on working just as hard, making up things to do when there was no work, like sweeping up a clean floor or sifting the sand for imaginary particles of metal. When that brass job had been finished there was a slack period and the extra men were laid off, so the following week, when I opened my pay-envelope and there was a curt dismissal-notice in it, I wasn't surprised. After quitting-time, when the other men had gone, I cleaned out my locker and put the things in a paper bag. Then I went out and walked slowly along the road toward the trolley-line. At the bend of the road I sat down on the ditchbank among the goldenrod and waited until the trolley had come and the men had gotten on and it had rattled away across the prairie toward town. Then I got up and went over to the small clapboard station, but when I entered I saw the Gaffer sitting there on a bench beside the window.

"I guess I'll walk," I said, and went out again and began to walk along the ties. After I'd walked a little way I heard his footfalls on the gravel a short distance behind me, but I paid no attention. . . .

The sun was still up and brilliant-winged grasshoppers, waxy red and black, were leaping across the roadbed, bumping and brushing my hands and face with their dry wings. The sad low trembling of dying crickets sang under the piercing shriek of a myriad of cicadas. A bob white perched on a fence-post called and called a simple liquid phrase. And all over the prairie the grass was fading, weed-pods had burst and shrivelled and the tattered sunflowers dropped their petals.

"You got fired?" the Gaffer said. He had come up beside me. "It was for your own good, believe me."

I kept walking and didn't say anything, but I looked sideways at him. He was plodding along, head down.

"You are young. You will get another job. But you work too hard. Don't be a fool like me. I know I'm a fool about work but I can't do nothing about it, I can't help it any more. When you have your nose down on the grindstone for forty years. . . ." He shook his head. "I tell you, don't do it, don't be a fool."

He didn't say anything more until we came to the outskirts of the town. Then I remembered that just before I had passed out and found myself sinking down into the molten brass a cool vision had passed in front of my eyes of a patch of blue sky, green earth and a few of the blue flowers that we called johnny-jump-ups and used to find in the dune country during the early days of spring.

When we reached the first grey stucco houses on the edge of town it was getting dark, the sun had gone down, and in the cool blue of the evening the flames from the open hearths along the lake showed up brightly and then a Bessemer was blown, a geyser of flame and red sparks. The taste of smoke was very strong in the air.

"I go this way," the Gaffer said. "Good-bye."

"Good-bye, Gaffer," I said.

Watching him go down the street all alone, I discovered with a little surprise that I didn't hate him any more.

The New Anvil Aug.-Sept. 1939

The Long Trip

DEL SMITH

"You sheep, you cowards, you're only fit to die then!" Linda McMurray jerked up from the wooden yard chair and slammed through the back door of the house.

"What's mamma sore about?" little Chuck asked, looking after her doubtfully.

"Something she ate, I guess." His father's face was hard, the easy-going lines were gone.

"You better watch out," Chuck warned, "or mamma won't let you go on the trip."

Worth McMurray sat on his heels, grinding the indoor ball into the sparsely-grassed ground. "That a fact, Chuck?" he asked seriously.

"Sure. I played in the road today, and she wouldn't lemme go over to Danny's."

"Yeah, well," his father said in a funny soft voice, "you don't wanna play in the road while I'm gone."

Chuck avoided a promise. "Whyncha throw the ball?" he asked quickly.

Worth looked for quite a while at the homely questioning face of the five-year-old. Then silently he rolled the ball toward him.

The ball rolled wide. Chuck made a frantic grab and sprawled out on his belly, arms outstretched. The ball tumbled lightly over his little hands and vanished under the brick supporting blocks of the porch. Chuck disappeared after it like a dog.

His father opened his mouth to protest, but then turned away. He walked slowly to the back of the lot and stood motionless. Far down below, across the gray Monongahela, smokes of a dozen hues—blue, black, yellow—rose lazily from the stacks of the great steel mill. As he watched, a toy engine wound out of the cinder-gray plant, drawing after it a string of tall orange ingots. Another deep boom echoed from the mill's big rolls as a new slab of steel started through. Listening closer, Worth could hear the steady rushing of the "three sisters"—the blast furnaces. He sighed heavily.

"I'm sorry, Worth. . ." Linda had come out silently and was standing there beside him. "This day's got my temper ragged."

"Oh well."

Together they looked down at the familiar motion and sound below.

"Missus Gildersleeve says there's talk of taking on at the mill next week," Linda said absently. "But of course it doesn't make any difference now."

"No, not now."

Eyes on the ground, they turned and walked back toward the house. Chuck was crawling out from under the porch, a seam of the indoor gripped in his teeth.

"Charles!"

"Drop it!" his father commanded sharply.

The little boy opened his mouth obediently and the ball rolled out ahead of him. He stood up, running one dirty hand through his brick-colored hair.

"Why?" he wanted to know.

"Don't always be asking questions," his mother ordered. "And go on in and wash your hands."

Chuck banged through the screen door.

"You'll have your hands full with him," Worth said. They walked to the wooden slope-back chairs and sat down listlessly.

"Say," Worth remembered. "About my set of dies. Anybody that wants to use them has got to use them right here. If they take 'em away, some'll get lost sure as hell. Especially old man Crown. Remember that now!"

"I'm not a five-year-old!"

Worth leaned back to roll a cigaret. "It's a good thing. One in the family is enough. Look at him!" Chuck had come out again, hands still wet from a sousing, and begun climbing on the sooty porch railing. Moist smoky grime took the place of the washed-off dust, Linda sighed, smiling a little.

Worth snapped his fingers. "And say! About the car, I forgot to tell you. The front wheels need packing every five thousand miles. I'll put that on the list."

Linda shifted nervously. "I should be driving it five thousand miles! Where've I got to go?"

"You got to keep the battery up!"

"All right."

"And don't let those dumb bunnies at the corner station touch it. Take it to Robinson's."

"All right."

Chuck clung to a post above them. "Daddy, why don't you go to see gramma in the car? Then me and mamma could go with you."

"Come down off that railing."

Chuck obeyed. "Why doncha?" He sat peering through the porch slats, little overalled legs dangling. "Danny's gramma," he added, "hasn't got no teeth."

"Remember that," Linda told him, "next time I catch you just wetting your tooth brush."

Chuck scrambled up and disappeared around the house.

Worth wandered back to look down at the river and the mill again. The blast had been cut off the third sister; they were tapping her now; he could tell by the thin fierce beams of light below. The penetrating scream of a crane floated up to him. He strained to catch the rising crescendo of the motor as the big machine swung out high over the floor.

Worth turned away bitterly. Running his hand over a small branch of the new-leaved apple tree, he hesitated a moment, then broke the branch off roughly. He went back to his seat, opened a knife, and began whittling the green wood steadily. Linda sat and watched.

After a while a rattling car pulled into the garage next door, and a long stringy man with weathered red face and neck got out. He came up to the wire fence.

"Hi there."

"Hello, Jones."

"When you leaving, Worth?"

"Train pulls out at five."

Jones cleared his throat. "No gettin' out, eh. . . ?" Linda snorted.

"Guess not. Linda and me talked over every angle we could think of, and I guess there's nothing we can do. Not a thing. They'd sic the police on me. G-Men, maybe."

Jones tapped his toe against the fence. "It's too bad you never took your papers out."

Worth stared at the ground dully. "Yeah, guess I was dumb about that. Me and the old man come down long ago. Toronto and Pittsburgh never seemed like two different countries to me. They was just two places. Why, I went to high school right up the street there! Every job I ever had I had right here in the Pittsburgh steel mills! I never felt like no foreigner."

"Christ," Jones said, "nobody's blaming you. Only, it would of come in handy now."

"Sure." Linda spoke sarcastically. "Too bad he wasn't born a few years earlier, too. Then he could sit back another month or so, waiting his turn to be called."

Worth looked at her uneasily. "A guy can always think of things he shoulda done, after it's too late," he said to Jones.

"You wait, Fred Jones," Linda went on. "When *you* start out, leaving *your* wife and kids home, I'll throw up to you the things you shoulda done!"

Jones glanced up, surprised. "Hell, *we* ain't gonna get into it!"

"That's what Worth thought about Canada, a year ago." She stared at him. Her voice rose, challenging, hysterical. "But no! You're so God damned sure your turn ain't coming—you don't care about Worth."

"Linda! . . . she's pretty upset," Worth apologized quickly.

Jones nodded. "No wonder." There was a long awkward pause. "Well . . . Got to patch a doggone tire before dinner. I'll be over this evening for a little."

"Okay."

Jones walked away from the fence.

Worth whittled at the green wood of the apple branch. "Jones is a good guy, Linda," he said gently.

She didn't look at him. "You're a good guy, too, Worth. What difference does it make?"

"Aw, now, Linda." He reached out to pat her shoulder help-lessly. "I'll come back. Somebody always comes back."

Linda didn't answer.

Chuck surged around the house corner suddenly on a rusty old scooter. Linda swiped at her eyes.

"Dad," Chuck said, "this here bolt is loose. You wanna fix it now, or wait'll you come back?"

"Now. Bring me my small wrench, Linda," he said, a little later, while Chuck scootered over the uneven ground, "I'm worried about the money. It won't be much I'll get to send you."

"Oh, don't worry about *me!*"

His jaw set doggedly. "We got to figure these things out."

"I'll get along all right. I can always go back to Southside with the folks."

His knife cut into the branch so deep it snapped in two. He stared at the ground for a minute, then spoke softly. "And then you'll be living in that little brick house by the J & L Mill, just like before I ever came along. Just like I'd never seen you. Just like I'd never stopped in that day and offered to fix your old man's gutters for a dollar. Like you never came out and asked me those dumb girl-questions about gutters."

"You were the dumb one. I was vamping you," she laughed nervously, "and you were too thick to know it."

". . . just like I'd never been alive."

"Worth. Remember that first little apartment? The kitchen all painted blue?"

"Yeah."

"You used to come rushing in from the mill and love me so much the dinner got cold?"

"Yeah. A couple months later we had all the time we could use for loving."

She got up to sit on the arm of his chair. "I didn't mind," she insisted, parting his sandy-red hair with her fingers. "Not even being on relief that whole two years you were out of a job. I had my man and I knew it." She stopped short, wiping her eyes.

"We had a lot of fun all right," Worth said hastily. "Remember those picnics at South Park? And I really got to play with Chuck when he came. When was that, anyway?"

"I'm five," Chuck volunteered, scooting past.

Linda gazed after him, blinking. Then she broke out, "Oh, Worth, don't go! I won't *let* you go!"

"Now Linda." Worth twisted his stick uncomfortably. "What's the use—"

"What's the use of me and Chuck living here by ourselves in this great big house? What's the use of being left alone, nobody to love, nobody to look after, nobody to tighten scooter bolts! What's the use—" She choked, sobbing.

"Christ, Linda, you think I want to go?"

Chuck braked the battered scooter sharply. His freckled face looked up at them, excited. "Well, golly, dad. If you don't *wanna* go, whyncha write gramma a letter? Tell her mamma won't let you go."

There was a silence. Linda blew her nose. "Well, see," she said in a controlled voice. "Daddy can't exactly do that now. It's too late now. They got all the plans made before he knew it."

"Well, but where was daddy when the plans was being made?"

"Yes!" his mother cried out. "Where are *all* the men while the plans are being made?"

Chuck took another spin around the yard. Then he pulled up again. "Well, gee, daddy. If *you* don't wanna go, why doncha send me? I could go! I could ride on the train!"

"No, Chuck. It's a long trip."

"Sure, I could go! *Please,* mamma! I wanna go!"

His mother's chin trembled. "Now Charles," she said sternly. "What does mamma tell you, when you tease to do things?"

Chuck screwed up his face to remember. "Wait till I grow up?" he ventured. He looked first to one, then to another, hopefully. After a moment he pushed off slowly on his rusty scooter.

"Now Linda. . . ." Worth turned to her as she began crying gently. "No sense getting worked up about *that*. Why, Chuck is just a kid." He looked off toward the river. "I only wish *I* was a kid. . . ."

"You were—once—and now you have grown up to be a soldier."

He stirred restlessly. "Is that my fault?"

"Oh, no! *Nothing* is your fault! *Nothing* is your fault! Just simply *nothing!*"

The New Anvil July-Aug. 1940

Sour Grapes

JESSE STUART

I don't know how I got into the world. I just remember being there. The first time I remember being in the world was when I tried to follow Ma out'n the cliff. She went out first and shoved me back. She closed the gate that kept me shut in the cliff. I cried and cried after Ma. She was the only person I ever saw then. All the light I ever saw came in at the mouth of the cliff.

I remember every piece of furniture we had in the cliff. We had a flat-topped stove. It had a pipe that run up straight, then elbowed and went out along the top of the cliff to the outside. We had a big flat rock inside the cliff for a table. Ma spread a white cloth over it. We had a bed-tick made of coffee sacks and filled with oak leaves. We slept on this together. I slept in Ma's arms then. We had two quilts that Ma worked for and carried home. We had a few pots and pans, and some dishes. Ma had a big wash-tub, a wash-kettle and a wash-board. The wash-board was bright and pretty with little ridges across it.

In the summertime I didn't wear any clothes. I had to stay in the cliff. I went naked. In the wintertime I wore a pair of pants and a shirt. The cliff was long. I used to go and go before I'd come to the end of it. There was dry sand on the bottom for my feet and some dry piles of oak leaves. At the door of the cliff Ma hung a quilt during the wintertime to keep out the wind. In the summertime Ma just kept a high gate fastened to keep me inside. Mister Seagraves used to keep his cattle in this cliff before Ma brought me here. Ma worked for Mister Seagraves now. He let us have the cliff.

I remember how Ma used to leave me. She would leave bread on the white cloth spread over the rock. She would leave a pitcher of water for me to drink. She would fasten the gate. She would twist a wire on the outside so I couldn't reach over and untwist it. I couldn't open the gate and get out. I had to stay in the cliff. It was the only place I'd ever been. I could tell you every piece of rock in the cliff from the gate in front, back to where the water dripped down. I could show you every pile of leaves. I could tell you about every dish we had and every pot and pan.

Ma used to come up the hill to the cliff. She would be nearly out'n breath. She would have a big sack of clothes across her back. She had brought them to the cliff to wash. Ma would wash them in the cliff. Snow would be on the ground outside. Ma was a big woman. She had big arms. She would come down with her weight on a dirty pair of overalls. The suds would fly. She'd rub and rub. Then she'd twist and twist the pair of overalls and the water would come out by squirts. When she'd wash the sack of clothes she'd hang them to dry on a grapevine across the cliff.

Before I went to bed Ma would take me in her arms and sing to me. The last I'd remember were the pretty words Ma'd sing. I'd wake up in the morning and Ma'd have breakfast. We'd eat again and Ma would leave. She'd be gone all day. I'd stay in the cliff. It was good and warm. The wind couldn't get to me. I'd sometimes go up to the door and pull the quilt to one side and look at the snow on the high hills. It was a white world. I could see the trees that stood dark and without leaves, in the snow. The winter would pass. Summer would come again. The trees would get green. The cattle would eat grass in front of the cliff. I would like to watch the cattle eat. I would watch them from the cliff. I'd hear the birds sing. I'd watch the butterflies fly from one blossom to another. They were pretty things.

I don't know how old I was. I don't know how big I was. I'd never seen anybody but Ma. I know she was big. But Ma let me get out'n the cliff. She watched me. She stayed close to me. I remember the grass was green. I remember the feel of the wind against my naked body. I remember the warmth of the sun. It was spring. The birds were singing. The grass was growing. The cattle were picking the grass with their big mouths. It was a big room. I couldn't run to the end of it. Ma was at my heels all the time. But I jumped around like a young calf in the spring. I tried to catch the birds. I nearly caught a butterfly on a purple blossom. After I ran around over the pasture on the steep hillside below the cliff, Ma took me back and put me behind the gate. She fastened me up.

Ma would let me go out now. She took me to a patch of berries. I picked them from the ground. Ma told me the names of things. She called them strawberries. They tasted good and sweet. I saw flowers in bloom on the hill. I saw honeybees. Ma told me about them. Ma told me everything. But Ma stayed right beside me. After we picked the strawberries and ate them and Ma brought an apron load to the house, Ma fastened me in the cliff again. We once heard a voice. It was a strange voice. Ma took me by the hand and run with me through the woods.

Ma would take me out from the cliff. She would tell me the names of trees, flowers, birds and plants. I would see rabbits. I would watch dogs run the rabbits. I would hear them bark. I would want to run after the dogs. Ma wouldn't let me. She would hold me. Life was different. It was big. I didn't want to go back and be fastened up in the cliff. I got tired of the cliff. I hated it. I wanted to get out. I wanted to stay out. I wanted to run after the snakes. Ma wouldn't let me. She told me the snake would bite me. I would die. I didn't know what she meant when she said I would die. She told me the black snake would hurt me. The black snake was the color of Ma's face.

But I didn't look like Ma. I warn't the color of Ma. My hair was another color. I warn't the color of the black snake. I was the color of the blowing viper. When I pointed to my face and to Ma's face and to Ma's hair, she grabbed my hand and run through the woods to the cliff with me.

I had been over the fields about the cliff now. I just hated to stay in the cliff. Ma went away to work. I climbed over the gate. I run off down over the hill to the strawberry patch. I was eating berries. I heard voices. I crawled on my belly thru the weeds and I saw something I had never seen before. I saw a man plowing. I saw two boys with hoes. They warn't the color of Ma. I laid in the weeds and watched them. Their dog started barking. He came toward me. He was growling and kicking up the dirt. I jumped up and started to run. The man plowing saw me. The boys saw me. The boys run after me hollering, with their hoes up in the air. They was trying to hit me. I didn't have on any clothes. I could outrun them. The man said: "What do you know about that! A wild youngin!" I outrun them to the thickets of green brush and green briars. I run back to the cliff.

One day Mister Seagraves came to the cliff. I'd heard Ma say that name. She had said it to me. He come on the outside and hollered to Ma. Ma went out. She says to me: "Adger, you stay in here. I won't be out but just a minute." I slipped up to the gate and listened.

"Mollie," says Mister Seagraves, "Adger has been slipping out. You can't hide him any longer. You are going to haf to send that boy to school. You are going to haf to do something about it. Lake Sperry and his two boys saw him down at the cornfield yesterday morning and it's going around here there's a wild youngin loose in the woods. People are a scouring the rocks and woods for this wild youngin."

"I know, Mister Seagraves," says Ma, "but he can't go to school here. What will I do? What will Mister Zeb do? Oh, I can't do it, Mister Seagraves."

"You will have to do something now," says Mister Seagraves. "I'll see Zeb about it. I'm going to town Saturday. I'll put Zeb wise."

I saw Mister Seagraves. He was a big man. He was the color of the man I saw plowing. He wore clothes like this man. He had a big stick in his hand that helped him climb the hill. He had a big bag of salt on his shoulder. He spread the salt on rocks. The cattle come up and licked the salt with their long tongues. Ma came back in the cliff.

Ma didn't go to school with me. Mister Seagraves sent me with his boy. I was afraid of the other boys. When I got to school all the children looked at me. They just kept looking at me. I was afraid of them. Ma had put clothes on me. I wore a white waist and a little pair of pants that buttoned to the waist. The teacher asked me my name. I says: "Adger." The children laughed. She says: "Is that all the name you got?" I says: "Yes." The children looked at one another and laughed. I saw things they called books. They didn't look like leaves. There was pictures in the books. I had seen things that looked like the pictures. There was little black things in the book. The boys and girls would look at these and say words I couldn't understand. We were two kinds of people. None was the color of Ma. A lot wore clothes like Ma. I'd never seen girls before.

When we went out of the house the boys gathered around me. I wanted to run. I didn't run until one of the boys started to bark like a dog. Then I run like a rabbit. The boys took after me. The boys were all barking. I started for the cliff. I didn't get to the cliff. They were getting too close to me. I climbed up a tree. The boys tried to climb up and get me. Many of them stayed under the tree and barked. When they tried and tried and couldn't climb up to get me, they started throwing rocks at me. Just one rock hit me. It hit me on the side of the head. The blood run down and made my white shirt red. The teacher come out and made the boys leave the tree.

She tried to get me to come down. She tried to find a boy who would climb up and get me. She couldn't find a boy who could climb the tree. I was afraid to come down. The teacher took the boys back to the school house. She went with them. I heard her ring a bell. I could look from the top of the tree. I saw the boys in one line, the girls in another. They marched into the schoolhouse. When they went in the house I came down out'n the tree. I ran hard as I could go back to the cliff to Ma.

Ma washed my head where I'd been hit with a rock. Ma cried when she took my white waist off. It was red with blood. I was glad to get my clothes off. I went out in the pasture field and laid down in the sun. I watched the cows come back and lick the rocks where Mister Seagraves put the salt. Ma says: "Adger, you won't haf to go no more to that school. You can stay here with me." I didn't know what school was. Just a lot of boys and girls in a house. The teacher was big like Ma but she warn't like Ma. The boys and girls warn't the color of Ma neither.

One day when I was dragging in poles of wood for Ma, the teacher and a big man come up the hill to the cliff. I saw Ma go out to them. The man was bigger than Mister Seagraves. He was getting his breath hard after he climbed up the hill. He was fat like Ma. He was the color of Mister Seagraves. The big man says to Ma: "I am the Superintendent of Schools of this County. I've come here to investigate. I've heard there was a wild boy loose out here. Then Miss Harkreader reported that a boy enrolled in school and wouldn't tell his name and the boys ran him away with rocks."

"He was hit with a rock," says Ma. "Yes sir, he was hit with a rock."

Ma was shaking like a leaf. Ma's eyes got big. I stooped down behind a bunch of blackberry briars. I watched them. I listened to them. I laid my two poles of wood down beside me.

"Is he your boy?" says the big man.

"No, he ain't my boy," says Ma.

Ma began to cry.

"The boy is white," says the teacher. "If you could see him— He just acts funny. He don't know how to play with children. He don't know what a book is. He is afraid. He acts like a wild boy."

"No wonder," says the Superintendent, "living in a rock cliff. I've come here to investigate this situation. He's in the school law, isn't he?"

"Yes," says the teacher, "he must be. He didn't know his age. I asked him. He didn't know what I was talking about. He just stood and looked at me. No one had ever seen him before. No one knew where he lived. I found out where he lived from Mister

Seagraves' boy, Erf. He said he heard his Pa tell his Ma that they lived in the cliff"

"What are you doing with this boy then," says the Superintendent to Ma, "if he's not your boy?"

"Oh, don't ast me that, Mister," says Ma.

Ma cried harder and harder.

"I'll see this boy goes to school," says the Superintendent. "I'll stop all this rock throwing if I have to put this situation in the hands of the County Judge. Where is this boy? I'd like to see him."

"I don't know," says Ma.

"Yes you do," says the Superintendent. "I want to have a look at him."

When the Superintendent said this I jumped up and run from behind the briars. I left my poles of wood there. I took off across the pasture field.

"There he goes," says the teacher.

"He looks white to me," says the Superintendent, "but he is wild as a quail. He's got red hair. He must be sent to school."

"I won't be responsible," says the teacher. "I'm afraid I can't handle the school the way the children act when he's there. You'll have to get another teacher."

I hid behind another bunch of blackberry briars in the pasture. I saw them come back down the hill. I heard them talking. The Superintendent was smoking his pipe. He was walking with a cane.

He says: "If that's not a white boy I'm fooling. He's white as I am. She's kidnapped that boy. We'll further this investigation. I'll put it in the hands of the Sheriff when I get back to town. That boy is big enough to be ten years old. Running wild without a stitch of clothes on."

They went out of sight. I heard them talking and talking but I couldn't understand what they were saying. I run back up the hill and found Ma laying on the bed of leaves in the cliff. She was crying and crying. I told Ma what I heard them say about the Sheriff. Ma got up and says to me: "Now you stay here until I come back. I won't be gone long."

Ma went over the hill toward Mister Seagraves' house. I waited in the cliff for her to come back. Night had come when Ma got back. Ma got my white waist and put it on me. She made me put my pants on. I didn't want to wear them. Mister Seagraves came up to the cliff.

"Where is the stove, Mollie?" he says.

"It's right over there," says Ma. "I'll take it, and my dishes, pots and pans, but I'll leave the bed tick. I'll take the quilts."

Ma took one side of the stove, Mister Seagraves the other. They carried it over the hill. Mister Seagraves had a wagon waiting. They lifted the stove on the wagon. Then they come up the hill to get the rest of the things.

"You're stout as a man, Mollie," says Mister Seagraves. "I've never lifted with a stouter person in my life."

Ma and Mister Seagraves got the rest of the things. I carried the stove pipes down to the wagon. We got in the wagon. Mister Seagraves set up front and drove the horses. Me and Ma rode back with the furniture. Ma held me in her arms most of the way. I remember the stars in the sky. I remember the moon in the sky. I remember the grinding of the wagon wheels on the gravel and the horses splashing water in the creeks.

I heard Mister Seagraves say: "I'm just doing this for old Zeb. He didn't have no business getting into this mess. He's a friend of mine. We were boys together."

Then he says: "Get-up!" to the horses. He slapped them with the lines. The horses trotted on and on through the night with the wagon. I don't remember all of the trip nor the way we went. I slept with my head on Ma's lap. I just remember waking up in front of a pretty little white house. It warn't daylight yet. Ma and Mister Seagraves lifted the stove from the wagonbed and carried it into the house. I carried the pipes in the house. Ma and Mister Seagraves carried in the rest of the things. Mister Seagraves left his lantern with Ma.

"I thank you so much, Mister Seagraves," says Ma as he got up in the wagon and drove away before all the morning stars had left the sky. Ma set up the stove. She fixed us a bed. We laid down for a little sleep. I couldn't sleep. The place was so strange. It warn't nary a bit like the rock cliff. There warn't no leaves on the floor. No water was dripping from the roof.

That day a man came to the house. He smoked a pipe like the Superintendent smoked and like Mister Seagraves smoked. He wore a black hat. He walked in the house. He just stood a long time and looked at me. I wanted to run. But I couldn't get out'n the house. Then he looked at Ma.

"Well, Mister Zeb," says Ma.

Ma looked at Mister Zeb.

"I see you've got here all right," says Mister Zeb. "Now you can start to work for the Missus today. She's expecting you up to the house this morning. This boy must go to school. You can't leave him here in the house."

"I know, Mister Zeb," says Ma, "but he tried that going to school out on Shelf's Run. The boys run him like he was a possum. They treed him. Then they throw rocks at him. Look at that place on the side of his head."

"I know about it," says Mister Zeb. "Charlie Seagraves told me the whole story. We'll try him in the other school. The one down here on the creek. You have a home here, Mollie. You can help my wife. You are far away from Shelf's Run now. Let the Sheriff go back there. You are in another county now. He will not find anything but the empty cliff."

Mister Zeb took his hat off. He fanned in the house. It was a little warm. I saw Mister Zeb's hair. It was red, too. It was like my hair. It warn't a bit like Ma's hair. Then Mister Zeb put his hat back on. He puffed on his pipe.

"Now you get up to the house, Mollie," says Mister Zeb, "and help the Missus. I told her I'd get her a woman to do the work the other day. She doesn't know you. You don't know me either."

"No, I don't, Mister Zeb," says Ma. "I don't know you. I've just come for work. I've come to live here."

"I'll get you a bed in here," says Mister Zeb. "I think we've got a old bedstead up in the garret you can have. I'll have it brought down to the house. I'll give you enough money so you can buy a few little things you need. I'll take this boy down and let Slim's boy take him to school. He can go with Slim's boy, Jeff, down to the school by the creek."

I wore my white waist and my pants buttoned to them. I went with Mister Zeb. I saw Ma go up the hill to the big brick house. It was bigger than our rock cliff. There was a lot of big trees in the yard. I saw the flowers in bloom upon the hill around Mister Zeb's big house. We walked down the road until we come to a little plank house by the road. I saw a boy coming out'n the house with his books in his hand.

"Jeff," says Mister Zeb, "take this boy to school with you this morning."

"He can't go to school with me," says Jeff, "he's going to the wrong school!"

"No, he's not," says Mister Zeb. "You do as I say, young man."

Jeff was the color of Ma. He was one of Ma's people. He was the color of the black snake.

"Take care of 'im, too," says Mister Zeb as he puffed his pipe and walked away. He stopped in the road and looked at us as we walked away together. We walked beside of a barbwire fence. Then we turned to our right and walked out a road until we crossed the creek. Jeff wouldn't talk to me. He just looked at me. He was like the boys I'd met before. Only Jeff was the color of Ma. He wouldn't walk close to me.

We walked up the bank to the schoolhouse. I saw a lot of boys and girls. They were all Ma's people. They were all the color of Ma. When I went up in the yard the children begin to laugh. They jumped up and down and laughed and looked at my hair. The teacher came out. He looked at me. The children begin to laugh. He tried to stop them. They wouldn't stop.

"You've come to the wrong school," the teacher says to me. He was a man bigger than Mister Zeb. He was the color of Ma. He was as big as Ma. "You belong at the white folks school down in town. What is your name?"

"Adger," I says.

"Adger, who?" he says.

"Adger," I says.

"No name," he says. "Where did you get him, Jeff?"

"Mister Zeb sent him down here with me," says Jeff. "I didn't want to bring him in. Mister Zeb told me to bring him and take care of him. I don't know nothing about him, Mister Porter. I've just brought him because Mister Zeb said for me to."

The children looked at one another. They started laughing. I was afraid. I was ready to run. Two big boys looked at me. They acted like dogs wanting to get to a rabbit. The big teacher walked back in the house. The children gathered around me and laughed.

"Get 'im, Slick," says Jeff. "He ain't our kind. He don't belong here nohow!"

"What do you say, Big Charlie?" says Slick to the other big boy that snarled his lips at me. "Let's get 'im."

"Pretty red hair," says Big Charlie, "where did you get it?"

I run down the road hard as I could go. I could nearly catch a rabbit before I left the cliff. I could outrun these boys. They was all after me. Big Charlie and Slick was close to me. I kept away from them. All the boys and girls was after me. Rocks whizzed past my head. I went out the road and turned the corner by Jeff's house and took up the road. I looked back. I heard the school bell. They started back across the creek to the school on the bank.

"Don't ever come back here, Red-Head," says Big Charlie.

"It won't be any good for you if you do," says Slick. "We'll get you the next time."

I went up the road. I went back to the little white shack. I went in and laid down on the bed and waited for Ma to come from Mister Zeb's house. I waited all day in the house. I didn't get out and hunt the butterflies. I was afraid. I was afraid of people. Mister Zeb was good to me. I warn't afraid of Mister Zeb.

"Why didn't you stay at school, child?" says Ma.

"They run me away," I says to Ma.

"Where was the teacher?" says Ma.

"He went in the house," I says, "and Big Charlie and Slick run me away. All of the children run after me. They throwed rocks at me. I outrun them. I came back to the house."

"No place in the world for you," says Ma. "Neither school will have you. I'll tell Mister Zeb about it. But you won't go to school no more. You will stay right here with me."

I didn't go to school any more. I started to work for Mister Zeb. I pushed the lawnmower and cut grass in the yard. I fed Mister Zeb's hogs. I learned to milk the cows. I learned to harness Mister Zeb's horses and drive them over the farm. I learned how to take them to town. When Big Charlie and Slick run along and tried to get upon my wagon I used the rawhide on them. I would crack the rawhide in their faces and lap it around their shoulders. They would run away cursing and screaming and I'd slap the horses with the lines and get away before they could hit me with a rock. I couldn't drive thru the town where Ma's people lived. They would holler at me and curse me. Then they would take after my wagon. They would holler something about my red hair and asked me how I liked my first day of school and when I was coming back.

Mister Zeb would come back from his office. He would be standing out watching me work lots of times when I didn't see him. He would be smoking his pipe. He would say to me: "I wish Young Zeb was as good to work as you. I'd give anything on earth. You don't mind to work. Here is some extra money for you. Buy yourself some clothes. Don't let Mollie know I give it to you. This is for you." Then Mister Zeb would go away.

Young Mister Zeb didn't work, he went to school. He was the only child Mister Zeb had. He would get in the big automobile and get Missus Zenophine in the front seat with him. Mister Zeb would set in the back seat and smoke his pipe. They would go

off every Sunday afternoon and drive around. Young Mister Zeb
wore good clothes. I wanted to dress like him. But I couldn't. I
didn't know how. He looked so much like Mister Zeb. He was the
size of Mister Zeb. He had red hair too. It seemed like a lot of us
had red hair.

I didn't know how to drive a car. I did know how to drive a
team. Mister Zeb showed me how. He showed me how to plow.
It was easy for me. I could do it just as easy. I would plow while
Ma worked in Mister Zeb's house for Missus Zenophine. Ma
would come to the shack and get my dinner. We would eat
together and then we would go back to our work. I didn't want
to ever go back to the rock cliff. I didn't want to ever leave Mister
Zeb. Ma didn't want to leave her job working for Missus Zenophine. We liked it fine here. Ma was happy but she was always
afraid of Missus Zenophine. I was always afraid of Young Mister
Zeb. He got so he didn't like me. I'd never done anything to him.
I washed his car. I done everything he told me to do. But he would
look hard at me. He would look at my hair. Then he would look
meaner at me.

I worked for Mister Zeb five years. He never quarreled at me.
I got to be as big as Mister Zeb. I was a lot stouter than Mister
Zeb. I was as stout as Mister Zeb and Young Mister Zeb put
together. I was stouter than Ma was. I got me a long suit of
clothes. I tried to dress like Young Mister Zeb. When I put my
first long suit on I went down through the town where Ma's
people lived. I saw Big Charlie. He come walking over to me. He
says: "You think you're something on a stick, don't you? Well,
you know what you are? Red-headed—ha! Well, I'm going to
color that hair for you right now!"

Before Big Charlie had time to change the color of my hair I
had him knocked cold on the ground. I hit him under the chin
with my fist. I run as hard as I could go after I saw what I'd done
to Big Charlie. I thought I'd killed him. I run back home. There
warn't no place for me to go but just walk around. Mister Zeb's
people wouldn't have me nor Ma's people wouldn't have me. I was
afraid of them. Just two people I warn't afraid of. That was Ma
and Mister Zeb.

When I went back to town again I met Slick. He saw me and
he came over where I was walking down the railroad tracks. He
run out to me and looked at me. He stopped in the railroad tracks.
He just stood there. His lips pulled apart like a dog's. He showed
his teeth.

"You whipped Big Charlie," he says, "but it ain't no sign you can whip old Slick. I aim to get you right. I'm going to tear you apart with my hands! You got purty red hair and a mighty purty suit you got on there. Where did you get that?"

He made at me. I grabbed a cinder. I held it in my hand. I hit Slick between the eyes with the cinder. It cut a long gash. The blood squirted. Slick fell down on the tracks. I pulled him off the tracks. He was bleeding. I run back to the shack hard as I could go. I never told Ma or Mister Zeb about it. I thought Mister Zeb would be mad. If I'd killed Slick nobody would know who done it. I never told. Slick got all right but he had a scar between his eyes. He never bothered me again. When he saw me he went the other way. Big Charlie did too.

Ma got her some new clothes. She looked good in her new clothes. She put them on one Sunday afternoon. She dressed up the best I ever saw Ma dressed.

Ma says to me: "Let's go to church, Adger. There's prayer meeting down to the church today. I ain't been to church in so long. You dress up in your new suit and let's go to church."

I put on my new suit. I dressed up too. Just Ma and me living in the little white shack down below Mister Zeb's big brick. We had a pretty little shack. Hollyhocks bloomed around the door. Birds built nests in the elm trees around the shack. Bees and butterflies lit on the hollyhock blossoms. I was so happy with Ma. I didn't care if she was another color. I warn't ashamed of Ma. I went to church with her.

I saw Big Charlie at church. I saw Slick there. He looked hard at me. Everybody looked at me coming in with Ma. They looked at my red hair. The women and men and children were all the color of Ma. I was among her kind of people. The women looked at me and whispered. The preacher got up to preach. He was a big man. He was bigger than Ma.

He says: "My text will be children: 'The fathers have eaten sour grapes and their children's teeth are set on edge.' Now this sermon will hit hard, Sister Mollie. But we all just like children and when the shoe fits one of us we got to wear it."

Ma says to me: "Come, Adger."

She took me by the hand. We got up and left the church. Ma cried all the way back to the house. We didn't go around the road. We cut across the field by the railroad tracks. We crossed the creek on the big elm tree that had blowed down by the swimming hole. Ma didn't want nobody to see her crying. I was glad to get out'n the church. I didn't feel at home there. I would rather be with people like Mister Zeb. Ma always wanted to get back to her people. But they didn't want Ma. They didn't like Ma. They didn't like me. I didn't like them.

The day after we went to church I looked at myself in the looking glass. I looked at my jaws. I looked at my eyes. I looked at my hair. I says to Ma: "You know I look a lot like Young Mister Zeb. I am bigger than he is now is all. I am a stouter man than he is."

Ma didn't say anything. I put on my old work clothes and went to the barn. Young Mister Zeb was at the barn where he kept the automobile. He says to me: "Adger, the car is muddy. Clean it up!" He looked hard at me when he said this. He gritted his teeth. I just stood there. I thought a whole lot. I didn't move.

"Hear me, Adger," says Young Mister Zeb. "Clean up that car!"

I didn't move.

Young Mister Zeb went in the barn. He came out with the rawhide whip that I used on the horses. He hit me around the legs. I didn't move. He hit me again. I didn't move. He hit me again and again and again and I didn't move.

The blood run down my legs.

"Can't you feel it?" he says.

"Not as hard as a weak kitten like you can use a whip," I says. "I could break you in two. But I won't. You look too much like me!"

Then he whipped me harder. He started crying. He threw down the whip. He run to the house. I looked at my legs. My pants legs stuck to my legs. The blood had wet them. It had soaked through. It was dripping off. I started to the house. Mister Zeb was away at the office. I saw Missus Zenophine running down to the shack. She run to the door. She went in. I saw Ma come out.

"Get out'n here, you old wench you," says Missus Zenophine to Ma. "I understand it all now. You get out of here! You old bitch you! You good for nothing wench! Get that bastard and get out of here! Go before I get a sheriff up here! Leave everything in this house. I want to burn it."

Ma run out'n the house. I went with her. We left the shack. I looked back at it when we got to the turn of the road. I saw the hollyhocks in bloom there. I saw the wagon under the elms. I saw the big horses in the barn lot. I saw Young Mister Zeb have Missus Zenophine by the arm. He was helping her up the hill to the big brick. She was crying. Ma was crying. I didn't have Ma by the arm. We didn't have a big house to go to. I didn't know where we'd go. I felt like helping Ma but she didn't need help no more than I did. The blood was still running down my legs where

Young Mister Zeb whipped me with the rawhide. I didn't have a change of clothes to put on. We took Missus Zenophine at her word and got out while times was good. Me and Ma could a whipped Missus Zenophine and Young Mister Zeb. But we didn't fight them.

Ma and me started down the road. I never asked her any questions. I just went with her. She was the best friend I had. If it warn't for Ma I didn't know what I would have done. But she stuck to me. I would stick to her. I was ashamed of her people. They were ashamed of me. I didn't like them. They didn't like me. Mister Zeb's people wouldn't have nothing to do with me. Mister Zeb was good to me. He was good to Ma.

"Well," says Ma, "there's not but one thing for us to do. We must go back to the cliff. Have you got any money with you?"

"I got half a dollar," I says, "that Mister Zeb give me yesterday."

"Give it to me," says Ma, "and I'll go in the store and buy us some cheese and bread. It'll take us all day and all night to reach the cliff. I know a way to go through the hills. I went that way many years ago."

Ma got the bread and cheese. We started on our way.

It was daylight the next morning when we reached the cliff. We found our old bed of leaves in the cliff. Ma says to me: "Adger, I'm sick. It's a fluttering. I feel hot. I want water. Go tell Mister Scagraves."

I went down and told Mister Seagraves. He come to the cliff. He looked at Ma. He says: "She's bad off. She's got the fever, I believe. I'll go back to the house. I'll get help. I'll let Zeb know about this." He went away. No one came back. Ma got worse. She made loud noises. Night came. It was dark on the outside. Ma laid on the leaves. I laid down beside her. I must have gone to sleep. After a while I didn't hear any more noises.

Next morning when I got up I tried to get Ma up. She was still. She wouldn't speak. She warn't getting her breath. Ma was dead. I was scared. Just me in the cliff with Ma and she was dead. I cried and cried. I remember Ma told me what it was to be dead. I didn't know then. Now Ma had come back here and was dead. Ma was run off from the shack. She'd walked all day and all night. She was sick a day and night. Now she was dead.

Missus Seagraves come up the hill to the cliff. It was the first time she'd ever been here. She looked at Ma. She says: "Poor Mollie. She's dead. She was a good worker." Then she says to me: "Adger, Mister Seagraves will attend to this. You stay here

until we can get a coffin." Missus Seagraves went away. Ma used
to work for Missus Seagraves. She went down over the bank to
the house.

That night Mister Seagraves, Mister Sperry and two other men
I didn't know come up the hill. They were carrying a coffin.
It warn't one made of planks. It was a pretty coffin with bright
handles. It was soft lined, prettier than any bed Ma had ever
slept in. They brought it up and set it down in front of the cliff.
Mister Sperry was carrying a lantern and Mister Seagraves was
carrying a lantern.

"Take Adger and go back down at the foot of the hill and get
the tools," says Mister Seagraves to one of the strange men.

I went with him down to the foot of the hill to get the picks,
mattocks and shovels. When we got back to the cliff Mister Seagraves and Mister Sperry had Ma in the coffin. Four men carried
the coffin. Mister Seagraves and Mister Sperry walked in front
and led the way with lanterns. I followed them and carried the
tools. We come to a high spot on the hill above the cliff. The
ground was loamy and soft. Mister Seagraves and Mister Sperry
come to a stop.

"This is the place," says Mister Seagraves.

They hung their lanterns up in trees under the green leaves
where the bugs made noises up among the leaves. They started
digging. They didn't talk much. I helped them dig. By midnight
when the moon was getting over on the far side of the hill, we
had the grave dug. It was a deep hole scooped out in the mountain
loam for Ma. There warn't another grave near. Not one of Ma's
people had ever lived here. Not one of them had ever been buried
among these hills. They let Ma's coffin down with rope plowlines.
They shoveled in the dirt. I cried and before they had the last
dirt shoveled over her, I run out through the woods the way we
had come with the coffin. I found the cliff. I slept there that night.

The next morning I found a piece of dry bread and some cheese
Ma and me had brought to the cliff. I ate the dry bread and the
cheese. I left the cliff. I didn't know where I was going. I walked
all day. I just walked and walked. When it got dark I thought
about sleeping in a haystack. I couldn't find one. I hated to sleep
in the weeds. I was afraid of snakes. I was afraid to crawl in a
barn loft and sleep. If the farmer found me the next morning he
was liable to do something to me. I walked to a river. There was
a covered wooden bridge across it. There was a loft in this covered
bridge. I heard the birds up in the loft. I saw a hole where a
man could go through. There was notches cut on the post leading

up to the hole. I clim up in the loft. It was dark. I couldn't see. I just went to sleep. I didn't know any more until morning.

I was so hungry. I couldn't think about Ma. I had to think about something to eat. I clim down the notched pole. I run down the road by the river. I took out'n a field and found a watermelon patch. I found ripe sugar melons too.

I says to myself: "Right here is where I stay."

I would slip melons up in the loft. I would pull green corn down in the bottoms and take it back on the hill and roast it. Then I would carry it up in the loft of the covered bridge. I lived in the loft two weeks. One night I heard two men walk across the bridge down under me. I heard one say: "Too bad about Zeb killing himself."

"What made him do it, do you reckon?" says the other man.

"I heard," says the first voice, "that he got hitched up with some old wench and had a child by her. Brought them right in under his wife's nose for five years. His wife found it out. She had a nervous breakdown. She sued Zeb for a divorce. Said this wench had a bastard baby by him. A right good scrapper. Cleaned up the town!"

"You don't say," says the second voice as they passed over the end of the bridge and walked down the road by the river.

I clim down out'n the bridge. I followed the river to the town. It was daylight when I got there. I slipped out on the hill above Mister Zeb's house. The graveyard where his Pa and Ma are buried is right above his house. I thought they would bury him there. I slipped through the woods above the graveyard. I watched the men dig his grave.

In the afternoon the hill was covered with people. They hauled Mister Zeb up in a big automobile. I saw Young Mister Zeb down by the grave. I saw Missus Zenophine. I stayed up on the hill and watched. I heard the preacher. I just had to think about the way we buried Ma. I didn't have to wonder where the coffin come from. It was a good coffin. I just wondered if Mister Zeb's own coffin was as good as Ma's.

But we buried Ma at night. It was dark. But Ma was dark too. She was the color of the black snake. They buried Mister Zeb in the day time. He was light like the day. We buried Ma in the dark woods by lantern light. The bugs made drowsy noises up among the dark green leaves when we buried Ma.

After they buried Mister Zeb and had all left the hill, I slipped down by his grave. I did know where it was. I could come back to it. But I couldn't go back to Ma's grave. I couldn't find it. I looked at the flowers heaped on Mister Zeb's grave. I was glad. Big wreaths of flowers covered the fresh dirt. I pulled a flower from one of the wreaths. I would keep it. There was something that I couldn't say. It was just in me. I ran across the road, took the path across the fallen tree by the swimming hole the way Ma and me had come from church.

I run to the railroad tracks. I waited for a freight train.

The New Anvil Aug.-Sept. 1939

Homecoming

TOM TRACY

A friendly brakeman in the sandwich shop alongside the yards told him that a special train would go through in about an hour.

"It's taking a bunch from along the line here down to the city for the game," he said. "It's homecoming down there at the 'U', and there's always a big bunch from the Falls and Clear Springs goes down. She makes her last stop here in Stanton a little before twelve, and if you can grab a blind you'll be in the city in about an hour."

"Sounds like my train all right," Harry said. "Home is just where I want to go."

"Well, you better mosey across the tracks pretty soon," the brakey said. "You can duck into one of the empties on the spur there and when she comes in you can grab her from that side and they won't see you from the station."

"O.K.," Harry said. "Thanks a lot."

He went up to the faded blue sheds of the canning factory and between piles of wet lumber to the end of the yards. A raw wind was blowing down the yards, spinning dust around the piles of old ties and driving dirty papers along the rails. Harry turned up his collar and ran along the spur until he was near the station again. An empty car that had been used for bricks had a heap of straw at one end, and he crawled in out of the wind. Kicking the straw together with his feet, he piled it high in one corner and sat down, worming his shoulders back into the straw. A red powder of brick dust rose from the straw and settled on his windbreaker. He pulled his collar closer about his neck, doubled up his knees, and folded his arms tight across his chest. Even with the straw it was not very warm, and he kept wiggling his shoulders back and forth to work up a little warmth.

"Hell of a day to watch a football game," he said to himself, and immediately thought of the street of plain frame houses with the elm trees along the curb that ran from the back of the Stadium.

In a couple of hours he would be walking along that street. At the corner of Ross Street he would turn and there would be the brown and white front of the bungalow where they had moved last year. He would push the door open and his mother and sister would look up surprised.

And "For heaven's sake, it's Harry!" his mother would say.

And it would be warm in the kitchen, and there would be hot food, bacon and eggs, maybe, cooking, and the smell of coffee perking on the gas flame.

There were voices outside the car and the sound of feet crunching the cinders. A head in a brown cap appeared in the doorway. "This looks O.K., Frank," the boy at the door said.

Two boys crawled into the car. Both of them wore overalls and leather jackets. One of them had a little canvas roll strapped on his shoulders.

"Hello," Harry said, "are you waiting for the special?"

The boys turned their heads to the end of the car.

"What's the 'special'?" the taller one asked.

"She just runs down to the city," Harry explained. "There's a big game on."

"We're hitting it south."

"Where yuh heading for?" Harry asked.

Both the boys shrugged their shoulders.

"We might hit it west," the tall boy said. "Where you heading for?"

"I'm grabbing the special," Harry said. "I'm beating it home— I just came in from the west—Oregon. It's plenty tough out there."

"We were figuring on Cal," the tall boy said.

"It's tougher there," Harry said.

"It's warm, anyway. . . ."

"You can freeze plenty there," Harry said, "and the bulls keep you on the prod."

"They keep you on the prod anywhere."

"They're worse in Cal," Harry said. "They're hostile as hell."

The tall boy shrugged his shoulders. "What the hell," he said. "We gotta go somewhere. You can't put in a winter in this country."

Harry nodded. "That's no s—," he said.

He was glad that he was through with it. Even if it was tough at home it beat this. You had a place to sleep and the bulls weren't always on your tail. Then if you picked up any lousy kind of a job it was so much to the good.

The wind blowing hard from the northwest made a high whining sound around the corners of the cars.

"It sounds like winter, all right," Harry said.

The two boys had sat down on the side of the straw heap. They both shivered a little when the wind hit the car. They sat close together, their arms folded across their chests.

"Listen!" the tall boy said. "Is that your rattler?"

The high running whistle of a passenger engine came down the wind.

"I guess that's her." Harry got up, shaking his shoulders and brushing the straw from his windbreaker. He put his head out the door and looked up the tracks. The tall passenger engine was pounding along the flat grade, her black smoke jets flattened by the wind and trailing in long streamers above the yard. "Well, so long," he said. "Hope you guys make out all right."

He spilled tobacco into a paper, twisting a cigarette. It would be his last smoke till he got to town.

"So long," the boys answered.

The tall one eyed the sack of tobacco. "How about a smoke, buddy," he asked. "We ain't had a smoke all day."

"Sure," Harry said. He tossed them the half sack of tobacco. "Keep it; I'll get some more in town."

"Thanks," the short boy said. "We sure wanted a smoke."

"Well, so long," Harry repeated.

He swung down to the cinders and crossed the tracks. The special was a short train and he scrambled up on the blind behind the baggage car. The two boys stood in the door of the box car watching him and he leaned out to wave at them. As the train began to move the wind came up between the cars and he flattened his body against the iron.

"Lousy day to ride the blinds," he thought as the train clacked past the low brick station and the humpbacked shafts of the grain elevators standing beside the tracks. Still it was only an hour. He could hang anywhere for an hour. The train was picking up speed, passing rows of frame shanties and square ramshackle houses set in big gardens along the outskirts of town.

Out in the open the wind was blowing hard. The train was running very fast and the suction scooped up the cinders from the roadbed and pelted them against the steel cars. Back in the yards the wind had seemed damp but now with the wind of the train it was really cold and he hunched his shoulders a little, pulling the collar of his windbreaker higher around his throat. By pressing close to the side of the car he could avoid some of the wind, but the iron was cold and the jolting of the train hurt his ribs and he had to lean back a little, holding tight to the iron bar. He turned his face away from the wind, looking out between the cars at the strips of bare field with their patches of plowed land and stripped trees that batted past the speeding train.

His fingers on the iron bar began to feel cold and he pulled a pair of old canvas gloves from his pocket. Hooking his arm through the iron bar he wiggled his fingers into the stiff cloth. He had not thought the wind was going to be so bad. Dead leaves and straw from the fields were being driven into the suction of the train and whipped back with the cinders along the coaches. Whenever he looked up he could see the dead leaves driving by and the brown grass along the fence lines bent flat in the wind. The smoke from farmhouse chimneys off in the fields was cut off sharp and whipped away and when now and then a jerkwater station flashed past, Harry caught a hasty glimpse of dust clouds swirling down the dirt streets and the awnings of country stores flapping in the wind.

Even with the gloves on, his fingers on the bar were beginning to feel cold and he let go of the bar with one hand to beat it against his hip. The roadbed was not in good shape and the train lurched on the tracks. It was bad hanging on with one hand, but it was better than letting his hands get numb. When he had slipped that day in the yards at Cheyenne he hadn't known his hands were slipping till he felt himself falling. Lucky that the freight was going slow. That was just a spill. If a guy ever slipped on a rattler like this it would be just too bad. He beat one hand hard against his leg and then shifted, holding the bar with that hand and beating the other against his leg. It seemed to be getting colder all the time. The wind whirling up between the cars blew through his windbreaker and flannel shirt and he seemed to feel it pressing on his ribs.

"Jesus!" he exclaimed soberly. "I never knew it was so cold."

It was too cold to ride the blinds. He was a chump not to have waited and grabbed a drag. Even when it did get cold, on a drag you could move around a little.

His feet were beginning to get cold. He squirmed his toes back and forth and then began to tap the toe of his shoe against the car. It was hard to move his feet. Standing on the narrow ledge he really needed both his feet planted solidly to keep his balance. Being able to hang on with only one hand at a time made it worse. He grabbed the bar with both hands and kicked his toes hard against the iron coach. His cold toes bumping against the stiff leather of his shoes began to hurt and he tried jumping up and down instead, lifting one foot and stamping the other. He stamped until his fingers began to hurt with cold and he had to stand still, beating his hands against his leg to get the blood back into his fingers.

Good thing it wasn't going to be far like that time on the Katy when he and Mason had held the blinds clear from Joplin to Oklahoma City. Now at least he was sure of a good hot meal when he did land. The first thing he'd do would be to cook up a potful of hot java. Jesus, but it would be good to have all the hot java you wanted again with real cream in it and not the cheap junk you got at sandwich shacks nor the slop they handed you out at the missions. Like that time in Frisco when they had stood in line for an hour and when they gave him that mug of gray-looking stuff he couldn't get it down. A guy was a chump to live like that. It was the lousiest kind of life.

The train rounded a long curve and the wind came in at a new angle, making him shift and face the other way. They were running along a lake with brown swamps and meadows along the edge and he could see the mounds of the muskrat huts above the brown grass.

"Must be Lake Wilton," he thought, "or maybe Fern Lake." He tried to remember how far the lakes were from the city, but could not be sure which came first, Fern Lake or Wilton. Anyway they couldn't be a hell of a way from town. Burton used to drive out there for a swim Saturday afternoons. It couldn't be so damn far. It was only supposed to take about an hour from the junction to the city. He began to count back. They had passed through a number of little stations and he tried to calculate the miles between stations. If the stations were ten miles apart it must be nearly forty miles now. If it was forty another ten or fifteen minutes ought to put them in the yards. If the stations were only eight miles apart it would take twenty minutes. It was twenty minutes at the outside then, and maybe less. She was hitting the ball all the time. He looked out between the cars at the trees—a grove batting past and then the houses of another jerkwater swept into the narrow frame of the car ends and batted out again as the train highballed through with a screech of its whistle and a brief clatter of wheels across the switch locks.

Fifty miles he counted—or up in the forties, anyhow. It couldn't be much longer now. If only his hands didn't get too cold. He beat them against his legs as fast as he could, but before he could get the numbness out of the flapping hand he felt the hand on the bar starting to hurt with cold. His feet were both numb but he had no time to move them; it was all he could do to keep his hands from getting too numb to cling to the bar.

He shivered; to control his shivering he squirmed his shoulders and beat his free hand up against his breast. For a while it helped, but he had to keep changing his arms and could not beat fast enough, and long shivers began to run up his back where the wind hit him.

"Jesus, they'd ought to be getting there pretty quick." He'd freeze right to the bar if he didn't unload. By Jesus, it was bad as that kid that got locked in the reefer. Only you could move around in a reefer.

Each time he slapped his hands on his chest his fingers pained as the blood flowed back into them, but before they could get really warm he had to change again to relieve the aching fingers on the bar. The best thing was not to think about it. If he could get his mind off the cold for a while maybe the time would go faster. He tried thinking of times he had been too hot like the day they rode the S.P. drag from Yuma to El Paso, and the Mex district of El Paso with the sun blistering hot on the dusty streets between the low adobe houses and the Mex girl in the shack by the canal who had sold them the home brew and stood there in her slip with her bare arms and legs, watching them drink and smiling all the time and saying something in Spanish, and afterwards in the stuffy El Paso jail when the bulls had picked them up, he had thought of her round bare legs and her heavy thighs under the cheap cotton slip. They had lain without a stitch on them in the cage at the jail that night and the sweat had just poured out of them and they kept wiping themselves off with their shirts.

His feet were cold as hell. They hurt worse than his hands did, but he couldn't take time to move them. Even frozen feet would hold a guy up. They didn't have to hang on to anything. What a damn fool he was to be in such a hurry. After ten months what the hell difference would another couple of hours make? If he hadn't been in such a damn fool hurry he could be taking it easy in a drag now. . . .

The feeling was going out of his fingers and he did not dare hold to the bar with one hand long enough to beat the circulation back into the other one. Holding with his left hand he hooked his right arm through the bar and leaned forward against the iron wall. The cold of the iron went right through his windbreaker and made his teeth chatter. He slapped his left hand against his leg a few times and then lifted it to squeeze the fingers of his right hand. The fingers were so numb he could hardly feel with them. Even when he squeezed hard he could not feel the fingers of his right hand and those of his left hand felt stiff and thick as corncobs inside the coarse glove. He swung the free hand, beating it against the hand thrust through the bar. The number fingers hurt from the thumping but there was nothing else for it. Hooked in like that his whole arm would get numb in a little while unless he could beat a little blood back into it.

The train made a sudden roar, going fast over a span of steel bridge and Harry, looking up quickly, saw a flat broken stretch of dumping ground studded with signboards and clumps of dead weeds and off beyond the broken ground the smoke of factories streaked low on a sky the color of wet asphalt. The sound of the whistle came back to him on the wind and he felt the speed slacken and there was a grade crossing with scattered frame houses along a muddy street and a suburban tram-car waiting beside the tracks.

"By Jesus!" he exclaimed happily, "there she is!"

He had never thought he could be so glad about anything— even a meal when he was very hungry. Beyond the crossing, spur tracks were beginning to branch out along the line and faded red and yellow boxcars stood on the spurs and then the blank walls of factories and warehouses, smoky and streaked with damp, cut out the sky.

"Jesus, I hope Ma's got a lot of coffee!" he was thinking, "and I'll boil up a whole potful with some hot grub, a slab of ham maybe with the eggs basted in the hot hamfat and some preserves or maybe a baked apple to top it off and then for a hot bath and a soft chair in the front room with maybe a book and a cigarette and a guy could be comfortable looking out the window at the cars on the street or the girls from the gym going along the side-walk. . . ."

Now was the time to unload. He rubbed his hands together hard, trying to flex them for the job of holding him while he sidled around to the step.

At the first move he made on the ledge he knew it was no good. He was too stiff. He'd have to ride her into the station and take a chance on the yard bull. He beat his free hand against his leg again, slapping it down hard so that the numb finger ends throbbed with pain. The train came to a dead stop before he dared to try to hold on with his hand. He was on the side away from the station elevators and the quay was empty. Lifting his stiff feet, he stamped them on the ledge. Then he unhooked his arm carefully and, holding the bar with both hands, slipped down to the cinders.

His feet were so numb he could hardly stand, and he leaned

against the side of the coach, stamping the blood back into them. Leaning against the car and stamping his feet, he couldn't stop the shivering. His teeth kept chattering together and the cold seemed to grip him right in the guts and ran up through his body making his arms shake against the car wall.

A baggage tractor with a string of trucks was rattling down the quays.

"I'd better get away from this train," he thought, and took a few steps still leaning against the car. He limped along the car towards the end of the train. His feet felt like chunks of ice and his legs were so stiff that he could only take steps a few inches long.

The baggage truck was coming up to him and he looked around. ". . . I hope this guy ain't hostile. . . ."

The baggage tractor slowed down and the driver hailed him.

"Hey, kid! Where yuh goin'?"

"I'm trying to get out of here," Harry said.

"The bull is up the line," the baggage worker said. "If he catches you, he'll sap hell out of you." He looked up the tracks. "Come here," he said.

Harry took his hands off the car and started across the track.

"What's the matter?" the baggage worker asked. "Are you lame?"

"I'm just about froze stiff," Harry said.

The baggage worker jerked his thumb towards a truck loaded with sacks.

"Get down in those sacks and take your cap off," he said. "I'm running up near the street and you can duck out."

Harry limped over to the truck and sat down between the bags, stuffing his cap in his pocket. "Thanks," he said, "it's swell of you to give me a lift."

"That's all right, kid, but keep to hell out of these yards. That bull has sapped up on plenty of kids around here. He's an ornery son of a bitch."

The tractor rattled up the quay and stopped alongside a car.

"See that wall, kid?" the worker said. "Cut around the end of it and you're right out on North Street."

"I know," Harry said, "thanks a lot for the lift."

"O.K., buddy!"

Harry crossed the last tracks to the wall. His legs had limbered up a little but he was still stiff and held on to the wall going down the embankment onto the dead end of North Street. He walked slowly along the cobbled street and past a string of ramshackle warehouses and rusty spur tracks overgrown with weed stalks.

A raw wind was blowing up from the river and Harry walked close to the walls, rubbing his chest with his hand to stop the shivers.

As he began to get into the University section there were big letters in the store windows draped with the state colors and placards hung across the fronts with big signs WELCOME HOME GRADS and occasionally 2-colored streamers stretched across the street. Beyond Monroe Street there were big new frat houses of stone and cream-colored brick set back from the street with enormous letters and decorations stretched across the stone fronts above the beds of stiff flower stalks and cold clipped lawns.

Vernon Street looked shabbier than he had remembered it. Most of the houses needed painting; the shingled roofs had a dingy weatherbeaten look.

He crossed the street and broke into a run. He dogtrotted two blocks to Ross, then slowed down.

"Will they ever be surprised!" he thought happily, and began to rehearse his entry. "I'll go right in," he told himself. "They'll be in the kitchen or maybe in the dining room sewing or something, and I'll just push the door open. . . ."

He turned the corner onto Ross, his eyes going ahead to the brown and white bungalow. Only the steps and the beams of the porch stood out from the house alongside and their plain homely look brought a sudden tight feeling around his heart.

He cut across the patch of lawn and came to the edge of the steps before he saw the litter of yellowed dodgers by the door.

"Jesus Christ!" he said out loud in a scared voice and looked anxiously up at the front window. It was perfectly blank, the shade pulled away down. Then he saw the FOR RENT sign tacked on the clapboards alongside. He stood still on the steps and put his hands in his pockets.

"For Christ's sake," he muttered, "can you imagine that?"

He went up the steps, kicking the faded dodgers out of the way, and tried the knob. Holding the knob in both hands he shook the door hard. The rattling of the knob made an empty sound in the hall. Shaking the knob as hard as he could, he raised his knee and thumped it against the door. It was no good. He knew it was no good. The house was empty. They were gone away. He had really known that when he saw the dodgers, but he didn't want to let himself know it. It was something that had never occurred to him. All the way on the long trip back from Oregon he had been thinking of opening the door and walking in on them. Now they were gone. He let go of the knob and stood still in front of the door. Taking off his cap he ran his fingers idly through his hair. He put his cap back on his head and went down off the porch, walking slowly along the wall of the house. The windows were blank, the shades pulled down. Old papers had blown into the yard and tangled in the lilac bushes. He pounded on the locked back door.

A man who was sawing old railroad ties in the next yard straightened up and looked at him. "Nobody living there, bud," he called.

Harry walked over to the fence.

"Do you know where they're gone?" he asked. "I mean the family who used to live here, the Connors?"

The man shook his head.

"I don't know," he said. "The place was vacant when I moved in here two months ago. The fellow who used to live on the other side was telling me they got put out last summer when they couldn't pay rent."

"Last summer . . ." Harry repeated mechanically. He leaned over the fence and tears came to his eyes. There was a post right in front of him and he put both his hands on it, pressing his fingers hard against the wood.

"They were my family," he said after a little. "I've been on the road. I was just coming home."

"Jesus," the man said, "that's a tough break!"

Harry nodded his head. "Well, thanks for telling me," he said.

Walking along the fence, he looked up at the shaded windows of the house where he had lived. The sun had blistered the paint on the window sills and it was beginning to peel. Tears pushed into his eyes again and he looked down at the sidewalk.

He walked slowly up Vernon toward the Stadium. It had begun to spot with rain and the wind had come up stronger and tore the dead leaves from some oak trees on the corner. He went on aimlessly putting one foot carefully in one square of the sidewalk, then lifting the other foot and putting it carefully in the square ahead. At the Stadium corner he stopped, looking at the long up-slanting street with its double row of elms and its stretches of wet asphalt faintly gleaming with rain.

He raised his hands stiffly and pulled the collar of his wind-breaker up around his neck. Then he began to move his feet slowly again, going down the long street toward the city. It had begun to rain harder and the house-boys in the big frat building were hurriedly folding up the WELCOME HOME banners and carrying them in out of the rain.

The New Anvil May-June 1940

An Interview with Domino Bashfield

JOSEPH VOGEL

Your correspondent has the distinction of being the first writer to interview Domino Bashfield, or to have thought of it, for that matter. I might inform readers who never heard of Bashfield that he is the eminent critic who startled the cultural world a few days ago by advancing a unique claim of "the lack of preponderance of vision in the artist's point of view," claiming that the creative artist should look neither to the right nor to the left especially, nor for that matter to the north or to the south. I happened upon Bashfield in front of his brownstone house just as he was turning west, and when in a few words I explained the purpose of my mission, he blushed pinkly, supposedly flattered, and said "I'm on my way to the N by E. If you wish, come along . . . although I can't afford. . . ." "I accept your kind invitation to lunch," I said, and we proceeded to the N by E.

For the benefit of readers who have never beheld Bashfield let me say that he is corpulent middle-aged man of about five feet two and a half with an exceedingly thin face compensated for by the large bulbous eyes of a man who loves his plate. In speech he hesitates often because of a slight stutter; these pauses lend an effect of profundity to his utterances. He wears a nine shoe but his glove is exquisitely small.

I had just come from a demonstration in front of a relief agency and I was ravenously hungry, which may account for my being dazed by the superabundant menu of the N by E. When the waiter approached, Bashfield asked me what I would have, but not having brought the contents of the menu into focus yet, I told him to order first.

"Half a cantaloupe and egg barley soup . . ." said Bashfield.

"Make mine cantaloupe and noodle soup," I said.

After a studious pause Bashfield said, "And steak with. . . ."

"Make mine steak with mushrooms," I said.

Bashfield looked at me from the top of his eyes, then dropped his menu with a gesture of finality and said, "That'll be all!" But I out-maneuvered him and ordered chocolate cake and coffee and ice cream too. In fact at the moment I felt pretty flat, and considering that out of pure free will I had let myself in for a session of Vision with Bashfield, it was imperative that I fortify myself with some extra heavy materialistic sustenance.

The first two courses passed reluctantly. What I mean is there was very little conversation on the topic so dear to our hearts, perhaps because first Bashfield had to satisfy those elementary pangs of hunger so cherished by the connoisseur. So with weighty monosyllables and pregnant grunts the meal progressed until we reached the steak, and at this point Bashfield began to warm up to his subject, vision and the artist. "What is the primary function of the artist?" he said at the end of a swallow. Cutting a piece of steak with painstaking casualness, he continued, "You would say to interpret the life about him."

"Exactly," I said, biting hard.

"That's where you are wrong! The artist—understand, I do not mean the journalist or the popular song writer—the artist has a higher goal, just as art has a higher purpose. Interpretation, of course, is necessary, but more so is comprehension in the searchlight of noble values. And therefore, what is fundamental—I can't emphasize this too much—what is fundamental is vision!" Bashfield looked at me sharply, then remembering the cut of steak on the tip of his fork he slipped it deftly into his mouth.

"This business of taking sides!" he exclaimed sarcastically, gazing with a smile at his plate. "This business of going left and participating in demonstrations and voting for Foster and getting one's head broken and writing pamphlets about Negroes in the south, what . . . ." he paused here, to neutralize a stutter, ". . . what relation has all this to art?"

"Absolutely none!" I said. "But what about humanity?"

"Ah! I was waiting for that, for that humanity," he said enthusiastically. "Well, what about this humanity? What is of more concern to you, your art or humanity? And how do you know that your program is one jot better for humanity than the capitalist program, how do you know your acquisitiveness is any the more desirable than that of a Rockefeller?"

I was flabbergasted at this, and beg the reader to note how viciously Bashfield referred to it as my program and as my acquisitiveness, and the reader will understand how greatly abused I felt—I who am a professor of the beautiful life, in whose soul vision and art blend so delicately.

"But what about Moholy-Nagy?" I answered heatedly. "Does not Moholy-Nagy, that famous artist, contend that expression is fruitful only when it carries with it, outside of mere personal satisfaction, an objective validity for the collective body of the human race? What have you to say to that?"

Bashfield swallowed. He smiled benignly. "Is this the new Marx?" he said with a mischievous twinkle. "Then why do you misinterpret him?" Then after a pause tense with significance, "But to return to the main point: the artist, by the nature of his calling, is a prophet. Deeds may be forgotten, but the word is immortal. The artist is a. . . ."

"My dear sir," I interrupted. "Pardon me, but I think you misunderstand me!"

"Oh, I don't misunderstand you at all," he said dropping his fork with unexpected fury. "I understand you only too well! I've seen your work, and excuse me for becoming personal but I think you are on the wrong path by posing as a hard-boiled writer, always digging in cesspools and sores and misery and filth. That's dirt, it's not art!"

This struck at the heart of my weak spot and when I replied I could summon up only a whine. "But what would you have me do? I write about the only thing I know, my own people."

Perhaps the tone of my voice touched him, for he calmed down and sympathy twitched across his face. He picked up his fork and cut another slice of steak. Holding the morsel to his lips he looked at me kindly and said, "You should be objective."

"Ah! So I should!" I said despairingly. "How difficult that is! To be frank with you, Mr. Bashfield, I am really frightfully sensitive. The suffering of my people touches me to the quick, and it makes me, I confess, it makes me a hot subjectivist."

He cocked his eyes at me, but said nothing until he finished masticating a morsel which in his excitement he had cut too large. "Your steak is becoming cold," he said.

"Aye, so it is."

"Well," he began, studying a hatrack off to a side, "I must say I've detected a trace of the prophetic note in some of your work. You are not entirely without promise. But you must always be on guard not to let the crass note dominate your thinking. Remember, life is short but art is long. The artist must place himself above the trivial conflicts of life, he must make his survey with an impassioned eye and project his spirit into the future."

The waiter brought my chocolate cake and coffee and ice cream. Bashfield asked the waiter to bring him the same.

"Art centers and derives from the spiritual," continued Bashfield. "Where the Communists make their mistake is by holding that the creativeness of the artist is influenced and shaped by social and economic institutions. What absurd logic! Is there nothing higher in life than the material? Is there no more fundamental cause? Has mankind, and the artist particularly, nothing nobler to look forward to than a full dinner pail?"

The waiter placed Bashfield's dessert on the table.

"Is it merely physical things that the artist. . . ." Bashfield suddenly stopped and stared at the ice cream. He summoned the waiter. "Did I order this ice cream?"

The waiter looked puzzled. "Yes, sir. You did."

"I know I did," snapped Bashfield. "But I did not order strawberry ice cream."

"I beg your pardon," said the waiter. He put out his hand to pick up the dish, but Bashfield stopped him. "Oh, never mind, never mind, I can't be bothered. As I was saying," he continued, "what your work lacks is a definite quality that distinguishes great writing. I may read your work day and night, let us say, yet it will never succeed in lifting me out of myself. Your point of view brings the reader closer to . . . what shall I say, like choosing a rowboat when you have the choice of a yacht."

"I'm afraid I don't follow you," I said. "What point of view would you have me adopt? What particular sort of vision would you recommend?"

"Vision? Do you think it possible for me to provide you with vision?" He mashed his ice cream lightly and laughed.

"No, but. . . . Perhaps you can help me, if you wish to, by defining your point of view. I mean your vision. What is your vision, to put it baldly?"

"Ah, silly, silly," he mused. "Have the masses ever understood the vision of our great artists? If you cannot detect a man's vision, if you cannot see it and feel it and make it your very own, how then can I explain? However, since you are not obtuse, perhaps I can make it clear to you somewhat. Vision is synonymous with religion. After a man's stomach is satisfied, he requires something more, something infinitely more needful than mere food. I refer to the spiritual needs of man. I refer to the unity of the universe, if I may put it broadly at first. The unity of nature, the unity of life . . . the completeness of parts into the whole. People usually call it beauty . . . but that is not enough. It is a man's spirit emerging from its prison, identifying itself with nature, becoming unified, complete . . . eh, eh. . . ."

Bashfield's face of a sudden turned purple. He stiffened and pushed himself down hard in his chair. Then with a little jerky jump he belched. After a moment of dullness he picked up his napkin and wiped his lips. "Gracious!" he said. "It must be those Brazilian nuts I ate this morning."

The Anvil Nov.-Dec. 1933

The Paid Nurse

WILLIAM CARLOS WILLIAMS

When I came in, Sunday evening, approaching eleven o'clock, there had been a phone call for me. I don't know what it is, said Floss. Mrs. Corcoran called up about an accident of some sort that happened to George. You know, Andy's friend. What kind of an accident? An explosion, I don't know, something like that. I couldn't make it out. He wants to come up and see you. She'll call back in a minute or two.

As I sat down to finish the morning paper the phone rang again as usual. No. His girl friend heard about it and is taking him up to her doctor in Norwood. Swell.

But next day he came to see me anyhow. What in hell's happened to you George? I said when I saw him. His right arm was bandaged to the shoulder, the crook of his left elbow looked like overdone bacon, his lips were blistered, his nose was shiny with grease and swollen out of shape and his right ear was red and thickened much beyond its normal size.

They want me to go back to work, he said. They told me if I didn't go back I wouldn't get paid. I want to see you.

What happened?

I work for the General Bearings Company, in Jersey City. You know what that means. They're a hard-boiled outfit. I'm not kidding myself about that but they can't make me work the way I feel. Do you think I have to work with my arms like this? I want your opinion. That fellow in Norwood said it wasn't anything but I couldn't sleep last night. I was in agony. He gave me two capsules and told me to take one. I took one around three o'clock and that just made me feel worse. I tried to go back this morning but I couldn't do it.

Wait a minute, wait a minute. You haven't told me what happened yet.

Well, they had me cleaning some metal discs. It wasn't my regular job. So I asked the boss, What is this stuff? I said. Benzol, he said. It is inflammable? I said. Not very, he said. We use it here all the time. I didn't believe him right then because I could smell it, it had a kind of smell like gasoline or cleaning fluid of some kind.

What I had to do was to pick those pieces out of a pail of the stuff on this side of me, my left side, and turn and place them in the oven to dry them. Two hundred degrees temperature in there. Then I'd turn and pick up another lot and so on into the dryer and back again. I had on long rubber gauntlets up almost to my elbows.

Well, I hadn't hardly started when, blup! it happened. I didn't know what it was at first. You know you don't realize those things right away—until I smelt burnt hair and cloth and saw my gloves blazing. The front of my shirt was burning too—lucky it wasn't soaked with the stuff. I jumped back into the aisle and put my hands back of me and shook the gloves off on the floor. The pail was blazing too.

Everybody came on the run and rushed me into the emergency room. Everybody was excited, but as soon as they saw that I could see and wasn't going to pass out on them they went back to their jobs and left me there with the nurse to fix me up.

Then I began to feel it. The flames from the shirt must have come up into my face because inside my nostrils was burnt and you can see what it did to my eyebrows and eyelashes. She called the doctor but he didn't come any nearer than six feet from me. That's not very bad, he said. So the nurse put a little dressing, of tannic acid I think she said it was, on my right arm which got the worst of it. I was just turning away from the oven when it happened, lucky for me, so I got it mostly on my right side.

What do I do now? I asked her. Go home? I was feeling rotten.

No, of course not, she told me. That's not bad. Go on back to work.

What! I said.

Yes, she said. And come back tomorrow morning. If you don't you won't get paid. And, by the way, she said, don't go to any other doctor. You come back here tomorrow morning and go to work as usual. Do you think that was right?

The bastards. Go ahead. Wasn't there someone you could appeal to there? Don't you belong to a union?

No, said George. There's nothing like that there. Only the teamsters and the pressmen have unions, they've had them long enough so that the company can't interfere.

All right. Go ahead.

So I went back to the job. They gave me something else to do but the pain got so bad I couldn't stand it so I told the boss I had to quit. All right, he said, go on home but be back here tomorrow morning. That would be today.

You went back this morning?

I couldn't sleep all night. Look at my arm.

All right. Let's look at it. The worst was the right elbow and forearm, almost to the shoulder in fact. It was cooked to about the color of ham rind with several areas where the Norwood doctor had opened several large blisters the night before. The arm was, besides that, swollen to a size at least a third greater than its normal volume and had begun to turn a deep, purplish red just above the wrist. The ear and nose were not too bad but in all the boy looked sick.

So you went back this morning?

Yes.

Did they dress it?

No, just looked at it and ordered me on the floor. They gave me a job dragging forty pound cases from the stack to the elevator. I couldn't use my right arm so I tried to do it with my left but I couldn't keep it up. I told 'em I was going home.

Well?

The nurse gave me hell. She called me a baby and told me it wasn't anything. The men work with worse things than that the matter with them every day, she said.

That don't make any difference to me, I told her, I'm going home.

All right, she said, but if you don't show up here tomorrow for work, you don't get any pay. That's why I'm here, he continued. I can't work. What do you say?

Well, I said, I'll call up the Senator, which I did at once. And was told, of course, that the man didn't have to go to work if I said he wasn't able to do so. They can be reported to the Commission, if necessary. Or better perhaps, I can write them a letter first. You tell him not to go to work.

You're not to go to work, I told the boy. O.K., that settles it. Want to see me tomorrow? Yeah. And quit those damned capsules he gave you, I told him. No damned good. Here, here's something much simpler that won't at least leave you walking on your ear till noon the next day. Thanks. See you tomorrow.

Then it began to happen. Late in the afternoon the nurse called him up to remind him to report for duty next morning. I told her I'd been to you, he said, and that you wanted the compensation papers. She won't listen to it. She says they're sending the company car for me tomorrow morning to take me in to see their doctor? Do I go?

Not on your life.

But the next day I was making rounds in the hospital at about ten A.M. when the office reached me on one of the floors. Hold the wire. It was George. The car is here and they want me to go back with them. What do I do?

Wait a minute, I said. What's their phone number? And what's that nurse's name? I'll talk to them. You wait till I call you back. So I got the nurse and talked to her: I hear you had an explosion down at your plant, I told her. What do you mean, she said. What are you trying to do, cover it up? I asked her, so the insurance company won't find out about it? We don't do that sort of thing in this company. What are you doing now? I asked her again. She blurted and bubbled till I lost my temper and let her have it. What is that, what is that? she kept saying. You know what I'm talking about, I told her. Our doctors take care of our own cases, she told me. You mean they stand off six feet from a man and tell him he's all right when the skin is half burned off of him and the insides of his nostrils are all scorched? That isn't true, she said. He had no right to go to an outside doctor. What! I said, when he's in agony in the middle of the night from the pains of his burns, he has no right to get advice and relief? Is that what you mean? He has the privilege of calling our own doctor if he needs one, she says. In the middle of the night? I asked her. I tell you what you do, I said, you send me the compensation papers to sign. You heard me, I said, and make it snappy if you know what's good for you. We want our own doctor to see him, she insisted. All right, I said, your own doctor can see him but he's not to go to work. Get that through your head, I said. And that's what I told him.

He went back to their doctor in the company car.

It was funny. We were at supper that evening when he came to the house door. I didn't have any office hours that night. Floss asked him to come in and join us but he had eaten. He had a strange look on his face, half amused and half bewildered.

I don't know, he said. I couldn't believe it. You ought to see the way I was treated. I was all ready to be bawled out but, oh no! The nurse was all smiles. Come right in, George. Do you feel all right, George? You don't look very well. Don't you want to lie down here on the couch? I thought she was kidding me. But she meant it. What a difference! That isn't the way they treated me the first time. Then she says, It's so hot in here I'll turn on the fan so as to cool you a little. And here, here's a nice glass of orange juice. No kiddin'. What a difference!

Floss and I burst out laughing in spite of ourselves. Oh every-

thing's lovely now, he said. But you're not working? No I don't
have to work. They sent me back home in the company car and
they're calling for me tomorrow morning. The only thing is they
brought in the man who got me the job. That made me feel like
two cents. You shouldn't have acted like that George, he told me.
We'll take care of you. We always take care of our men.

I can take it, sir, I told him. But I simply couldn't go back to
work after the burning I got. You didn't have to go back to work,
he said. Yes, I did, I said. They had me dragging forty pound
cases around the floor—

Really? he said.

He didn't know that, did he? I interposed. I'm glad you spoke
up. And they want you to go back tomorrow?

All right, but don't work till I tell you. But he did. After all,
jobs aren't so easy to get nowadays even with a hard-boiled firm
like that. I won't get any compensation either, they told me, not
even for a scar.

Is that so?

And they said they're not going to pay you, either.

We'll see what the Senator says about that.

He came back two days later to tell me the rest of it. I get it
now, he said. It seems after you've been there a year they insure
you, but before that you don't get any protection. After a year
one of the fellows was telling me—why, they had a man there
that just sprained his ankle a little. It wasn't much. But they kept
him out on full pay for five months, what do you know about that?
They wouldn't let him work when he wanted to.

Good night!

Geez, it was funny today, he went on. They were dressing my
arm and a big piece of skin had all worked loose and they were
peeling it off. It hurt me a little, oh, you know, not much but I
showed I could feel it, I guess. My God! the nurse had me lie
down on the couch before I knew what she was doing. And do
you know, that was around one-thirty. I didn't know what happened to me. When I woke up it was four o'clock. I'd been sleeping all that time! They had a blanket over me and everything.

Good!

How much do I owe you? Because I want to pay you. No use
trying to get it from them. If I make any trouble they'll blackball
me all over the county they tell me.

The Heel's Progress

MILTON U. WISER

The headlights of the bus cut a long wedge in the darkness of the highway. Inside, the tiny bulb on the dash was one lone bright spot, but our eyes were used to the dark now, six hours out of Rochester. Whitey leaned forward in his seat across the aisle, and I knew that the long thin scar that disappeared under his heavy moustache was twisting the corner of his mouth.

"I said we were a bunch of dopes," he said.

On the seat ahead Connelly roused. "All right, Whitey. We're a bunch of dopes. Now shut up and go to sleep. Or let the rest of us get some sleep, anyway."

"Sure. Sleep on a stinking bus. If we weren't a bunch of dopes we'd be in bed tonight."

Connelly didn't answer. Someone snored.

The older man pulled his cap down over his face, making noises behind his teeth. Next to me, at the window, the kid leaned forward to look across at Whitey.

"Never mind him," I said. "He's always shooting off his mouth. Don't pay any attention to him."

Whitey snorted. "Sure. Don't pay any attention to me, kid. Don't pay any attention to the old crackpot. Why, you young squirts that think you're so hot, I could tell you——."

Connelly spoke without moving. "Lay off, Whitey, for God's sake. We got to work when we get in, and if we don't get some sleep, we'll be all pooped out."

"Sure. We'll be pooped because we're riding on this damn bus that should have been run over a cliff and burned two years ago. What the hell! All I want to know is why."

The kid was tense.

"All right. This is why," Whitey answered himself, not speaking loudly. "Because there ain't a company or a driver that'll do it. We get a scab bus and a scab driver, and we got to ride in this thing that some guy pawned off on another guy sitting on his can at a desk somewhere, and who didn't give a damn whether we

199

were pooped or not when we get in, as long as he gets his fee and can stay right there on his can without worrying about it."

Connelly breathed deeply, faking sleep. The kid was still leaning forward. I was sore at Whitey; I had been sleepy before, but now I was wide awake from his noise.

"So what?" I said.

"So we're the dopes. Ten years ago we'd have laughed in their faces and told them to go to hell."

"That was ten years ago," I said.

"Yeah. You had to be good then. I remember I went up there to Buffalo when they were running the street car strike. They said, 'Can you run one?' and I said, 'Has it got wheels on it?' I drove that damn street car for two months, and when I got through and the punks came back, I still didn't know one end of it from the other."

Connelly faked a snore.

"No. We didn't go riding around on a stinking bus. And they paid, too. You would get a job and clean up and then you could loaf for two or three months until the next one broke somewhere."

The driver slowed the bus, stopping it finally far over on the shoulder of the road. He said, "Look. There's a schoolhouse over there. You guys better try it because this'll be the last stop, and I gotta be dumpin' some of this gas."

We climbed out slowly, stretchingly, mumbling sleepily. Whitey walked beside the kid and me as we hopped the ditch and felt our way through the dark toward the white blur of the schoolhouse. The frost was heavy, the grass high around our legs. We stood in line outside, waiting, shivering.

"They give us a treat now," Whitey said. "You don't have to find a tree like a dog any more or squat in a field somewhere, because they've found a nice, convenient schoolhouse for us now."

Some of the fellows didn't wait. Connelly kept saying, "For God's sake, don't make a mess of it. There's kids got to use this place. We gotta lot of time while that driver dumps the gas. Wait in line, can't ya?"

"All right," I said to Whitey. "You know they wouldn't let us in a gasoline station, because they know we're coming by this time. They wouldn't even sell us any gas now, you know that. What you think we got those cans rolling around in there for?"

"I know it," he said. "That's what I'm squawking about."

When we climbed back in, Whitey tried to take my seat next to the kid, but I shoved him away. Whitey's all right, see, but he

gets his hair mussed once in a while, and the kid was young and
green and still ashamed.

The road began to edge down off the hills. The motor stopped
laboring. It was three o'clock.

"You young guys that think you're some stuff. When they came
in the gate back there, what were you going to do? Say, 'Okay,
boys, help yourselves, make yourselves at home'?"

Connelly turned around. "So you let 'em have it with that piece
of pipe that I told you to throw away. And that guy's still in the
hospital with a busted knob."

"What you want? They say, 'Guard the place' or 'Get out a
little stuff to keep the customers satisfied until this blows over.'
So I hit a guy and they howl."

"You didn't have to use that pipe. I told you to throw it away."

"Sure. I could have hit 'im with my sock. I could've combed
his hair, too. They make you a heel and then they don't want
you to act like a heel. They ain't no sissies either. You don't
think I wear this mattress on my puss for fun, do you? Where
half the lip is gone? Where the guy at the mine down in Pennsylvania sliced it off?"

Connelly shrugged. "All right. Shut up."

"No. We used to be strikebreakers. We were all right. We
were honest scabs. But now we're heels. You tell your kids and
your neighbors that you're a traveling salesman or something so
your family won't be ashamed of you. So I been a traveling salesman for fifteen years, and I'm a heel. I gotta stop in a field or a
country schoolhouse because I'm a heel and I ain't got no right
to use a decent bathroom."

The kid spoke quietly. "My girl thinks I'm a public accountant.
I had to tell her something, with all this traveling around."

"Sure," Whitey said. "Why didn't you tell her you were a
strike-breaker, a scab? Because she'd have spit on you, that's why.
You can't even be a private detective or a plant guard any more.
You gotta be just a dirty, stinkin' scab."

The kid leaned back quickly.

Whitey stood up in the aisle, pitching with the roll of the bus.
"So we're dopes. We're a bunch of dirty goddam heels, that's what
we are."

Someone in the rear of the bus spoke above the noise of the
empty gasoline cans rolling around. "Get that guy off the stump.
He don't need to tell us. What's he want? A strikebreakers' union
so he can get to use a regular can?"

Whitey's voice was loud. "Yes. Yes. That's what I want. So I can tell my kids I'm no damn dirty heel."

Connelly got up fast and shoved Whitey into his seat. "All right. Now shut up. There ain't nothin' you're goin' to do about it. Your kids gotta eat even if you gotta be a traveling salesman. You guys get some sleep so we won't be corked when we get there."

There was silence for a long time, except for the cans banging. Everyone sat up straight, his eyes wide open. It was cold. The kid's face was buried in the lapels of his coat. He sat very quiet and motionless.

Whitey lighted his pipe, sucking the flame hard. Then he said, quietly, "I just want to know what it's getting us. A guy don't want to be a heel all his life."

The kid made a funny noise. I looked at him, but he turned his head quickly to the window, searching the edges of the darkness for the first faint streak of dawn.

The New Anvil May-June 1940

The Thunder of God

FRANK G. YERBY

You never can tell about a river. I have seen the Savannah in late August with the mud flats on the bottom showing through the water and then in November I've watched it smash the iron railings on the Center Street Bridge by hurling tree trunks against them. Those railings are usually forty-odd feet above the water line, but when the river has a mind to, it can reach them. And river people are queer too: they pile up levees and squat down behind them and forget the river is still there until it takes a notion to remind them. Then they get all panicky and begin to work like hell, piling up sandbags, dynamiting to relieve pressure— that is, they dynamite the levee so that the water flows into the Negro section and saves the business places on Broad Street—and guarding their overgrown mud-piles with guns.

In 'twenty-nine, it rained in the watershed above Augusta for three weeks without stopping. The water backed up in the sewers and flooded the lower end of Gwinett Street and covered the Commons like a pale sheet of muddy yellow glass. Inside the dormitory at Haines was almost as wet as outside so we couldn't do anything but play cards with a damp deck that stuck to the table and wouldn't shuffle. We plowed through acres of mud to our classes and sat huddled and miserable while the water dripped from the ceiling and sprinkled all over us. Then we went back from the damp classrooms to the wet dormitory and played wet cards until we got tired and climbed into the wet beds and slept. Outside the rain slanted down in hard lines and we watched it until we got sick of it but even when we closed our eyes and stuck our heads under the covers we could still hear it making a dull roar on the leaky tin roof.

We all knew that the river was up, but we were all river born so we didn't give a damn: not even when the news got out that it was up to forty-seven feet and was spilling over the top of the levee at Campbell Street. The next day it was still rising and we all cut classes and went down to see it. We couldn't get any further than Calhoun Street on Jackson because the sewers had backed

up and flooded a section of five blocks between the Negro section
and "Town." So we just stood there and watched the outboards
splutter up and down Calhoun until a man came up on a raft
and offered to take us to Town for a quarter apiece. But we
didn't have a quarter so we just stood there and watched the
dirty yellow water creep up for another hour before we turned
and went back to the campus.

We went to bed early that night: there wasn't anything else to
do. We had all won and lost back again all of each other's money
playing blackjack and we were sick as hell of cards and everybody
was beginning to get a little frightened by then anyway, so—we
went to bed.

About eleven the bottom dropped out. The rain was a solid
white sheet of water that you couldn't see ten feet through and
the drumming on the roof had become so loud that you had to
shout in order to be heard by a fellow in the same room. The
wind caught at the edges of the old building and shook it like a
terrier shakes a rat. You could read a newspaper by the lightning
flashes and the thunder sounded like hell itself had broken loose.
We sat up in the beds and hugged the covers and shivered, waiting for the building to fall in. It didn't, but hell popped loose just
the same.

I was just about to get back to sleep when Joe piled into my
room. He was so scared that he couldn't talk and his thick lips
kept flapping up and down like Stepin Fetchit's in the movies until
I laughed. He got awfully mad and that stopped him from being
scared so he got his voice back again.

"Aw right," he squeaked, "laugh! But the Law is arresting
everybody in th' building!"

"What for?" I began, but a big red-faced cop had Joe by the
shoulder and was saying to me: "All right, boy, pile out o' there!"
I started to argue, but the cop slapped me clear out of the bed and
my head hit the wall on the other side of the room. He grabbed
me by the shoulder and stood me up.

"You do like I say, nigger," he roared, "and you won't have
no more trouble!"

He hustled us downstairs and there they had the rest of the boys
lined up. Nobody dared say anything and after a while the Black
Maria rolled up and they loaded us into it and we squashed
through the mud in the direction of town. We were crowded all
over each other but every time we tried to whisper to find out what
it was all about one of the cops would yell: "Shut up!" So we

shut up and the patrol wagon splashed through the flooded streets toward Broad Street. After we had passed Broad Street, we knew they weren't taking us to the station, and we got scareder than ever. Then the wagon stopped and they hauled us out.

The first thing we saw was the big black hulk of the levee with gangs of Negroes working on the top with the cops guarding them with guns. The cops punched us in the back with their clubs and made us scramble to the top. By the time we got there we were muddy all over. They marched us up to the section boss. The big red-faced cop grinned and said: "Here's another bunch o' volunteers reporting for work!"

The section boss looked at us. "You boys'll get paid for your work," he said. "This is an emergency; if the levee ain't strengthened the whole city will go. Anybody here who don't want to work?"

Fats muttered something and one of the cops cracked him across the behind with a club so hard that he went to his knees. Nobody else said anything.

"That's good," the boss said, "I'm glad all o' you are willing to work." The cops laughed. Joe put his mouth close to my ear.

"The bastards!" he said, "the dirty stinking bastards!"

We lined up and they gave us wheelbarrows and shovels and set us to work filling sandbags. We would fill the sandbags at the bottom of the levee and roll them up an incline and pile them at the top. It wasn't raining so hard now but in spite of the fact that it was cold and we were wet through and our clothes were sticking to us, we could still feel the sweat running down our faces. The mud stuck to the wheelbarrows and the sandbags weighed tons. My arms were one big ache and my head was whirling so I couldn't see where I was going. I wanted to let go and slump down into the mud, but I didn't because one of the other fellows did and they kicked him until he got up.

Every time I went down to get more sandbags the river would be out of sight but I could hear it rumbling and roaring through the wall of the levee. The levee was more than ten feet thick but already the water was beginning to strike through. When I had pushed and grunted my way to the top again the roar of the river would rise to a furious scream. The surface was nearly covered with debris; one of the boys swore afterwards that the floor of Mike's liquor joint came floating down the river with the electric piano playing "Nearer My God To Thee." If it did, I didn't see it. Ever so often a huge tree or part of a barn would hurl itself half way across the bridge and hang there, grinding and crashing, until the river would tear it loose again. Each time that happened another section of the iron railing would go with it.

On top of the levee the blinding spray stung your eyeballs; the mud clasped your feet; and the rain smashed down in torrents. Now and then, around the bend of the river, a plume of black smoke and clods of earth would leap up into the sky and afterward would come the dull, slow boom of the explosion. And we knew that some of the fellows wouldn't have any homes to go back to, because that bend looped around the colored section, and the engineers were relieving pressure.

Down the levee from us another gang of Negroes was working. They were the men whom the policemen had rounded up from Norris' liquor joint, and they were plenty tough. They did twice as much work in thirty minutes as we did in two hours and it didn't seem to faze them in the least. Our section boss had charge of them, too, and hard as he was on us, he was twice as hard on them. He cussed them and kicked them, and they rebuilt a levee that was washing out from under their feet while they worked.

Then it began to thunder again, and we could see the white ribbons of lightning curl over the surface of the water. The rain came down faster and the thunder was one continuous roll. The lightning came closer and closer to where we were work-ing. The boss ordered us to move down and help the other gang because the levee was washing away down there faster than they could build it back. We went over and pitched in with the lightning flickering in and out between us. Then a bolt struck the levee not ten feet from where we were working. It tore loose the sandbags and the river came howling through the gap. Some of the men were knocked flat by the explosion. The boss was wild.

"You bastards!" he screamed, "You gawddamned black sonofabitches! Get in there and stop that water! Get in there! For Christsake do something!" One of the men jumped to the edge and started hurling sandbags in. The river bore them away like chips. Then the ground on which he was standing gave way and the torrent hurled him down the levee into the street and smashed his head against a lamppost. We saw him lying in the street, not quite covered by the yellow water. Then a dozen men took his place and kept hurling in earth and sandbags until the torrent subsided to a trickle then ceased altogether.

We worked like the devil and finally we evened up the pressure on all our section of the levee, but still the boss wouldn't let us rest.

All the time the lightning kept getting worse and worse, and the men began to mutter among themselves. Then one huge black fellow threw down his shovel. The boss rushed up to him.

"What tha hell do you think you're doing?" he shouted and struck at the big Negro. The big fellow caught his hand and held it, then he said in a voice that rumbled deep as the thunder itself:

"Listen, whitefolks, dat's God talking out dere now. An' when God talks, I listens!" Then he released the boss' hand and stepped back. The boss stood stock still, then one after another the boys threw down their shovels and slumped wearily down in the mud. The boss started to say something, but thought better of it. He knew he couldn't do anything now that the cops were gone.

He let us relax while he thought up a way to get us back to work. As for me, I didn't give a damn what he thought of, I just wormed my way deeper into that mud and let the whole world howl around me. After a while, I heard his voice coming from over my head. I couldn't make out what he was saying, but it sounded awfully grim and quiet, so I rolled over and looked up. He was standing close to me, his legs spread wide apart, his body slanting up into the mists until he looked gigantic. Dark as it was, I could see a gleam of light play along the barrel of the shotgun which he held in his hand.

"All right boys," he said very quietly, measuring the words as he spoke so that they came out very slow and dangerous and deadly calm. "It's my turn now. The first man that refuses to pick up a shovel and go back to work gets my personal ticket to hell. Get going now!"

Nobody felt like arguing with a shotgun even in that storm. The shovels were heavier than ever and the thunder made our ears ache. After a while the boss stopped pointing the shotgun at us, but he kept it in his hands so nobody stopped working. Finally I couldn't stand it any longer; I turned to Joe and started to say something when a blue-white ribbon of lightning curled in from over the river and struck right in the middle of the men. I saw green and red and white and my head crashed louder than the thunder so that the peal that followed sounded far off and faint as though it were coming from an immense distance. Then I was dead and floating and everything was peaceful and quiet, and then I was alive and being pulled apart with red hot pincers and the boss was hanging over the edge of the levee and crying like a woman and saying: "Help me, for Christsake help me somebody, won't somebody help me?"

But I was numb all over and couldn't move. And he kept hang-

ing there with the great tears running down his face and moaning:
"Help me, for Gawdsake, I'd do as much for you."

But everybody else was out, and three of the men were dead,
so no-one could help him. He kept slipping until the river caught
at his legs, and just before it whirled him away he screamed:
"Why won't one of you damned black bastards get up and help a
white man? Damn you all to hell!" Then, as the water caught him:
"Help me—please, boys—for the love o' God—" Then he was
gone and there was nothing but the booming of the river and the
crash of the thunder and the steady roar of the rain.

After he was gone, one of the men stood up and in a couple of
minutes two or three others got up until they were all standing
except the three dead men. It came to me that if they could get
up that quickly they could have got up before—but I didn't want
to think that, so I called to them and Joe and two other men
rubbed my legs until I could walk. We started down the levee
when Joe said:

"If we leave now the levee'll give way 'fore morning."

The man who had got up first turned and looked toward the
invisible gap where we knew the river was pouring into the colored
section of town. "Let it," he said.

We turned and walked down the incline and waded through the
flooded streets and all the time the rain kept whipping at our
backs.

The New Anvil April-May 1939

Makers of Music

The city is a sleeper, without a friend:
Walk slow past a million friendless faces,
Avoiding a million friendless hands.
Who will play Lenin to Chicago,
Touching faces, touching hands?

Wake, the city is a hurled grenade.
Wake, the city streams its fire.
Walkers, Sleepers, Paupers, Fakers,
At night, in Chicago,
There is no hope.

Watch the slow movers, the half-asleep drinkers,
Tell the burleycue queen there is no hope,
Argue all night with the last pimp alive,
Yet who will cry "He Is Risen!" at the Marigold Gardens
For the punchdrunk welterweight from Cincinnati!
Getting onto one knee for the fifth and last time?

O Sylphs and Paralytics on the last local south,
Straphangers to Success on the last Shopper's Special,
Sears & Roebuck sleepwalkers remembering where to transfer,
Hopers from Home reading all about it.
Sellers, Creepers, Gropers, Sleepers,
Yours is a drunken city,
A laughing fairy in a Clark Street car;
A woman weeping on a flyspecked bar.

Movers, Sleepers, Drifters, Drinkers,
Makers of Music and all tavern-keepers:
Close up the bar. Put away the glasses.
Put the chairs on the tables and have one last shot.
Within the city the last dawn breaks.

NELSON ALGREN

The New Anvil April-May 1939

Program for Appeasement

In the event of fire, consult your program
Then walk, do not run, to the nearest exit.
We can all get out: If nobody runs.
And even if somebody should get excited,
Most of us will get out into the air again just the same.
Even if only half get out,
That's better than they've done at some other fires.
Or the time the *Eastland* turned on her side in the river.
Or the time somebody decided to picket a block from Republic
    Steel.
But even if all the rest are stricken with panic
You and I are going to keep calm the whole while—
Say, you and I are almost sure bets to come through without a burn.
Unless you too should get frightened of fire.
(I feel I could make the street by myself in that case—
With the use of your coat.)

BUT IF THE EXITS ARE BLOCKED, IF WE'RE ALL HEMMED IN
IF THE USHERS WERE BOUGHT DURING INTERMISSION
IF THE HEAD-USHER PERSONALLY BARRED EACH DOOR
IF IT'S GOING TO BE LIKE THE EASTLAND ONLY A LITTLE WORSE
IF IT'S GOING TO BE LIKE REPUBLIC STEEL ONLY A LITTLE WORSE
IF IT'S GOING TO BE LIKE BADAJOZ
IF IT'S GOING TO BE LIKE DURANGO
IF IT'S GOING TO BE
IF IT'S GOING TO BE
IF IT'S GOING TO BE—

Then jump, do not run, every man for himself
Get down from the balcony on someone else's head
Pick up two burning seat-cushions and burn your own way out
Get down through the mezzanine and don't let them pin your arms
If you're strong if you're cool if you can just use your knees
If you can be first to the one darkened door that all the rest forgot
To the one darkened door left half an inch ajar
In the farthest corner of the last unlit cellar—
Maybe they don't know, don't point where you're going—

Let yourself into the open, slam it fast in their faces—
And slip stealthily past everyone all the way down
To the farthest exit of the deepest corner of that last unlit exit
That all the rest forgot.
But never look back
Never look back
O never look back.

NELSON ALGREN

The New Anvil April-May 1939

A Walk in Time of War

Spread now the soft explosions: spring
That aches with rumor in the trees,
While he goes plodding drunk to bring
Some willow to its battered knees.

He shakes the grove: the echo's real!
Coronas flame the pond's black mirror;
With rites of death the wood, the field
Reamplify his private terror.

He would go shadowless and proud
Up the plateaus of new earth,
Knowing this glory for a shroud,
Knowing his fear prelude to birth.

Who treks within the headsman's park,
Ghosted with the wreaths of spring,
Must break his pact with passive dark,
Return to struggle, trumpeting.

JOHN MALCOLM BRINNIN

The New Anvil June-July 1939

Hurry

Hurry.
The Germans are in a bad way.
Hurry Stimson and Mellon to London
They need money and more money.
Banks are failing,
People starving,
Declare a moratorium.
They are reaping the whirlwind.

Hurry some one to Brazil,
They are dumping coffee into the sea.
They did dump it on land and burn it
To raise the price
To starving wretches,
But some few grabbed a bit from the burning
And had food.
Now the sea gets it.

Hurry some one to the plains.
Farmers are plowing their wheat under
(Wheat will not pay for the cutting)
No modern Ruth must garner it free.
Plow it under, tho the poor starve.

Cattle are dying in parched pastures.
Hurry some one to the ranges.
Cattle are too weak to ship
And bring little on the market.

Hurry some one to the cotton fields.
Cotton is thrown from the wharves
(As potatoes were one year)
Or burned in bon-fires
Celebrating no victory.

Silk hose are cut in two or three with shredders
And used for packing,
While miners' women go unshod in the street.

Hurry some one to the factories.
Men are unemployed,
Eight million of them, and that means
With their dependents
Some forty millions unfed,
Not knowing where the next meal is coming from,
They need money and more money.
They have strong willing hands,
Skilled eager hands . . . and no work.
Banks are failing, people starving.
They are in such a bad way!
No one suggests a debt-rest for the jobless.
They too reap the whirlwind
Even if they did not raise the wind.

Hurry!

MARGARETTE BALL DICKSON
The Rebel Poet Aug.-Sept. 1931

Confidential
(An old man)

I was a forceps child, an orange juice brat;
My father's belly girth was greater than
My mother's ever reached at all.

When I was young we whipped Yale once;
We tore down picket fences, drinking beer,
And later whored in Boston until dawn.

In '29 the family pot
Was drained to emptiness, and now
My angered sons are prison hands.

They have been grieved to learn that I
Go down some afternoons to ask
Questions of the very poor.

ALVIN FOOTE
The New Anvil April-May 1939

The Kiss of Spring

Here in the marble peace of the museum
We stop before the sculptured sigh of Spring
Pressed into permanent posture by Rodin.

The young man almost breaks her back with ardor;
I see your face break with a brittle smile—
Recalling similar feats—
Like timing love to the rhythm of a key in a lock
Because your sister gets home from work at five,
And the park is still too cold.

MIRIAM HERSHENSON
The New Anvil May-June 1940

Ballad of Lenin

Comrade Lenin of Russia,
High in a marble tomb,
Move over, Comrade Lenin,
And give me room.

I am Ivan, the peasant,
Boots all muddy with soil.
I fought with you, Comrade Lenin,
Now I have finished my toil.

Comrade Lenin of Russia,
Alive in a marble tomb,
Move over, Comrade Lenin,
And give me room.

I am Chico, the Negro,
Cutting cane in the sun.
I lived for you, Comrade Lenin.
Now my work is done.

Comrade Lenin of Russia,
Raised in a marble tomb,
Move over, Comrade Lenin,
And give me room.

I am Chang from the foundries
On strike in the streets of Shanghai.
For the sake of the Revolution
I fight, I starve, I die.

Comrade Lenin of Russia
Speaks from the marble tomb:
On guard with the fighters forever.
In death—behold our room.

LANGSTON HUGHES

The New Anvil April-May 1939

well, well, blind man. . . .

a blind man
    playing a guitar
    and moving slowly
    thru the crowds

means something

just as a poet
    singing songs between
    life and death wants
    to say something and
    you are astonished
    that a coin, rattling,
    doesn't let you understand

well, well, blind man,
    we both must eat, let us
    say thank you in chorus
    (but not too loudly)

BORIS J. ISRAEL

The Rebel Poet June-July 1931

July Twenty-eight, 1932

On July twenty-eight, nineteen thirty-two
the real war began for you,
fellow worker.

Bayonets were stuck in hero behinds
by the world's best scientific minds,
fellow worker.

The legal lights of the Cabinet
ordered the rookie against the vet,
fellow worker.

On July twenty-eight, nineteen thirty-two
the bones of Woodrow Wilson rose to you,
the lies of Wilson were Hoover's to you,
fellow worker.

Woodrow Wilson in his skeleton
walked once more through Washington,
the ghosts of the bugles, the ghosts of the drums
left Pennsylvania avenue for Anacostia slums,
fellow worker.

On July twenty-eight, nineteen thirty-two,
they declared the war in China and the war in Peru
were a war on you,
fellow worker!

ORRICK JOHNS
The Anvil July-Aug. 1934

Let Me Laugh

You remember when you worked nightshift under the glare of the
   cold blue neons
and the strange warmness of peaches on the belt that made you
   think they were alive with a heart

and how the grader keeps pounding inside you the belts keep
    slapping and the checkers keep shouting
then everything melts and it feels so nice just to let go and sink
    down on nothing
you wake up in the first aid room
    your body all aching and throbbing
and you try to go to sleep like before but the company nurse keeps
    putting fire under your nose
you don't know how you do it
    but you go back to the bins and the boy opens the gate
and in rush the halves with that queer heat that flows through your
    mind like an embrace
then the grader slows down
    and the peaches stop coming and the belt stops jerking
and the shift is done as girls pour out of all kinds of steaming
    places

you take a deep breath
you become electric with the hope of seeing your boyfriend again
you rip off your gloves and laugh with the others as you
snake out of your smock and dash out to the street
for don't think of tomorrow don't think of the next shift
for jesus jesus you say let me laugh let me laugh let me laugh. . . .

GEORGE KAUFFMAN
The Anvil June-July 1939

The Wolves

Walking at nightfall while the stubble crawls
Brown under the last light and the slow November rain
Lips the scarred orchard boughs, we stop by woods
Where the late leaves are shadow-grey on grey:
A wet-fur odor steams from the rank earth pelt
Wrinkling to muscle when the wind stirs, folding
Back on the blurred limbs when the shadow closes.

And we are afraid, though the home lamp
Burns steady and warm from the hollow: old fear
That pricks the spine cold (the dark imagined beast
Lies docile to the hand's touch here, bedded with sleep)
But the warned blood remembers, the prescient ears
Strain to the twig's snap; the least night cry
Sweats in the palms, grips stiff the set heel. Listen!

The wolves are there—ranging another land:
Hot from the timber's edge, their hairy throats
Horning the spent fern, they leap snarling, their claws
Sabres to the ripe grain, slashing the walled amber:
They tear the rocks like flesh: the pasture bars
Are down, the keepers fled, the unhoused taken
Screaming like cattle from the night's dark rim.

That was a land like ours, where the leaves shone
Brown in November rain and paths led home
To the winter pear's flecked russet. That was a land
Where the valley sheep fed quiet in the full years,
Where dusk brought peace to the willow by the river,
And the small shining houses circled the round hills
Like amulets for love bound sweet to the wrist.

Then the invaders, violence in the green light
Of burning eyes: the peasant, the gnarled old man
Beard stained with blood, fell broken: the fleeing townsman
Left in the stripped bones on the cobbled street
His heritage; another, exiled, wept
Under foreign roofs; and the woman whose child lay dead
Still holds in her empty arms the shape of grief.

Are we safe here—is anywhere safe when the killers
Tongued fresh with death, bay from the echoing hills?
Here is our land: the fields, the slow rain falling,
The trees bare in the thick light, the heavy leaves
Stirred by the night wind, shadow-grey on grey,
Fur-deep over the flexed haunches, the muscled flanks
Ready to leap . . . Run, run from the woods! The wolves!

RUTH LECHLITNER

The New Anvil April-May 1939

Penance

Yesterday
A mob
Tarred, feathered,
And hanged from a tree
A black man.
Satisfied,
The good people
Went home to their dinners.
No doubt God
Will overlook the incident
For today
The good people
Sent a bale of old clothes
To Africa
To cover the heathen's
Sinful nakedness.

ROBERT CRANSTON LEE

The Rebel Poet Oct.-Nov.-Dec. 1931

Liberal

While social tremblors rock the scene
And sift us, man from man,
He rides the bounding fence between
—As only a eunuch can.

H. H. LEWIS

The Rebel Poet Oct.-Nov. 1931

Drought

I have seen drought singe Arkansas, as sun dries an apple.

The corn stalks are young in August, and as earless as moles.
Dogs are infested with fleas and the wells are dry.
The river has hushed its gossiping and has humped its back.
Small brown fish crowd in mudholes stupidly,
While the water shrinks above them in a narrowing ring,
The oak tree is barren of leaves, its branches look like roots.
Goats look pertly inquisitive.

An old woman told me drought is a monk in a brown cassock,
Who walks forth on sandled feet over the hills and prairies
Inflicting penance on white men and black men alike—
Unhitch the horses! Put away the shining plow!
Prop pitchfork and spade against the empty silos!
Slaughter the cow, for her udder is dry!
The monk is coming toward you mumbling a litany of penance.
At night the frogs are silent beside the dusty pond bed,
The katy-dids rattle their glassy wings like castanets.
Insects tick like clocks.
The brown garbed monk is advancing, head low, lips moving.

Turn away your face at noon!
The sun is a new minted penny
Cemented in the bottom of an overturned fish bowl.
Beneath it
Children sprawl in the dust-bitten grass before shack doors.
Men who have ceased to worry about crops
Sit munching cuds of tobacco, spitting hard into space.
Their hopes are broken in half, prideful chatter is of yesterday—
I saw her rocking, rocking, rocking—
For three days she kept her baby naked on her lap—
It lay limp and white, mouth open.
Her eyes wrapt in stupor stared at the sky.
(God, I wish I could forget the way her hands stroked at her knees!)
Pray for rain—pray for wind—pray for rain—
(A cyclone would have been welcome had it brought rain).
But not even a dust drift.

I saw the monk pause at the woman's door. I heard her weep.

Garb the young ones in gunny sacks!
In October they will eat puckering persimmons
And play ball with stunted pumpkins.
The sun is a new minted penny which can not be spent.
The horn of plenty is an ash can.

ROSA ZAGNONI MARINONI
The Rebel Poet Aug.-Sept. 1931

poem to be nameless

we were the exiles. find our names on the stones.
the park benches knew us. the lilac lanes
echoed once more with our footsteps and now no more
wake to our laughter or the sensuous air
lave us with warmth or wet or weft of spring.
we were exiles. look on the stones for our names.

you do not remember. you do not remember our names.
the marks on the trees are ours. in cornerstones
some notes have been left lost. no more
of us remains but the dead words and the air
turns the paper to ashes. in never spring
will we return now. you may forget the names.

I will say how it was. the year was spring
but a short time and at night. autumn was air
like the loose hair of a girl. the winter more.
a long time cold. and we had names.
one was for love. we lacked it. and there were names
for war for want for waiting. and on stones

the proud names of our death in the proud air
and the names of our proud destroyers and these were more.
perhaps they are still there perhaps the stones
remember. but you with the princely exultant names
come with flowers never. or memory. in flowering spring.
in march. in may. writing I love these names.

I say how it was here. it was cold. the air
sparkled with cold in the long winter. our names
were thick in the morgues. and we would look for spring
under newspapers. wrapped in the proud names
we slept over ventilators. we got no more.
we were always homeless. we slept on the cold stones.

we were always homeless. even in spring
(remember us. remember our useless names)
was no place even for love. in the quiet air
we took positions on benches. the calm stone
steps by the river knew us. we carved our names.
we were exiles from tomorrow. we wanted more.

we were exiles. Comrades remember our names.
we fought too. remember us when your spring
is a proclamation of love in the living air.

                                    THOMAS McGRATH

                            The New Anvil May-June 1940

Lenin

Choir, sweet voices of a thundering dawn.
(Hills are reddening on the fringe of desolation.)
Lips, dumb with prophecy, are moving,
        moving to the sternness of a dream;
Waving plumes of sound are advancing
        on the glory of his voice;
In the ashes of his tomb the sturdy feet of a nation
        are stirring in their shackles.
From the nostrils of his faith is blowing the fire
        that shall melt the chains of man.

                                KENNETH PATCHEN
                            The Rebel Poet Oct. 1932

and never never need they know

i think regretfully of all the modest clerks
who so much tempted by the glamor of their work
they do not care to know
how fast the worlds outside their hearing go

nor as they dream of every raise in pay
or fill the lucky floors of downtown stores
how the menace grows around them
that soon will come with unkind face
and take them to a ghastly meeting-place

nor as alert they squat in motorcars
with hurried scan of billboard and beginning page
to tell them what is best for decent folk to buy

no rude one ever asks about the underhanded deals
that send the bombing planes to other lands
while workmen smile because they have their meals
forgetting how or why so many armies die

i think continually of all the faithful clerks
who come importantly and go with little talk
and in their narrow glasses to and fro
they have no further need to look or know

for they have just so much of hope
as the desk has shining duties and the clock allow
of what is doing Sunday on the radio
and how the comic-strip will make out better in the end
and they need never be without a penny or a friend

WILLIAM PETERSON

The New Anvil July-Aug. 1940

Property

To build a bridge they cleaved clean as sweep of giant plow in
    loose loam
A mile of solid city,
Bursting to sun the once sealed home
And baring the garden secret at the back,
Sending away forever the roomers and their broken children.

Like camera eye
But not pure of pity
I click click the shutter of sight,
Taking at odd angles the bitter scene,
The cornice cracked
The turned-over tree
And like wires down
Dangling ivy.

Devalued now for houses this property lacks all that reflected
A sweet slow century,
The ornate habits of another country,
The cast-iron lion and the mansard roof,
And of owners the self-quietus of ownership.

Built upon privilege this area was quietly honored;
Pride was its legacy and peace compounded
Till on heavy facades it hung hushed and heavy as death.

Now nowhere are those tenants to be found
Who bestowed on later citizens their oldest sections,
But north of the city in their English valleys
Their sons and daughters
Continue the management of a large inheritance
Of joy and fashion.

KARL JAY SHAPIRO
The New Anvil Dec. 1939

Social Worker

We had a most successful year.
You, gentlemen of the finance committee, will be gratified to know
That we furnished thirty thousand good, simple meals to aban-
doned mothers and their children at a total cost of $3,111.07;
That our thirty beds gave these noble, unfortunate women a total
of ten thousand nights' reposes;
That we procured a hundred good, simple jobs as scrubwomen and
dish washers for widowed, needy mothers so they could know
the thrill of being self-supporting;
That we had two hundred neglected children baptised into the
Catholic and various Protestant creeds;
That our charges, employees and staff attended a total of five
thousand inspiring religious services;
That we paid expenses for ten of our younger staff members to
take summer courses in social work;
That we enabled five of our older staff members to visit social
settlements in other cities, Canada and Europe and study
various modern welfare methods.

Several young social workers who had radical tendencies, caused
  by reading Bolshevik books at universities,
Have been brought to see the errors of their ways and now ap-
  preciate the benevolent goodness of our men of great wealth.
We hope to send these girls on European inspection trips next
  season.
Yes, we certainly had a most successful and enjoyable year for a
  small institution.
We hope you charitable gentlemen of the finance committee
Will increase our next year's budget by thirty thousand dollars
To enable us to continue the great work lying before us.

WALTER SNOW

The Rebel Poet Oct.-Nov. 1931

Next Summer

He asked for bread,
  They promised instead,
A job—next summer.

Then congress met,
  They voted—you bet,
A job—next summer.

Big business said,
  With nodding head,
A job—next summer.

If this will check,
  I'll have—by heck,
A dozen jobs—next summer.

T. A. STANCLIFFE

The Rebel Poet May 1931

Contributors

NELSON ALGREN was born in Detroit in 1909, but soon moved with his family to Chicago—the setting for much of his writings. His third novel, *The Man with the Golden Arm*, won the first National Book Award for fiction in 1950. Both it and *A Walk on the Wild Side* (1956) appeared in movie versions which provoked the author's strong disapproval. *Somebody in Boots* (1935) and *Never Come Morning* (1940) are novels and *The Neon Wilderness* (1947) is a short story collection. *Who Lost an American?* (1963) and *Notes from a Sea Diary* (1965) are travel diaries. *Conversations with Nelson Algren* (1964) contains interviews taped by H. E. Donohue. Algren's *The Last Carousel* (1973) is a collection of stories and sketches.

SANORA BABB began her literary career when a young teacher in a one-room country school in Kansas, writing verse and prose that appeared in a number of literary magazines. Her short story "The Wild Flower," was translated into 20 languages after it appeared in *Best American Short Stories of 1950*. *The Lost Traveler*, a novel, was published in 1958. The autobiographical *An Owl on Every Post* (1970) recalls her Kansas childhood. She has long been a resident of Hollywood, where she is the wife of famed movie cameraman James Wong Howe.

J. S. BALCH, born in Russia, was living in St. Louis when he began writing short stories subsequently printed in various periodicals. *Lamps at High Noon* (1941) is a novel inspired by a writers' strike at the St. Louis office of the Missouri branch of the Federal Writers' Project, where Balch was assistant state supervisor. At various times he has been a dramatic critic, program director of a television station, and editor of a theatrical magazine. Within recent years he turned to painting in New York City and has had several well-received exhibitions.

JOHN MALCOLM BRINNIN, the son of United States citizens, was born in Halifax, Nova Scotia, in 1916. While a student at the University of Michigan in the late 30s, he edited with John H. Thompson two issues of *Signatures*, a magazine devoted to "work in progress." *The Garden Is Political* (1942) was the first of several volumes of verse. *The Selected Poems of John Malcolm Brinnin* appeared in 1965. Brinnin was long a friend and agent of Dylan Thomas, and wrote *Dylan Thomas in America* (1951).

MILLEN BRAND's novel *The Outward Room* (1937) was dramatized by Sidney Kingsley as *The World We Make*. A graduate of Columbia University, he conducted for ten years a writing class at New York University. His other works include *The Heroes* (1939), *Albert Sears* (1947), *Savage Sleep* (1968), and *Fields of Peace* (1970). He is an editor for a well-known publishing company.

ASHLEY BUCK trod the Broadway boards as a boy actor and later, after he moved to California, appeared in some of the first talking motion pictures. His stories were printed in *Esquire* and other magazines. In Hollywood he wrote scripts for various coast-to-coast shows in the "Golden Age" of radio and also directed many programs. Before his "reformation," as he puts it, he wrote scripts for TV and motion pictures. *Beyond Laughter,* a novella, was published "smack between Pearl Harbor and Christmas Day," and, though recommended by the Book of the Month Club, was generally ignored by the reading public. During World War II, Buck was an agent of the OSS in the China-Burma-India theater.

ERSKINE CALDWELL's candid and frequently Rebelaisian chronicles of people and mores in Dixie have been exhibited in a great many novels and short stories since *Tobacco Road* (1932), a novel that seemed doomed saleswise, was dramatized by Jack Kirkland to enjoy the longest continuous run on Broadway to that date, and ultimately sold millions‾of copies in paperback. Recent in his long list of novels are *The Weather Shelter* (1969) and *The Earnshaw Neighborhood* (1971). *Deep South* (1968) is a nonfiction work describing the author's return to the scenes of his youth after an absence of 50 years.

JACK CONROY's novel *The Disinherited* (1933) was reissued in 1963 as an American Century paperback. In 1967 he shared the James L. Dowd Award with Arna Bontemps for their *Anyplace But Here,* a history of Negro migration in the United States. This was an updating and expansion of *They Seek a City* (1945). With Bontemps, too, he wrote *The Fast Sooner Hound* (1942) and two other juveniles. In 1968 the Louis M. Rabinowitz Foundation gave Conroy a grant to assist in the preparation of his autobiography. The first section of this, "The Fields of Golden Glow," appeared in the Autumn, 1972, issue of *New Letters* (University of Missouri at Kansas City).

PAUL F. COREY was born on an Iowa farm and was graduated from the University of Iowa. In 1928 he married the poet Ruth Lechlitner, and a year later they bought an abandoned farm in Putnam County, New York, where they built a house—largely with their own hands. They later built two other houses in New York and one in the Valley of the Moon, California. *Three Miles Square, The Road Returns,* and *County Seat,* published in the 40's, are novels comprising a trilogy about the Mantz family of farmers. Corey also wrote other novels, juveniles, and nonfiction.

AUGUST W. DERLETH was one of the most prolific (and work-manlike) writers the United States has had. He began at age 15 to write science fiction, later wrote verse, detective stories, serious novels, memoirs, nature studies, and biographies. The locale of several of his novels is the fictional town of Sac Prairie, Wisconsin. *Walden West* (1961) and *Return to Walden West* (1970) are autobiographical. Before he died in 1972 at age 62, Derleth had written about 100 books.

MARGARETTE BALL DICKSON was born in Little Rock, Iowa, in 1884. She contributed verse to a wide variety of periodicals and was on the editorial board of several. She was for a long time professor of poetics at Valparaiso University in Indiana. Her book collections include *Gumbo Lilles* (1924), *Thistledown* (1928), and *One Man With a Dream* (1936).

STUART DAVID ENGSTRAND was born in Chicago in 1905. During the late 1930s he was a supervisor at the Illinois branch of the Federal Writers' Project there. Some of his later novels were more successful than his first, *The Invaders* (1937), but not spectacularly so. Two of these were *The Sling and the Arrow* (1947) and *Son of the Giant* (1950). A prey to increasing despondency, he walked fully clothed into the water in Los Angeles' McArthur Park on a September day in 1955 and kept going until he submerged and drowned.

JAMES T. FARRELL was born in Chicago in 1904. He studied for a total of three years at the University of Chicago, his attendance having been interrupted by an interval spent in New York City as cigar clerk, advertising salesman and filling station employee. While an expatriate in Paris, he sold his first novel, *Young Lonigan* (1932), beginning the Studs Lonigan trilogy completed with *The Young Manhood of Studs Lonigan* (1934) and *Judgment Day* (1935). Since then Farrell has published more than a score of novels, a dozen collections of short stories, and a volume of verse. He departed from his customary South Side of Chicago milieu with *The Silence of History* (1963), set in a small Midwestern community called Valley City. This began a trilogy ending with *A Brand New Life* (1968). *Invisible Swords* (1971) is a novel exploring a familiar Farrell theme—an unhappy marriage.

LEONARD FEINBERG was an English instructor at the University of Illinois in Urbana when he wrote "Fingers," his first published story. He soon abandoned fiction writing to devote his time to teaching.

ALVIN FOOTE, a Colorado postman, contributed verse to a number of reviews.

MICHAEL GOLD has been called, with some justification, the Father of Proletarian Literature in the United States. He was born in 1883 in New York City's lower East Side ghetto. His life there gave him material for *Jews Without Money* (1930), a novel which was the only one of his books to attain any sort of success. Gold was long a columnist for the *Daily Worker* and, in later years, for the San Francisco *People's World*. Failing eyesight and poor health forced him to relinquish the latter post shortly before his death in 1967.

MIRIAM HERSHENSON, a Brooklyn nurse, began writing verse at the age of eight. Setting aside school publications, *The New Anvil* was the first magazine to publish her work.

LANGSTON HUGHES, born in Joplin, Missouri, in 1902, won distinction in many fields of creative endeavor. When only 14 he was elected class poet for grammar school graduation in Lincoln, Illinois. In the 1920s he took part in the Harlem Renaissance and won poetry prizes from *Crisis* and *Opportunity*. His published works include several volumes of verse, short stories, novels, and memoirs. His play *Mulatto* enjoyed a long run on Broadway and on tour. Hughes died in 1967. Donald C. Dickinson's *A Bio-Bibliography of Langston Hughes, 1902-1967* (1967) is a valuable source of information about Hughes and his work.

BORIS ISRAEL edited two issues of *Nativity: An American Quarterly* in Columbus, Ohio, and wrote verse and short stories for "little" magazines. Adopting the pseudonym of "Blaine Treadway," he journeyed to the South as an organizer of sharecroppers and wrote about their conditions for the radical press. He died under mysterious circumstances, presumably murdered.

EUGENE JOFFE wrote short stories for a number of periodicals and did considerable work on a novel which was never published. He was for some time a member of a small jazz combo.

ORRICK JOHNS was born in St. Louis in 1887. He was a member of the group associated with William Marion Reedy's *Mirror*. His books include *Asphalt and Other Poems* (1917) and *Black Branches* (1920). *Time of Our Lives: My Father and Myself* (1937) is autobiographical. Before his death in 1946, Johns was New York director of the Federal Writers' Project.

JOSEPH KALAR spent most of his life in northern Minnesota as lumberjack, mill worker, and union official. He wrote verse, fiction, and criticism for a wide range of periodicals and his poetry was included in a number of anthologies. His verse was joined with that of Edwin Rolfe, Herman Spector, and Sol Funaroff in *We Gather Strength* (1933). In the fifties Kalar moved to Minneapolis to do public relations work for a lumber firm. He died there in February, 1972, at the age of 66.

GEORGE KAUFFMAN left the staff of the San Francisco *People's World* to do military service in the Pacific theater during World War II and published a novel about his experiences. He also wrote several volumes of verse.

I. L. KISSEN, a Brooklynite, wrote for *New Masses, Windsor Quarterly* and other publications before he entered on what he called a "period of vegetation."

RUTH LECHLITNER (Mrs. Paul F. Corey) writes of the Corey farm in upper New York state in the 1930s: "We built a small house, mostly from old stone fences, grew our own vegetables and fruits, raised chickens, and earned what we could by writing." She wrote prose and verse for many publications and was poetry reviewer for the *New York Herald-Tribune Books* for 25 years. *A Changing Season* (1973) is her fourth volume of verse. The Coreys subsequently moved to California where they now live in their fourth self-built house in the Valley of the Moon, north of San Francisco.

ROBERT CRANSTON LEE had his verse published in a number of literary magazines.

ARKADY LEOKUM, a Brooklynite, was graduated from New York University. His stories appeared in *New Masses* and elsewhere. His first novel, *Please Send Me Absolutely Free,* reflected his experiences in the advertising "game."

MERIDEL LeSUEUR, short story writer, teacher, and editor, was born in Iowa and has lived most of her life in the midsection of the nation, from Texas to Minnesota. She has taped millions of words gathered in the course of her extensive travels among the folk and has spent considerable time in New Mexico, but her base is always Minneapolis, Minnesota. Among her works are *North Star Country* and *Corn Village* (1970), an autobiographical memoir.

SAUL LEVITT was a contributor to the old *Anvil* and had his work printed in many other periodicals before a term in the military service. His first novel, *Only the Sun Is Silent,* reflects his military experiences.

H. H. LEWIS, the rambunctious Plowboy Poet of the Gumbo, functioned as flies in the soup of many East-of-the-Hudson esthetes and Marxian polemicists. To those who complained of the barnyard flavor of his verse, he explained: "Here I am, hunkered over the cow-donick, earning my dollar per and realizing, with the goo upon overalls, how environment works up a feller's pants-legs to govern his thought." Lewis was more than a doggerel-spouting eccentric, however. A group of his poems won the Harriet Monroe Award in *Poetry: A Magazine of Verse* and a laudatory article on his work by William Carlos Williams precipitated an acrimonious exchange between *Partisan Review* and *New Masses,* which published it. B. C. Hagglund printed a series of booklets for Lewis, and H. L. Mencken ran a Lewis story in *The American Mercury.* Lewis' base was always the ancestral farm near Cape Girardeau, Missouri, whence he would sally forth on hoboing trips or on pilgrimages to scourge Communist Party pundits in New York. In the fifties he fell silent on the farm insofar as versification or disputations are concerned.

LOUIS MAMET, a New Yorker, had "The Pension," a story from *The Anvil,* reprinted in Edward J. O'Brien's *Best Short Stories of 1934.* His work was presented in several literary magazines during the 1930s.

THOMAS McGRATH, a native of South Dakota, had his Rhodes Scholarship cut short by World War II. He later did graduate work at the University of Louisiana and is now teaching at Moorhead State College, Minnesota. Among his most recent collections of poems are *Letter to an Imaginary Friend* and *Movie at the End of the World.*

ROSA ZAGNONI MARINONI was born in Bologna, Italy, in 1888. The wife of a professor of Italian at the University of Arkansas in Fayette-ville, she had verse published in a wide variety of periodicals, had several collections published, and was poet laureate of Arkansas and of the Ozarks.

KENNETH PATCHEN was born in Niles, Ohio, in 1911. His early collections of verse included *Before the Brave* (1936) and *First Will and Testament* (1939). His poetry gained wider attention in the fifties, when he began reading it with jazz band accompaniment in night clubs, the sessions being recorded and sold as records. He was awarded a Guggen-heim Fellowship in 1936, and in 1967 the National Foundation of Arts and Humanities presented him with a $10,000 grant for his "lifelong contribution to American letters." For the most part of 13 years before he died in 1972, Patchen was bedridden with spinal arthritis. *The Journal of Albion Moonlight* (1941) and *Memories of a Shy Pornographer* (1945) are novels by him. His *Collected Poems* was published in 1968.

WILLIAM PETERSON, a Los Angeles poet, was one of the "as yet unknown young writers" who contributed to *Crescendo,* "a laboratory for young America," issued in Waco, Texas, 1941-44.

ROBERT RAMSEY was born in Memphis in 1912. Most of his early life was spent alternately in Memphis and Eastern Arkansas. He worked for some time as advertising and publicity writer for a Memphis radio station. "Fingers" was his first published story. Ramsey has been a member of the English faculty of the University of Arizona at Tucson for a number of years. His novels include *Fire in Summer, The Mockingbird,* and *Fiesta.*

Of YASHA ROBANOFF, Meridel LeSueur writes: "He is dead now. He was an organizer for the Non Partisan League . . . An I.W.W. when he was young and people still talk about what a great street speaker he was and how they got their education from him on a soap box in cities all over the country. . . . He wrote only when incarcerated in jail or poverty pocket and was a great story teller. . . . All his great stories planted directly in the folk militant mind and spouting, I am sure, in many strange fields. He had a story in the *Dial* which I quote in *North Star Country* almost in its entirety."

JOHN C. ROGERS manifests his creative abilities in art, prose, and verse. He has exhibited art and photos in the Corcoran Gallery of Art in Washington, D. C., where he graduated in fine arts and taught children's classes. His photos and art have been exhibited also in galleries from New York to Oklahoma and North Carolina. For many years he contributed articles, cartoons, and drawings to the Washington *Daily News.* Open-heart surgery caused his retirement as an illustrator for the federal government, but he still has prose, art, and photographs published in such periodicals as *North Country Anvil* and *The West Virginia Hillbilly.*

MARTIN SAVELA, a Finnish-American writer of Chicago, contributed to *Scribners* and other periodicals, and, while in the army during World War II, won an Armed Services Award from *Direction* magazine. For several years he wrote copy for advertising agencies in Chicago before becoming a post office employee.

KARL JAY SHAPIRO was born in Baltimore in 1913 and first became well-known for his poems of World War II. *V-Letter and Other Poems* won him the 1945 Pulitzer Prize. Shapiro was editor of *Poetry: A Magazine of Verse* (1950-56) and of *Prairie Schooner* (1956-63). *Poems 1940-1953* (1953) contains some of his best work. *Essay on Rime* (1945) and *Beyond Criticism* (1953) are critical works. His essays on modern poetry are collected in *In Defense of Ignorance* (1960).

DEL SMITH is the pen name of a husband-and-wife writing team, Clint and Dorothy Smith. Natives of the Pacific Northwest, they moved to Oklahoma during the Dust Bowl period described by John Steinbeck in *The Grapes of Wrath.* They worked for some time on a play dealing with the Green Corn Rebellion of Oklahoma farmers, an abortive revolt against the 1917 draft law in World War I, but never were able to get it produced.

WALTER SNOW, born in Gardner, Massachusetts, in 1905, worked from age 16 to 20 in the Willimantic, Connecticut, textile mills. Going to Greenwich Village, he was for a half season a stagehand and "flats" painter at the Provincetown Playhouse before becoming a reporter on the old *Brooklyn Eagle*. He wrote verse and mystery stories, and was New York editor of the *The Anvil* before its merger with *Partisan Review*. He joined the staff of the *Willimantic Chronicle* in 1957, retiring from that newspaper in 1971. *The Glory and the Shame* (1973) is a collection harvesting his verse from the 1920s to the 1970s. He calls attention to the anachronistic flavor of his "Social Worker," asking that it be remembered it was written before "mass pressure forced the introduction of State Welfare departments partially supported by the U.S." He died of a heart attack in June 1973.

T. A. STANCLIFFE wrote "agit-prop" verse for the radical press.

JESSE STUART, a Kentucky hill boy, first attracted national attention with his 700 sonnets in *Man With a Bull-Tongue Plow* (1934). Since then he has published a great many books: verse, autobiographies, stories, novels, and sketches. With *Land Beyond the River* (1973), a novel, his published books approached the three dozen mark.

TOM TRACY, a Californian, had his stories published in *Pagany* and other periodicals. Harry Hansen chose his "Homecoming" for inclusion in *The O'Henry Memorial Award Prize Stories of 1940* and it was also dramatized for a nationwide radio broadcast.

JOSEPH VOGEL was born in New York City in 1904. He was at various times associated with such "little" magazines as *Blues, Morada, Front,* and *Dynamo*. His novels include *At Madame Bonnard's* (1935), *Man's Courage* (1938), and *The Straw Hat* (1940).

WILLIAM CARLOS WILLIAMS (1883-1963) was born in Rutherford, New Jersey, where he spent most of his life as a practicing physician. His *Poems* (1909) and succeeding volumes established him as one of the foremost practitioners of Imagism. *White Mule* (1937), *In The Money* (1940), and *The Build-Up* (1952) are novels comprising a trilogy about the adjustment of immigrants to life in the United States. *The Knife of the Times* (1932) and *Life along the Passaic River* (1938) are short story collections.

MILTON U. WISER, an accountant who was graduated from the University of Buffalo, wrote for *American Prefaces, Manuscript, Tanager,* and other periodicals.

FRANK G. YERBY was born in Augusta, Georgia, in 1916 and was graduated with an M.A. degree from Fisk University in 1938. While a field worker on the Illinois branch of the Federal Writers' Project in Chicago, he wrote "The Thunder of God," his first published material aside from poetry in college magazines. According to Jerre Mangione, Yerby told some of his fellow projecteers: "You intellectuals can go ahead and write your highbrow stuff. I'm going to make a million." And he did just that with a long string of popular historical novels, beginning with *The Foxes of Harrow* (1946), in which Negroes customarily are minor characters. In 1968 he published *Judas, My Brother,* a costume novel like his others, but dealing with the origins of Christianity and written in anger as an attack upon blind faith.